RAGING WITH COMPASSION

RAGING *with* COMPASSION

Pastoral Responses to the Problem of Evil

John Swinton

WILLIAM B. EERDMANS PUBLISHING COMPANY
GRAND RAPIDS, MICHIGAN

Wm. B. Eerdmans Publishing Co.
2140 Oak Industrial Drive NE, Grand Rapids, Michigan 49505
www.eerdmans.com

23 22 21 20 19 18 17   9 10 11 12 13 14 15

ISBN 978-0-8028-2997-9

The author and publisher gratefully acknowledge permission granted to reprint material from the following sources:

Extracts from *Psalms of Lament* by Ann Weems. ©1995 Ann Weems. Used with permission from Westminster/John Knox Press.

Extracts from *Hasidic Tales of the Holocaust* by Yaffa Eliach. Copyright © 1982 by Yaffa Eliach. Reprinted by permission of Miriam Altshuler Literary Agency, on behalf of Yaffa Eliach.

All scripture quotations, unless otherwise indicated, are taken from the HOLY BIBLE, NEW INTERNATIONAL VERSION®. NIV®. Copyright © 1973, 1978, 1984 by International Bible Society. Used by permission of Zondervan. All rights reserved.

Contents

CONTENTS

Acknowledgments

Writing a book about evil is difficult. It is difficult not only because of the intellectual dilemmas and challenges that surround this area of human experience but also because thinking about evil and concentrating on human suffering for extended periods of time inevitably affects you. As I have worked on this text I have found myself dealing with some of the darkest regions of human experience and behavior. One cannot but be moved, concerned, and changed as one recognizes the depths of darkness that human beings are capable of sinking to. Such an exploration leaves a psychological and spiritual mark that needs healing. I could never have completed this book without the healing friendship and prayerful support of my brothers and sisters in Christ. I am eternally grateful to those in my home church, Oldmachar Church in Aberdeen, Scotland, for their prayerful support and faithful friendships. It is not coincidental that this is the fastest growing church in Scotland. The spiritual energy of the community and the tireless ministry of hope, encouragement, worship, and praise have enabled me (and many others) to see God in new ways and have sustained me as I have worked on the difficult things in this book. Thank you, Jim, my pastor and my friend. I am also deeply blessed by having a family that have put up with my physical and psychological absences during the process of writing this book. Thanks for welcoming me back even when I insisted on spending more time with a laptop computer than with you. Thank you, Alison, my wife and my finest friend.

I am also very grateful for the help and guidance I have received from other friends and colleagues. Thanks to Stan Hauerwas for flagging the importance of creating communities that can absorb evil and suffering and ensure perseverance until the Lord returns. This vital insight sits at the heart of this book. Thanks to Ray Anderson for helping me work through some complex thoughts about the nature of evil and suffering. Thanks also to all of my other colleagues who acted as welcome dialogue partners as I worked through the complex and troubling issues of evil and suffering. I am also very grateful to the good folks at Eerdmans, in particular Sandy De Groot for her guidance and wisdom and Linda Bieze for her excellent editorial work as well as her patience and concern.

Of course, the final responsibility for this book, for better and for worse, lies with me.

Introduction

Why does God allow evil and suffering? Among the many complex and fascinating questions that face believers and non-believers alike, probably none is as enduring and perplexing as this. How can a God who is all-loving and all-powerful allow the tragedy, suffering, and evil that leave such profound marks on our world? For those who believe in a meaningless universe comprised of nothing more than a random series of cause-and-effect events with no fixed direction, purpose, or telos, evil is not really a problem at all, it is just the way the world is. We might not like it, but there is no one to blame. Bad things just happen to people whether they are good or bad!

For Christians, however, the question is not that simple. For those who believe in the loving God whom Jesus called Father, a God who, it is claimed, is actively involved in the world and who, in and through the life, death, and resurrection of Jesus, is transforming and healing that world, the problem of evil is deeply perplexing. If the claim is true that in Christ God has overcome evil and suffering and that even now, the world is not the way it has to be or indeed the way it will be,[1] then the problem of evil and suffering becomes both a mystery and a paradox. How can we live as if Christ's victory were real when all around we see strong evidence that such a claim is at best an exaggeration and at worst simply not so? It is difficult to see signs of victory in the midst of the suffering, brokenness, and

---

1. "When you were dead in your sins and in the uncircumcision of your sinful nature, God made you alive with Christ. He forgave us all our sins, having canceled the written code, with its regulations, that was against us and that stood opposed to us; he took it away, nailing it to the cross. And having disarmed the powers and authorities, he made a public spectacle of them, triumphing over them by the cross" (Col. 2:13-15).

I

evil that surround us. How can we claim Christ as victor in a world in which goodness seems so frequently to be overpowered by evil? What does it mean to hold onto the hope of Christ and to remain a faithful people in the midst of so much suffering and evil?

The Question of Theodicy

One response to evil and suffering that has recently gained credence within theology and the philosophy of religion is to develop a theodicy. Put simply, *a theodicy is an intellectual defense of God in the face of evil and suffering.* Theodicies attempt to explain evil so people can hold onto the possibility of God in the midst of pain and suffering. Theodicies seek to provide complex philosophical and theological arguments to justify and sustain the idea that it is logical to believe that God is perfectly good, all-loving, and all-powerful even in the face of the reality of the world's pain.

Not coincidentally, the theodical task to provide explanations for the existence of evil sits well with the needs and expectations of post-Enlightenment western cultures. In an age when science and technology have made major claims regarding the ability of human beings to discover, explain, and understand most of human experience, it is not surprising that our culture strives to explain the existence of evil. Within a culture that assumes that all problems can eventually be solved, particularly when that culture is enjoying relative prosperity, that is, when suffering is no longer seen as an inevitable dimension of life, theodicy appears to be a necessity. We need theodicy to ask questions of God, suffering, evil, and death in the same way as we need science to help us answer the questions in other dimensions of our lives. The problem of evil is, we assume, just like every other problem we encounter: *solvable.* All we need is to expend enough mental energy on this problem and it will, eventually, yield to us the secret of suffering.[2]

---

2. The fact that theology has become caught up in this culture of problem-solving indicates the interesting tension between theology as a mode of knowing that challenges cultural assumptions, and theology as a mode of knowing that simply responds to the challenges thrown up by the questions society asks. In the former mode theology is radical and countercultural; in the latter it is reactive, often defensive, and keenly sensitive to issues of context, cultural change, and the epistemological challenges to the gospel offered by shifting moral structures, values, and worldviews. Theodicy falls into the latter, reactive mode.

Is Theodicy Necessary?

In an age that finds problem-solving profoundly important, the idea of solving the problem of evil appears natural and indeed necessary. The idea that living faithfully might mean learning to live with unanswered questions seems dissonant and odd. We need the comfort of believing that eventually the problems of cancer and AIDS will be solved. We need the solace of thinking that through our continuing efforts to find peace in the world peace will in fact become a reality. We need the psychological assurance that science will eventually cure all of our ills, including that ultimate ill: death. We need the temporal security of being able to explain precisely why it is that God allows suffering and evil. We may well find cures for AIDS and cancer, but will we find solutions for the other problems?

Yet, despite our desire to solve problems and chase after happiness and peace, over the past hundred years more human beings have been killed by other human beings than at any other period in history. AIDS continues to devastate millions of lives with no obvious solution emerging. The intellectual arguments of the theodicist struggle to carry the great weight of the evil, pain, and suffering that seeks to engulf the world. The way the world has been and *actually* is sits in an uneasy tension with the way we would *like* the world to be. Life is *not* fully comprehensible, controllable, or fixable. We constantly find ourselves as individuals, as communities, as nations, forced to live with unanswered questions. Where is God when it hurts?

The Thesis of This Book

In this book, I develop a Christian response to the human experience of evil and suffering. This response will not, however, be expressed in the form of a theodicy, at least not in the traditional sense that this word has acquired. Rather, I argue that standard philosophical and theological approaches to theodicy not only do not work, but can also be dangerous and have the potential to become sources of evil in and of themselves. Rather than seeing evil and suffering as simply philosophical and theological problems to be solved, I begin in a different place, by recognizing that the problem of evil is a deeply meaningful and often spiritual human experience before it becomes an object for theological and philosophical reflection. The problem of evil becomes a philosophical conundrum only in response to real, living human experiences. In other words, theodicy is a second-order activity; experience comes first and reflection on that experience follows. As one reads various theodicies that are put forward, one could be forgiven for supposing that theodicy was in fact a first-order activity. Rarely do the specifics of the lived reality of the human experience of evil, pain, and suffering enter into the philosophical equation. If they do, they tend to be portrayed through hypothetical "case studies" that neatly reflect the central tenets of the philosophical or theological discussion without actually having to deal with the complexities of real people facing real experiences. Such theodicies deal with evil as an abstract, generalized concept that needs to be brought into line with the supposed reality of an abstract (and abstracted), generic "god," a god whose character and goodness, it is assumed, we can understand quite apart from any specific actions by this god within history or in relation to any particular individual or group of individuals. Such theodicies take human pain out of the world of experience and into the world of ideas. They may offer some useful and perhaps helpful intellectual insights into the problem of evil, but they make little impact on the experience of suffering as it is lived out in the lives of Christian communities.

In this book I offer an alternative perspective. I maintain that theodicy should not be understood as a series of disembodied arguments designed to defend God's love, goodness, and power. We require a different mode of understanding, a mode of theodicy that is embodied within the life and practices of the Christian community. Such a mode of theodicy does not seek primarily to *explain* evil and suffering, but rather presents ways in which evil and suffering can be *resisted* and *transformed* by the Christian community and in so doing, can enable Christians to live faithfully in the midst of unanswered questions as they await God's redemption of the whole of creation. The focus of such a community will not be on why evil exists, a question that is ultimately unanswerable, but on, as Stanley Hauerwas puts it, how we can build communities that absorb suffering and enable faithful living even in the midst of evil.[3]

---

3. Stanley Hauerwas, *Naming the Silences* (Grand Rapids: Eerdmans, 1990), p. 49.

Outline of the Book

In chapters one and two I explore the shape of contemporary theodicy and some of the reasons for the ways in which it has developed historically and culturally. In these chapters I show that the problem of evil is not the same through time and across cultures. The questions we ask today and the problems we seek to solve are specific to our culture and are the product of particular cultural and philosophical assumptions. As such, the way in which we frame the problem of evil is open to critique and reconstruction. These chapters pick up on this challenge and seek to rebuild our understanding of theodicy and the problem of evil.

Chapter three explores the nature of evil. The concept of evil is rather vague and open to multiple constructions. In this chapter I begin to reframe evil in the light of God's redemptive movement towards the world in Christ, and in so doing I develop a specifically theological understanding of evil and the problem of evil that will guide the remainder of the study.

In chapter four I pull together a revised model of theodicy that I call *pastoral theodicy*. Pastoral theodicy is a theodicy of action and resistance. It focuses on specific pastoral practices that the church must learn and embody as it seeks to resist evil and to remain faithful in the midst of suffering. Here I argue that the task of the church is not to attempt to explain evil and suffering, but rather to offer modes of embodied resistance, such as listening to silence (the first five key theodical practices), that provide critical and countercultural ways of encountering and dealing with evil. Theodicy carried out in this way seeks to embody and gracefully mirror the habits of God as God encounters and seeks to redeem the reality of evil and suffering in the world.

In chapter five I examine the "forgotten" theodical practice of lament. Lament is a dimension of the church's life and worship that has lost its appeal to the contemporary church. Our failure to embody and regularize sadness and lament into the life and worship of our churches means that we often have few resources to deal with sadness and the impact of suffering. We have no language to express our sadness. This chapter explores the importance of lament for resisting evil and dealing faithfully with suffering and reflects on the impact that the learning of such a practice can have for the church's ability to cope with evil and absorb suffering.

Chapter six explores the pastoral significance of the practice of forgiveness, which sits at the heart of the gospel. At one level it is the source of all Christian hope and an aspect of faith that brings hope and healing. However, at another level it is scandalous. Why? Because God's forgiveness is open to *everyone*. Even the worst perpetrator of evil, the mass murderer, the child abuser, the rapist can find forgiveness and salvation. This is scandalous for victims, yet vital for liberation from the impact of evil. The chapter examines the breadth of God's forgiveness and shows how, properly understood, forgiveness can be healing and liberating for both victims and the perpetrators of evil.

In chapter seven I look at the practice of thoughtfulness. The idea that thinking is a formal practice of the church is rather unusual in many ways. However, if we take seriously the apostle Paul's urging for the renewal of our minds (Rom. 4:2), then it becomes clear that there is something important about thinking correctly in the light of the gospel. The chapter reveals a close connection between a lack of critical thought and the perpetration of evil actions. More than that, it shows that many of us are unthinkingly involved in actions and attitudes that are profoundly evil but culturally acceptable. One does not need to be actively involved in evil to participate in it. All a person or a culture has to be is to be thoughtless and inattentive. When people become thoughtless and inattentive, it is easy for them to become implicated in aspects of evil that, while normalized within our cultural thinking, can be devastating for some of the weakest and most vulnerable members of our communities, in this case, people with disabilities..

In chapter eight I explore the radical nature of Christian friendship and the potential for this apparently straightforward, everyday human relationship to resist and transform evil in significant ways. Through an exploration of the experiences of refugees and asylum-seekers, I try to develop a Christ-like, challenging, and transformative mode of understanding and ministering to the victims of profound acts of evil.

Taken together these four Christian practices form a foundation for building communities that will resist and transform evil and provide reservoirs of grace that will sustain people until Christ returns and evil and suffering will no longer be a part of our horizon.

Practical Theology: A Brief Note on Method

Before moving on, let me briefly explain something of the methodology that underpins this book. Most of the academic discussion that surrounds the problem of evil has emerged either from the philosophy of religion or systematic theology. These disciplines, through the creative use of theology and philosophy, have attempted to square the existence of evil and suffering with the reality of a good, all-loving, all-powerful God. With some notable exceptions,[4] practical theology, the discipline that forms the foundational theological perspective underpinning this book, has been strangely quiet in its response to the problem of evil. This is unfortunate as it has allowed the debate about the problem of evil to carry on, for the most part, in abstraction from the life experiences of those who experience the problem of evil primarily as a *practical* problem that profoundly impacts their lives, the lives of their families, and their communities, rather than a theoretical dilemma that leads to clarity of thought without any necessary corollary of action.

Put simply, *practical theology is critical, theological reflection on the practices of the church as they interact with the practices of the world, with a view to ensuring and enabling faithful participation in God's redemptive practices in and for the world.*[5] Practical theology finds its focus in the impact of the narrative of the death and resurrection of Jesus Christ as it finds its embodiment within living, worshipping communities of faith. To suggest such a focus on the practical is not to suggest that practical theology is atheoretical. Practical theology is rooted in the scripture and tradition of the Christian faith and takes theology very seriously. However, the theological reflection carried out by the practical theologian is never for its own sake; it is always for the sake of developing practices that faithfully reflect the actions and character of the triune God, as God has revealed God's self in the life, death, and resurrection of Jesus.

Understood in this way, the term "practice" as it relates to the task of practical theology has a very specific meaning. I will discuss this meaning in more detail as we move on. Here it will suffice to observe that the term "practice" relates to specific forms of actions carried out by Christians in community, which embody and perform theological knowledge and understandings. Practices emerge from specific theological understandings and feed back into them in a dialectic process which enables revelation

4. James Poling, *Deliver Us from Evil: Resisting Racial and Gender Oppression* (Minneapolis: Fortress Press, 1996); Alistair Mcfadyen, *Bound to Sin: Abuse, Holocaust, and the Christian Doctrine of Sin* (London: Cambridge University Press, 2000).

5. For a further development of this idea see John Swinton and H. Mowatt, *Practical Theology and Qualitative Research Methods* (London: SCM Press, 2006).

and faithful living. The task of practical theology is to both reflect critically and theologically on the practices of the church, and to offer perspectives and insights which will enable these practices to be carried out faithfully. Practical theology therefore has the particular goal of enabling faithful living and the authentic performance of the gospel.

In line with this methodological perspective, the book includes various narratives and shared experiences. It is important to understand the role that these experiences play. They are not simply illustrations or case studies. Rather they are integral dimensions of the process of practical theological reflection. Indeed, they are the beginning point for theological reflection. In taking experience seriously, I allow fresh questions to be asked of the Christian tradition and try to stimulate fresh responses and challenging modes of practice. In this way the reflective movement is from experience to theory and back to experience.[6] It is my hope that this approach will give the book a challenging relevance that is both theologically sound and practically transformative.

---

6. Swinton and Mowatt, *Practical Theology,* chapter one.

The Problem with the Problem of Evil:
Pastoral Perspectives

I remember it as if it were yesterday. It was six A.M. when I received the call from my neighbor. He was deeply disturbed and only barely able to speak. "She's gone," he whispered.

"Who has gone?" I asked; I was still half asleep and not at all sure what was going on.

"Gemma," he said, "Gemma has gone."

"What do you mean she has gone?" I replied, slowly beginning to realize that something awful had happened.

"Gemma . . . she's . . . she's dead. She was walking home after skating with her friends and she just dropped down dead! She was only eleven! Why has this happened? Why has God taken my Gemma? Why?"

I sat up in bed in stunned silence. What could I say? The little girl whom I had watched grow from a baby to a toddler and into a lively, vibrant child was gone. All that remained were devastation, sadness, and the question *why?*

What was I supposed to say to this man, my friend, who had had the heart of his life ripped out in an instant? The doctors had no idea why she died; "it was just one of those tragic mysteries," they said. Her parents had no idea why she had died. I had no idea why she had died . . . but . . . surely, as a theologian, I should have *something* to say. Was this loss punishment for something the family had or had not done? Was it a test of their faith? Had God "taken Gemma home" for purposes that are beyond human understanding, purposes vague and unclear in the present but that will become clear in the grand scheme of things? Or was Gemma's death nothing but a totally meaningless incident that has little real impact on a meaningless world ruled by cause and effect, a world within which the death of one small child will make little difference in the long run?

What could I say to Gemma's parents, George and Martha? All of the formal resources I had studied, which claimed to enable me to explain and interpret suffering and evil, seemed like straw in the wind in the face of the raw pain of George and Martha's experience. How could an all-loving, all-powerful God allow this to happen? The logic of formal theodicy, arguments to justify God's goodness in the face of evil, floundered and was irreparably smashed on the rock of George's lament: *"Why, Lord?"* The agonizing flow of his unrelenting anguish silenced me. I often wonder if I could have said more, if I should have told him that God loved him and told him that it was going to be all right . . . but it wasn't going to be all right! It could never be all right; what had happened seemed inexplicably wrong, painful, and confusing. How *could* a God of love and power allow this to happen? I had nothing to say because there was nothing to say, at least nothing that would make sense or create logic in the midst of such apparent unreason.

For George and Martha, that day changed their lives. Things could never be the same. But it was also a day that changed my life. It was the moment when I suddenly and quite powerfully was forced to recognize that the theodical framework that I had built around me to protect me from the reality of pain, suffering, and evil was in fact the emperor's new clothes. I thought the framework was there, real and sound. I tried to persuade others that it was real and effective, but when it came down to the wire, when it entered that very public world of pain and suffering, it vanished. Something was fundamentally wrong with the way I had been conceptualizing and dealing with the problem of evil and the reality of suffering.

Bad Things Happen to Good People

We live in a world that is profoundly marred by suffering and evil. Some of it seems "just to happen"; people get ill, they suffer, they die. Gemma's death and her parents' anguish are but small teardrops that reflect the reality of the daily rounds of suffering and evil that go on within our world. There appears to be no one to blame other than, perhaps, God.

But then again, much of the evil and suffering that goes on in the world is not "natural"; it does not have to happen. It exists only because human beings choose that it should exist. Bad things happen to good people because people behave badly. Much of the evil and suffering of the world is of a moral nature and human beings are solely responsible for its existence. Such suffering is, as Wendy Farley describes it, radical (unmerited) suffering.[1] Radical suffering refuses to be explained simply as punishment that is somehow deserved or as the just retribution for sin. Radical suffering is deliberately inflicted on one human being by another. When a company deliberately withholds information from its employees that the substances they are working with are carcinogenic, these people experience radical suffering. When a woman is raped as she returns from a shopping trip with her children, she experiences radical suffering. When a terrorist explodes a bomb in the midst of a group of innocent strangers, the terrorists are initiating radical suffering. When a child is abused by a stranger, its suffering is radical, unmerited, evil. Farley shares the following story of a Chilean torture victim, which illustrates well the nature of radical suffering:

> At one point, I realized that my daughter was in front of me. I even managed to touch her: I felt her hands. "Mummy, say something, anything to make this stop," she was saying. I tried to embrace her but they prevented me. They separated us violently. They took her to an adjacent room and there, there I listened in horror as they began to torture her with electricity! When I heard her moans, her terrible screams, I couldn't take it any more. I thought I would go mad, that my head and my entire body were going to explode.[2]

Bad things very often happen in the world because people do bad things.

Why, Lord?

Our immediate response to such suffering is to ask why. "Why would an all-loving, all-powerful God allow this to happen?" "Why is there suffering in the world?" "Why does evil exist?" When we start to ask such questions, we are beginning to engage in the intellectual enterprise of *theodicy.*

---

1. Wendy Farley, *Tragic Vision and Divine Compassion: A Contemporary Theodicy* (Louisville: Westminster/John Knox Press, 1990), p. 21.

2. From "Women and Torture," *File on Torture* (Amnesty International, July 1985), quoted in Farley, *Tragic Visions and Divine Compassion,* p. 1.

Put simply, theodicy concerns intellectual defense of the love, goodness, and power of God in the face of evil and suffering in the world. Practicing theodicy is a way to cope with the anxiety provoked by the reality of evil and suffering by using the intellect as an explanatory tool.[3]

At one level, the questioning of the goodness and power of God that comprises theodicy is an obvious response to the human experience of suffering and evil. Our world is ripped apart by a constant stream of pain, suffering, and struggle; evil and suffering are real, awful, frightening, and confusing. The question, "Why does God allow such things to happen?" appears to be a natural response to our tragic experiences in the world, so much so that we rarely doubt the legitimacy of the question.

Problems with Theodicy

Questions such as these are, of course, completely understandable and quite legitimate. Raw pain inevitably inspires hard questions. The problems arise when we try to answer them. When we attempt to create explanations that justify the goodness of God in the face of evil and radical suffering, we encounter aspects of theodicy that are theologically questionable and pastorally dangerous. As Farley points out in her commentary on the story of the torture victim mentioned above:

> [T]he obscenity of such an event annihilates the possibility of soothing ourselves with theories that justify the ways of God in an evil world. In the wake of such wanton cruelty, defenses of a divine order of justice become bitter mockeries.[4]

---

3. We might liken theodicy to the defense mechanism of *intellectualization*, which uses reasoning to block out emotional stress and conflict. Freud describes intellectualization as a "flight into reason" wherein a person seeks to avoid uncomfortable and anxiety-provoking experiences by focusing on facts and logic to the exclusion of emotion and experience. One interesting feature of intellectualization is the use of jargon to avoid emotional engagement. Using complex terminology draws our focus to words and argument rather than how human beings are affected within a particular situation. This is precisely how theodicy works.

4. Farley, *Tragic Visions and Divine Compassion,* p. 21. Farley's critique of theodicy falls within the category of "practical theodicy." Although her theological framework and conclusions differ in significant ways from the ideas presented in this book, a common strand running between the two works emphasizes the unsatisfactory nature of traditional theodicy and the need for practical rather than theoretical responses.

If we were to offer the mother of the torture victim a well thought-through theodicy that explained clearly the significance of human sin, the fall of humans, and the importance of human free-will as the reasons for her experience, what good would it do? Even if she does ask why God allowed this to happen, would the answer really help her? Would it draw her closer to God, her only source of hope, or would it push her even further away?

Again, if we offered the idea that suffering is sent into the world to test us or to make us better people to the people of Sudan, who are trapped in the midst of a famine, torture, rape, and genocide, what good would this idea do? Would it draw them closer to God or take them further from God? Indeed, what *sense* would it make?

To tell a mother whose baby is dying of starvation that it is really for the good and that she will learn valuable lessons through the experience is to develop a theodicy that may be theoretically interesting, but that in practice is evil. What kind of God are we left with if we manage, through clever intellectual moves, to fit such obscene forms of cruelty and evil into a framework that somehow justifies it and draws it within the boundaries of the love and righteousness of God? When we try, we blame either the victim, for making bad choices (either her choices or the choices of others: free will), or God and in so doing reduce both God's love and God's power. Normally, the former, blaming the victim, is the safest and the easiest option. The pastoral implications of such a move will become clear below.[5]

In the light of these initial, intuitive reflections, we can note two fundamental ideas:

1. The traditional enterprise of theodicy is meaningless.
2. Practicing traditional theodicy does not bring healing and a deeper love for God but is, in fact, a potential source of evil in and of itself.

Given these ideas, then what might be a faithful alternative to traditional theodicy, and how can we resist this mode of evil and find a form of deliv-

---

5. The point, which I will develop more fully as we move on, is that intellectual theodicy can never do what it claims to do. We can and always will speculate about why there is evil and suffering in the world and what God's relationship is to it. However, in reality, we can never know the answers to the questions that so deeply trouble us. Indeed, attempting to know the unknowable can actually create fresh suffering and evil.

erance that will enable us to develop practices that will lead to resistance and redemption?

One of the main problems with theodicy is that, particularly in its academic form, it deals with a primarily intellectual dilemma. Suffering is viewed, first and foremost, as a theological and philosophical problem to be solved and only secondarily as a human experience to be lived with. For the most part, the theodicist attempts to answer the questions raised by the existence of evil. She would not consider it her role to respond to evil in an embodied, practical fashion.[6] Consequently, the academic theodicist cannot experience the vital aspects of applying theodical thinking.[7] Theodicy, then, assumes responsibility for producing convincing answers to the complex problem of evil, but it need not be responsible for reflecting on the actual impact of evil on the lives of real people or for developing active ways to resist evil and deal compassionately and faithfully with suffering.

Thus, the approach and assumptions of theodicy stand in stark con-

---

6. Note that my argument is with intellectual theodicy, that is, the type of theodicy that is commonly done in abstraction, usually within some sort of academic setting. There is, of course, the whole question of the role of "personal theodicy" and its significance for the types of issues that I am discussing here. I cannot address personal theodicy in detail in this text, but I note that it emerges from a particular social context. The ideas, thoughts, and concepts that we use to develop a personal theodicy are not discovered in a vacuum. They emerge from our knowledge of God as we learn who and what God is from our families, friends, pastors, and others. At the heart of the enterprise of personal theodicy development lies the local Christian community. For most Christians, at the heart of that community stands the pastor. And most pastors are trained in universities or seminaries — the very places where intellectual theodicies are constructed, taught, and legitimized. This being so, even though my focus is on academic theodicy, clearly my argument has important implications for the development of personal and communal theodicies beyond the boundaries of academia.

7. An exception to this might be Gustavo Gutierrez's *On Job: God Talk and the Suffering of the Innocent* (Maryknoll, N.Y.: Orbis Books, 1987). This work clearly emerges from a context of solidarity, engagement, and struggle with evil and suffering. It wrestles with the vital question of whether there is such a thing as unmerited suffering by using the experiences of Job as a paradigm of suffering that is clearly undeserved. However, I question whether Gutierrez's work is in fact an academic theodicy or a form of practical theodicy along the lines of the schema being worked out in this book. Likewise, Daniel J. Lowe's work on theodicy, *Meaning in Suffering: A Theological Reflection on the Cross and Resurrection for Pastoral Care and Counselling* (Frankfurt: Peter Lang, 2000), emerges from a pastoral context and aims at critical pastoral engagement.

trast to the experiences of most of the world's population. Those of us who live in the world of bodies and sentient experiences do not experience evil and suffering primarily as problems to be solved through the clever use of the intellect without any reference to particularity or context. Rather, we experience them as meaningful and painful human events that are profoundly spiritual and that often threaten to separate the sufferer from the only source of real hope: faith in a loving God who will bring liberation and redemption. In other words, the problem of evil for most people is not simply that it exists, but what it means for their lives, for the lives of their families, their communities, their nation. The problem, then, is not only why evil exists, but what it *does.* The issue, then, is that traditional theodicy is primarily an intellectual enterprise, while for most people in the world theodicy (their personal and contextual "study" of the problem of evil and how it affects their understanding of and relationship with God) has a relentlessly *practical* impact and meaning.

Important cultural and philosophical reasons explain why this split between the theory and practice of theodicy has come about. We will examine these in detail in chapter two. Here we will prepare the ground for that discussion by highlighting and reflecting on the limited and narrow way in which we have come to perceive the problem of evil. Could it be that by putting our faith in the explanatory powers of theodicy we have been coerced into looking at the problem of evil in the wrong way? In looking wrongly, have we been encouraged to focus on the wrong things? As we explore this suggestion, let us look at a concept that will help raise our consciousness to some important issues: *reframing.*

Reframing Theodicy

To reframe something is to look at it from a different angle, to change the frame of reference. By doing this, we often see things that we had never noticed before. As Stewart Govig puts it,

> To "reframe" means to change the conceptual and/or emotional setting or viewpoint in relation to which a situation is experienced and to place it in another frame which fits the "facts" of the same concrete

situation equally well or even better, and thereby changes its entire meaning.[8]

Reframing changes both the situation and the responses to that situation. Reframing renders the familiar strange and the strange familiar. Sometimes, when we reframe something, our original understanding is radically and unalterably changed.

When we change the frame of reference in which we see an event, we change the meaning of the event.[9] The concrete facts of the situation remain the same, but the meaning alters significantly. Once the meaning has been changed, the range of our responses towards a particular event, action, or situation expands. Christ's death on the cross is a good example of reframing. What appears to be suffering ending in failure, when reframed in the light of the resurrection, is seen to be victory and the defeat of death. The same facts have a radically different meaning when they are reframed in the light of the resurrection.[10]

The idea of reframing raises the question, Could it be that the problem of evil might look quite different if viewed from within a different frame of reference than the one chosen by traditional theodicy? Of course, evil and suffering are real. No amount of reframing will alter this tragic fact. Nevertheless, if we change the frame in which we view evil and suffering, they might begin to look different, and that difference may be crucial for faithful living.

In this chapter, we have begun the process of reframing by taking theodicy into the realms of human experience and examining whether it has the potential for good or for evil. Beginning in human experience is important. First there is pain, and then there is reflection. Theodicy is a by-product of, or perhaps better, a response to the human experience of evil. It is, however, a second-order activity of the intellect that tends to mas-

---

8. Stewart D. Govig, *Souls Are Made of Endurance: Surviving Mental Illness in the Family* (Louisville: Westminster/John Knox Press, 1994), p. 78.

9. Donald Capps, *Reframing: A New Method in Pastoral Care* (Minneapolis: Fortress Press, 1990), p. 10.

10. Conversion is another good example of reframing. Once a person becomes convinced of the truth of the gospel and uses that new knowledge to reflect on his life past and present, he begins to see himself and his history in ways that are fresh, new, challenging, and sometimes disturbing. His history hasn't changed, nor has the world in which he now lives, but the new lens through which he now views and assesses himself and the world makes him see everything quite differently.

querade as a first-order activity of experience. Philosophical theodicy tends to forget its roots in the lives of real people and to carry out its reflective activities in abstraction from the lived experience of evil and suffering. Consequently, many apparently logical theodicies make little sense when they encounter the reality of evil and suffering as people experience them in "real time." When this happens, rather than solving the problem of evil, theodicy can easily become a source of evil in and of itself.

In chapter two, we will continue this process of reframing by exploring some of the cultural and philosophical reasons that have allowed theodicy to masquerade as a first-order activity. In the remainder of this chapter, we will lay down some necessary foundations by examining the pastoral dangers of theodicy. In testing theodicy against the raw reality of human pain and the experience of evil, we will highlight some significant problems with theodicy and in so doing begin the process of reframing it.

Theodicy in the Context of Pastoral Care

The narratives that opened this chapter indicated some of the ways in which theodicy could be impotent, unhelpful, and even dangerous when it is carried out within a pastoral context that seeks to deal with the lived experience of evil rather than the theory of evil. Theodicies that attempt to explain evil and suffering and to justify God's involvement in them can be problematic within a pastoral context in at least three ways. They can:

1. justify and rationalize evil;
2. silence the voice of the sufferer;
3. become evil in themselves.

We will examine each of these points in turn.

Theodicy Justifies and Rationalizes Evil and Suffering

Certain approaches to philosophical theodicy end up denying the reality of evil. Take for example John Hick's influential Irenaean theodicy, which he developed through reflection on the theology of Irenaeus of Lyons. Hick justifies the existence of evil, arguing that it is necessary for human beings to experience the realities of pain, suffering, temptation, and sin in order to develop into the type of people who are worthy of sharing life with God.[11] Hick puts his position this way:

> God has set us in a world containing unpredictable contingencies and dangers, in which unexpected and undeserved calamities may occur to anyone; because only in such a world can mutual caring and love be elicited.[12]

Human beings, Hick argues, are created, in some sense, at a distance from God.

> In order to be a person, exercising some measure of genuine freedom, the creature must be brought into existence, not in the immediate divine presence, but at a distance from God.[13]

In other words, if we were immediately to come into the presence of God in all of God's fullness, we would be overwhelmed by the reality of God. This being so, Hick says, it is necessary that a cognitive distance be created and maintained between human beings and God. If we did not have evil to veil God's irresistible beauty, it would not be possible for human beings freely to choose to love God. This theodicy views life as a journey on which one gradually gains knowledge and love of God as one encounters life's trials. Without the presence of evil and suffering, people would not be challenged to overcome and would therefore have no effective context for the development of their godly character. Evil and suffering provide human beings with the necessary challenges and problems that enabled them to participate in what Hick calls "soul-making."

Thus, according to Hick's theodicy, evil is not really evil at all! It just looks like evil. It is, in fact, a mode of goodness, or at least a means of achieving goodness. The presence of evil and suffering in the world enables the process of perfecting a human being's love for God. Evil is really a force for good, or at least it acts as a way of accessing that which is good. Such a theodicy makes sense intellectually only insofar as it preserves the goodness, power, and love of God and provides a clear explanation for the

---

11. Hick, *Evil and the God of Love,* revised edition (New York: Macmillan, 1985).
12. Hick, *Evil and the God of Love,* p. 50.
13. Hick, *Evil and the God of Love,* p. 43.

existence and purpose of evil. Evil exists because of its potential to develop goodness in human beings. Suffering is not meaningless, pointless, or without value. Indeed, suffering is necessary for human beings to achieve their ultimate goal: "to glorify God, and fully to enjoy him forever."[14] At one level, this theodicy seems intellectually and theologically quite sound.

However, when one takes such a theodicy into the concrete experience of suffering and evil, that which seems logical and helpful soon proves to be neither. Ray Anderson provides an illustration of the pastoral inadequacy of such a theodicy when it is brought down from the level of universal, general theory to the particularities of a human experience of suffering. Anderson tells the story of a woman who came to him for counseling after a personal disaster:

> Her story was tragic and disturbing. Six months prior [to her coming] to me for pastoral guidance, her 7 year old daughter had died of a brain aneurysm on a Sunday evening while she and her husband were attending a service in their church. The child had been left home with a babysitter and they were summoned out of the service by paramedics who responded to the call for help. Tragic as this sudden death was . . . what happened next was disturbing and the cause of outrage directed against God. The funeral service for her little girl was held in the church with the pastor officiating. During the service, in an attempt to bring some meaning and comfort to the parents, he suggested that God wanted to bring spiritual renewal to the members of the church and had selected one of their most prominent families and had taken their daughter home to be with the Lord, where she was much better off than to live in this world. God's purpose in doing this, the pastor went on to say, was to cause the members of the church to reflect upon the brevity of life and to call them to repentance and renewed commitment to the Lord. He then gave an invitation to those who wished to acknowledge their new commitment to Christ to come forward for a prayer of dedication. Following the service she never went back to the church.[15]

This story illustrates well the dangers of theodicies that deny or fail to fully acknowledge the reality and horror of evil and instead attempt to spiritual-

14. Westminster Larger Catechism.

15. Ray Anderson, *Dancing with Wolves, Feeding the Sheep: Musings of a Maverick Theologian* (Eugene, Ore.: Wipf & Stock Publishers, 2002), p. 100.

ize away the pain of suffering. For this woman, suffering was real, confusing, and painful. The suggestion that what had occurred was in fact a loving and graceful action of God, carried out *because* of the strength of the faith of her family, is more than a little odd! Such a theodicy makes God the author of evil (or perceived evil, as, of course, it "wasn't really evil" at all), silences the voice of the sufferer, and presents a dissonant picture of God and God's love. Rather than answering the question of why a good, loving, all-powerful God would allow such suffering, this theodical response to personal tragedy actually raises precisely these questions, only in a slightly different theological frame. As the bereaved mother herself put it: "I could never worship a God who would do that!"

For some, encounter with the tragic can be character-building. Suffering can be a productive teacher. But for many others, it is totally destructive. In what way would the love and compassion of God have been revealed to the people whose stories opened this chapter if someone responded to their situations by telling them that their suffering was really a good thing and that it would enable them to love God even more? I suspect they would simply say that they would rather have their children back safely in their arms than to love a God who behaves in such a way towards his creatures. Certainly, in the present we can only see things through a glass darkly,[16] so perhaps there is goodness in evil. Or perhaps there is not. We simply do not know. The inadequacy of our knowledge is a good argument for *not* trying to offer explanations. Of course, the suggestion that we should learn to live with unanswered questions jars with our cultural expectations. Every question should have an answer! In chapter two, we will explore more fully why we think this way and why to think this way is dubious and deceptive. Here it will be enough to note the tension and dissonance we feel when we are faced with unanswerable questions and the danger of trying to answer questions that, ultimately, only God can answer.

Another problem with Hick's approach to theodicy has significance for our discussion. The idea of suffering-as-character-building may have an appeal within a relatively safe and prosperous Western context. But it would, I suspect, hold little resonance for the millions of people tortured and killed in Auschwitz, murdered in the killing fields of Rwanda and Cambodia, slaughtered by their own countrymen in the Sudan, and raped

---

16. "Now we see but a poor reflection; then we shall see face to face. Now I know in part; then I shall know fully, even as I am fully known" (1 Cor. 13:12).

in the camps of Bosnia. In what sense did the pain and humiliation of those caught up in the horrors of the slave trade build their character? While some theodicists would argue that even these types of atrocities work for good in God's overall plan,[17] Hick's theodicy seems strangely culturally bound and does not sit comfortably with the mass of suffering and evil that presents itself in the world. Arguing that evil is "all for a good cause" does not ease the suffering of the world. God's character and person are not defended by developing a picture of a God who has such a lack of imagination that the only way that God can teach us to grow is through the apparently random infliction of tragedies and atrocities on men, women, and children. How or why one would wish to worship a God who appears often to be surpassed in love and mercy by God's own creatures?

The main problem with this form of theodicy is the way in which it appears to justify that which scripture says God detests: evil.[18] While such attempts to make sense of suffering and evil may be understandable and may function well at an intellectual level, the lived truth is that the evil that exists in the world can never be a good thing. Evil is tragic, awful, painful, and personal, and it should be acknowledged as such. If a theodicy urges us to forget or ignore that fact, it loses its relevance for addressing the relentless pain of the world.

Theodicy Silences the Voice of the Sufferer

A second important pastoral problem with certain forms of theodicy is well illustrated in Anderson's vignette above. By seeking to apply general and universal explanations of suffering and evil to situations that are profoundly unique and particular, theodicies often end up silencing the lamenting voice of the sufferer. Worse, they may even end up *blaming* the sufferer for her suffering. This is especially so for theodicies that directly attribute suffering to the individual or to original sin.[19] If we turn briefly

17. Richard Swinburne, *Providence and the Problem of Evil* (Oxford: The Clarendon Press, 1998).

18. A. Farrer, *Love Almighty and Ills Unlimited* (London: Fontana Library, 1966).

19. Note that the following discussion is not necessarily an argument against the idea of original sin. The doctrine may well provide useful insights and revelation. The problem arises when this doctrine is used as a theodicy in the sense being developed here, that is, as a way of explaining what is happening to particular individuals in quite specific circum-

to the thinking of St. Augustine, this point will become clear. Augustine viewed evil not as a thing in and of itself, but as a deprivation of the good creation of God.[20] The idea that evil exists is metaphysically false.[21] Drawing on the doctrine of creation, Augustine sought to affirm that all that God has created is necessarily good.[22] Since God is not capable of creating that which is evil, said Augustine, evil can have no ontological status within God's good creation. This being so, evil is not an entity, a "thing" with substance and purpose. Rather, it is a deprivation of the good, what might be described as a hole in the goodness of God's creation. Evil does not have a positive nature. Evil is nothing more than the loss of the good.

> For the Almighty God, who, as even the heathen acknowledge, has supreme power over all things, being Himself supremely good, would never permit the existence of anything evil among His works, if He were not so omnipotent and good that He can bring good even out of evil. For what is that which we call evil but the absence of good?[23]

God created the world and made everything within it good. Evil was thus not created by God. Evil is primarily a turning away from that which is good. As all goodness comes from God, evil is ultimately a turning away from God.

> For when the will abandons what is above itself, and turns to what is lower, it becomes evil — not because that is evil to which it turns but because the turning itself is wicked.[24]

Augustine wanted people to recognize that God is unquestionably good and is not the author of evil.

Understanding evil as a deprivation of the good is, in principle, helpful and will partly form the basis of the definition of evil to be presented

---

stances. This was not Augustine's intention when he defined original sin, but it is clearly the way in which theodicists use his thinking.

20. St. Augustine, *City of God* (London: Penguin Classics, 2003), 11, chapter 9.

21. See St. Augustine, *The Confessions* (Oxford: The Clarendon Press, 1992), 7.12.18.

22. "God saw all that he had made, and it was very good. And there was evening, and there was morning — the sixth day" (Gen. 1:31).

23. St. Augustine, *Enchiridion* (South Bend, Ind.: Gateway Editions, 1996), chapter 11.

24. Augustine, *City of God,* book 12, chapter 6.

in chapter three. God is good, and evil is undoubtedly a movement away from the good towards that which is not good, a movement that has tragic consequences. Augustine thoughtfully preserves the goodness of God in the face of evil and opens the way for believers to trust and relate to God despite the presence of evil. Human free will is the primary source of suffering. Therefore, God cannot lack goodness. More than that, the doctrine of original sin, pastorally considered, flattens the hierarchy of human sin, which has significant implications for the ways in which we conceptualize and practice forgiveness. If all have sinned and fallen short of the glory of God, then we are all in this together; we are all fallen, broken sinners in need of God's redemption. God loves sinners and despite the way that the world is, God longs to redeem all of creation.[25] We are all sinners, but also we are all loved by God who is reaching out to us to offer hope. Understood in this way, the doctrine of original sin has the potential to be pastorally healing. In this reading, the doctrine makes it clear that there is no moral high ground where certain of us can stand and pass judgment on others. *All* of us are sinners and *all* of us fall short. Consequently *all* of us need forgiveness, irrespective of the specific nature of our sins. We will pick up on this important dynamic later in the book when we explore forgiveness.

Problems emerge when this understanding of original sin (which, in its original context, emphasizes the inherent goodness of creation and ensures faith and trust in the goodness of God) is developed into an intellectual theodicy that attempts definitively to explain the origins of all evil and suffering.[26]

25. "For the creation was subjected to frustration, not by its own choice, but by the will of the one who subjected it, in hope that the creation itself will be liberated from its bondage to decay and brought into the glorious freedom of the children of God. We know that the whole creation has been groaning as in the pains of childbirth right up to the present time" (Rom. 8:20-22).

26. While Augustine is frequently used as an example of theodicy, such theodical activity was not his intention. He did not develop a theodicy in the way that we use that term today. His primary intention was to help people love and trust God more fully, not to defend intellectually the goodness of God. In other words, Augustine's original intention was *practical* and *contemplative* rather than theoretical; he aimed to develop people who could love God more fully, not to solve an intellectual conundrum. Problems occur when theodicists assume that Augustine and Iranaeus are speaking in the voice of post-Enlightenment Western reasoning, taking them out of their own historical context (Kenneth Surin, *Theology and the Problem of Evil* [Oxford: Blackwell, 1986]). The danger in using Augustine and

Difficulties emerge when Augustine posits human free-will as the source of evil. For Augustine, evil entered the world with the primal fall of humans, who chose, in the Garden of Eden, to exercise free will and turn from good. Evil, pain, and suffering are the products of original sin. Evil and suffering, as results of this turning away, are seen as *retribution* and sometimes *punishment* for original sin. All humans have been "infected" by this original sin. Thus, the presence of evil and suffering is explained and justified as the result of human disobedience.[27] When it comes down to it, evil and suffering are merely the inevitable product of disobedience and wrong choices by human beings. In other words, the fault lies squarely with human beings. Had we been obedient, sin and evil would not exist, but we were not, so we reap the consequences in our experiences of evil and suffering. Therefore, no such thing sufferer is innocent and no suffering is unmerited. Within the Augustinian tradition, as Smith puts it, "suffering is always in some sense of the word *deserved*. It may not be deserved by the sufferer per se, but if not, then it is deserved by someone."[28] Such an approach to theodicy solves the problem of why God would create a world within which suffering and evil exist. He didn't. Human beings cause evil through their wrong turnings and poor choices.

There may well be truth in Augustine's position, and it is not my intention here to attempt to discard or discredit the doctrine of original sin *per se*. Indeed, as I have suggested, used constructively it can become a powerful leveler that has pastoral utility. Nevertheless, the doctrine of original sin becomes highly problematic if we attempt to use it as a mode of theodicy within a pastoral context. By universally laying the

---

Irenaeus's perspectives as theodicies, as Larrimore observes, is that "Irenaeus and Augustine *seem* to be 'doing theodicy' as they wrestle with Gnostic and Manichee dualisms, but arguably their statements were never intended to be taken out of polemical and catechetical contexts" (Mark J. Larrimore, ed., *The Problem of Evil: A Reader* [London: Blackwell, 2004]). Augustine was not attempting to solve an intellectual dilemma about "*a* God." Rather, he wanted to encourage people to have faith in a very specific God, so that they could learn to love and relate *with* that God (turn back to him).

27. This disobedience need not be conscious. Augustine tied the fall closely to sex precisely to show how it is the uncontrollability of the will and the body that marked the fall and its consequences.

28. David H. Smith, "Suffering, Medicine, and Christian Theology," in Stephen E. Lammers and Allen Verhey, *On Moral Medicine: Theological Perspectives in Medical Ethics* (Grand Rapids: Eerdmans, 1987), pp. 255-66.

blame[29] for evil and suffering on the human race, the doctrine of original sin takes little account of the particular realities of human suffering and the lived experience of evil. Paul Ricoeur, in his reflections on the practical implications of the doctrine of original sin when it is used as a theodicy, notes that

> the scandal of suffering is overlooked in two ways. First, it is diluted and defused by the very expansion of negativity beyond the human predicament. Second, it is silenced by the substitution of reconciliation (of contradictions) for consolation addressed to human beings as victims.[30]

The doctrine of original sin effectively blames evil and suffering on human beings rather than on God. However, the scandal of human suffering is that not all human beings suffer equally. Surveying the world's suffering, we soon realize that it is the poorest and the most vulnerable who suffer the most. It is all very well to argue at an intellectual level that evil is caused by an original sin for which we are all responsible, but why is it that some people appear to be held more responsible than others? Why would a just God who wishes to punish humans for their disobedience not ensure that all humans were equally punished? The doctrine of original sin causes significant dissonance between theory and practice, theodicy and the experience of evil.

Even if the doctrine of original sin is correct, when it is drawn into the theodical enterprise and used to answer questions about the nature of God, questions that are asked with no reference to the unique lived experience of evil and suffering, the explanatory power of this doctrine becomes oppressive.

Suffering is always scandalous, and a theodicy that attempts to ameliorate that scandal by simply shifting blame from God to humans is inev-

---

29. The idea of free will as an explanation for the origins of evil doesn't function particularly well as a theodicy. If we grant that human beings have free will, then we must also acknowledge that God must, if only temporarily, have given up or limited his omnipotence. This being so, presumably God is not all powerful, even if that lack of power is only temporary and self-imposed. If this is so, the answer to the theodicists' question "is God all-powerful?" must be no. Augustine, of course, did not intend to develop a theodicy, so this limitation of God's power may not have been an issue for him. It is, however, an issue for a theodicy that seeks to use Augustine's thinking.

30. Paul Ricoeur, "Evil, a Challenge to Philosophy and Theology," *Journal of the American Academy of Religion* 53, no. 3 (1985): 643.

itably pastorally problematic. If my daughter, Micha, is suffering from incurable leukemia and my "comforters," like Job's counselors, inform me that an omnipotent God, who *is* love, is allowing this to happen for the purpose of some higher good, the pastoral logic of the theodical formulation quickly disappears. If these same "comforters" tell me that Micha's condition is the justifiable consequence of sin, my own or someone else's, I am going to sense injustice, anger, and outrage rather than divine love, comfort, and consolation. Worse, if suffering is the direct product of sin, then surely repentance should bring healing. If it does not, in order to protect God's omnipotence and justice, I must presume that Micha suffers because I or someone close to her remains in sin. In other words, Micha's condition is either her own fault for not being faithful enough, or my fault for not having enough faith on her behalf. Worse still, I have no right to complain about any injustice I might feel. In God's mind, what is happening is right and just; there is no such thing as "innocent suffering." I have no option other than to accept our fate. If Micha's pain and suffering are nothing more than the just consequence of original sin, then, as Ricoeur points out, "the unanswered protest of unjust suffering" is condemned to "silence in the name of a massive indictment of the whole of humanity."[31] How can I cry out to God at the injustice of the world's pain if my situation is in fact the product of divine justice and retribution? If Micha's pain is caused by my sin, then I am condemned to a lifetime of guilt, a deep, destructive guilt that brings devastation to me and prevents me from caring fully for the suffering person in front of me. Theodicies that use the doctrine of original sin to explain evil and suffering silence the voice of the innocent victim and choke the cry of lament. When theodicy functions in such a way, it becomes a *source* of evil rather than an explanation of it.[32]

31. Ricoeur, "Evil, a Challenge to Philosophy and Theology," p. 640.

32. It could be argued here that I am allowing human experience, and in particular human emotions, to determine the nature of doctrine. However, to suggest this is to misunderstand the point I am trying to make. My point is not that Augustine is wrong. It may be that in the eschaton he is proved to be totally correct. My concern is not with the authenticity of the doctrine, important as that may be (although the issues raised do offer important questions to the doctrine), but rather with its practical usage. My point is that when, within the type of cultural context outlined in chapter 3, we use Augustine to develop theodicies, which, in turn, we use to definitively *explain* the problem of evil, there are often unnoticed practical, theological, and pastoral "side effects" that can be highly problematic and destructive within the Christian community and that can, in and of themselves, lead to the creation of evil.

Theodicy Becomes Evil in Itself

In his book *The Evils of Theodicy*, Terrence Tilley argues that abstract, theoretical theodicies engage in a practice that "disguises real evils" and actually create evil.[33] Tilley suggests that theodicists are like the whispering friends of Job who torture rather than help. Their theoretical arguments hide real evils rather than lead people to a concrete response to the sufferer. We have already begun to see how such a suggestion might work itself out. In reconciling the goodness and power of God with the existence of evil, either by denying the existence of evil or by blaming human beings, the theodicist begins to develop ways of thinking that can easily become destructive rather than life-enhancing.

Richard Zaner provides a good example of the dangers inherent in certain types of theodicy. He tells the story of a two-year-old boy born with short-gut syndrome, a condition that involves either an anatomical or a functional loss of more than seventy percent of a person's small intestine. This leads to malabsorption of nutrients, which, until relatively recently, led inevitably to death. Zaner notes that the boy's parents were fundamentalist Christians who had conceived and given birth to the child out of wedlock. When it was discovered that the baby had this condition, their religious community informed them that it was a punishment from God for their sins. In response to this theodicy, the parents became withdrawn from their son. Zaner continues:

> Little wonder, we all thought when this story became known, that these young people had been acting oddly. They had to contend with their child's condition and continuous hospitalization, their own sense of having possibly done something to make it happen, and then the constant accusations from both families that they had indeed been sinful and made to suffer God's wrath.[34]

In this case, the particular mode of theodicy intensified the suffering of the couple and significantly impeded their ability to care for their son.

33. Terrence Tilley, *The Evils of Theodicy* (Washington, D.C.: Georgetown University Press, 1991), pp. 221-57.

34. Richard M. Zaner, *Troubled Voices: Stories of Ethics and Illness* (Cleveland: The Pilgrim Press, 1993). Quoted in Wendy Farley, "The Practice of Theodicy," in Margaret E. Mohrmann and Mark J. Hanson, *Pain Seeking Understanding: Suffering, Medicine, and Faith* (Cleveland: The Pilgrim Press, 1999), p. 43.

The consequence of the theodicy was not a greater understanding of God and the possibility of loving God more fully. Instead, it served to place a significant barrier between them and their son and between them and God. Functioning in this way, it challenged rather than supported perceptions of the goodness and forgiveness of God in the face of the pain and suffering of their situation. Wendy Farley suggests that this is a good example of theodicy becoming evil.[35] She has a strong point. If theodicy blocks people's access to the loving heart of God and the hope of experiencing God's redemptive power, goodness, and mercy as a living reality, then it functions in a way that can only be described as evil.

Beyond Theodicy

Our reflection thus far has indicated that when used within a pastoral context, theodicy can be a highly problematic and sometimes even dangerous enterprise. Developing rational conclusions that actually manage to justify evil and suffering as a coherent dimension of a God of love may satisfy the rationalist, but it is more likely to inspire hopeless resignation in the sufferer.[36] If God somehow desires or allows evil for a higher purpose, then surely our response should be to do the same. Is not healing suffering, therefore, in principle, an act of unfaithfulness? If good is impossible without evil, then surely we should not battle against evil but should actively encourage it in order that more good might enter the world. If the Holocaust was a good thing because it provided opportunities to be caring,[37] then why would we contemplate social and political actions that might prevent similar occurrences? Why not just let the evil of the world increase in order that God's goodness can become clearer? If Gemma's dropping dead on her way home from skating was for a higher purpose, then surely her parents have no right to mourn or complain. Indeed, to do so would be to admit to a lack of trust in the goodness of God. Viewing theodicy in the light of such questions and conclusions, we find it to be at best pastorally lacking and at worst, when taken to its logical conclusion, a rather odd and dangerous enterprise.

35. Farley, "The Practice of Theodicy."

36. My point here is not that ultimately we won't understand. The point is that we cannot in the present reach a coherent understanding through human logic.

37. Swinburne, *Providence and the Problem of Evil.*

By thus reframing theodicy, we have seen clearly the pastoral difficulties of approaching the problem of evil in this way. Nevertheless, the enterprise of theodicy is ingrained within our cultural psyche. The idea that there may be another way of framing and responding to the problem of evil and suffering does not obviously come to mind. Why is this? Why is the philosophical frame in which we have come to understand and address the problem of evil so appealing and apparently "natural" to us? Before we can begin to offer a different perspective on the problem of evil and offer an alternative response, we need to understand why theodicy seems like such a good idea.

CHAPTER TWO

The Problem with the Problem of Evil: From Philosophical to Practical Theodicy

In chapter one, we explored some pastoral problems caused by the traditional formulation of philosophical theodicy. We have seen that theodicy is pastorally problematic and offers promises that it can never keep. In this chapter we will examine the suggestion that theodicy is also questionable theologically. The heart of the argument here is that the very question theodicy seeks to answer is, in fact, the *wrong* question to ask about the problem of evil. "Why does an all-loving, all-powerful God allow evil and suffering?" may appear to be an appropriate question, but if, as I will show, theodicy is, in fact, asking the wrong question, then the actions that the question inspires may also be wrong. Challenging the validity of this question and offering alternatives can help us see clearly and live faithfully, even in the midst of evil and suffering. The task then is an important one.

Formulating the Problem of Evil

In the eighteenth century, philosopher David Hume offered an influential formulation of the problem of evil. He summed it up in a way that has come to define many philosophical approaches to theodicy:

> Is God willing to prevent evil, but not able? Then God is impotent. Is God able to prevent evil, but not willing? Then God is malevolent. Is God both willing and able to prevent evil? Then why is there any evil in the world?[1]

1. David Hume, "Enquiry Concerning Human Understanding," in *Dialogues Concern-*

Hume's formulation clearly draws out the key issues that concern the theodicist. Wrestling with the dilemma inherent within Hume's questions and propositions, developing satisfying intellectual responses to them, and reflecting critically on these responses form the essence of the philosophical task of theodicy.

At one level, such reflection and discussion might appear to be a sensible and even necessary task. All of us wrestle with the apparent incongruity between God's love and the reality of evil and have probably asked questions like Hume's. Surely there can be nothing wrong with a theological enterprise that seeks to answer such relevant questions? However logical as this may appear, if we ask another question, things begin to look different: *Why* is it so important for us to find answers to these questions? To which we might respond, "Isn't it obvious that the existence of evil and suffering in the world is a problem that requires answers and solutions? How could we *not* ask questions like these?" We live in an age when science and reason have taught us to expect to find answers to all our questions. Asking questions and solving problems is accepted practice in every other aspect of our lives; why should it not also be the case in our faith? If there is a problem, let's solve it! Framed within our cultural expectations, answering questions about the goodness and love of God in the face of evil and suffering appears to be logical and beneficial. However, as we have begun to see, the apparent benefits of such questioning may be deceptive. Does it not seem rather strange for Christians, who believe in a *created* world[2] and who believe that in Christ creation is being *redeemed,* to suggest that questioning the love, goodness, and power of God is an appropriate and "natural" response to the existence of evil and suffering? Crying out to God in hurt and pain yes, but questioning God's love? The early church did not seem to ask questions about the existence of evil and suffering in the way that Hume and the enterprise of theodicy do. Could it be that there is something about modern Western culture and its assumptions about God, evil, and suffering that makes the algebraic questions of theodicy *appear* to be the only set of questions one could ask?

---

ing Natural Religion, ed. Norman Kemp Smith (London: Thomas Nelson & Sons, 1947), p. 66.

    2. In other words, a world which is not simply a random series of meaningless events, but a created entity with order and telos.

Cultural Constructions of the Problem of Evil

The way we frame the problem of evil emerges from deeply rooted cultural assumptions about the nature and purpose of God and human beings and the meaning of evil and suffering. Our culture places great faith in the idea that, given enough intellectual reasoning and scientific knowledge, "all problems can be solved." By using science, reason, and intellectual endeavor, we assume, humans can solve most, if not all, problems. But why do we think this way?

The Enlightenment

In cultures that have been impacted by the Enlightenment, such thinking is typical. Put simply, the Age of Enlightenment was that period in European cultural history that moved away from a theological worldview, which understood God, church, and religion as central, and moved towards a worldview determined by science and reason. In his essay "What Is Enlightenment?" Immanuel Kant defined Enlightenment as

> man's leaving his self-caused immaturity. Immaturity is the incapacity to use one's own understanding without the guidance of another. Such immaturity is self-caused if its cause is not lack of intelligence, but by lack of determination and courage to use one's intelligence without being guided by another. The motto of enlightenment is therefore: *Sapere aude!* Have courage to use your own intelligence![3]

The Enlightenment assumed that human beings have "come of age," that the bonds of religion should be overthrown so that humans could be liberated to use their intelligence as the primary way to encounter the world. Through the proper use of reason and intelligence, and with the assistance of science and technology, human beings were deemed to be free, autonomous, reasonable individuals who could take responsibility for their own lives and, indeed, for the whole world. No longer did human beings require the tutelage of religion. Within the public sphere, God was replaced by an increasingly anthropocentric understanding of salvation

3. Quoted in Margaret C. Jacob, *The Enlightenment: A Brief History with Documents* (Boston: St. Martin's Press, 2001), pp. 202-8.

through human progress. God was frequently reduced to the ultimate principle of human reason, the one who set things in motion and then made human beings responsible, through the use of science, reason, and intellect, for perfecting the world.

During the Enlightenment, people began to understand *Creation* as *"the world,"* a demystified and desacralized space that had to be understood, tamed, and controlled so that humans could progress towards fulfillment and perfect order. People assumed that the universe was rational, orderly, and essentially comprehensible and that it could be controlled through reason by means of science and technology. Everything in the universe, including "God," was open to being broken down, analyzed, and explained. The mysteries of the universe and the complexities of God became acceptable loci for the ever-expanding gaze of science and human reason.[4]

Within this cultural context of belief in human progress and the growing assumption that all problems could be solved, the idea that one should frame the problem of evil in the same way as one would frame any other question appears completely natural. If all problems can be solved by science and reason, then why should theological problems not yield to the same intellectual forces? In a culture based on such assumptions, the ideas that mystery may be significant, that all problems may not be solvable through the use of reason alone, and that an important dimension of fruitful human living may involve learning to live with unanswered questions, sounds alien, disturbing, and foolish.

Understood in terms of the Enlightenment, the problem of evil appears to be just one more of the problems that humans frequently encounter and strive to solve through reason and intellect. Once we answer the questions and solve the problem, the use of human reason verifies and legitimizes faith in God. Once we are intellectually satisfied that God is worthy of our praise, we can then get on with the job of loving a God who is clearly rational and orderly and whose ways are fully comprehensible and accessible through reason and logic.

---

4. One of the clearest and most helpful texts to examine the shape, nature, and implications of these cultural changes for church and mission is David Bosch's *Transforming Mission: Paradigm Shifts in Theology of Mission,* American Society of Missiology Series, no. 16 (Maryknoll, N.Y.: Orbis Books, 1991). I would refer readers specifically to his masterful analysis of the impact of the Enlightenment on the church and its mission and the implications of this for contemporary church practices.

Before the Enlightenment: Living with Unanswered Questions

Because this approach appears so "normal," we tend to overlook the important fact that the problem of evil has not been formulated in the same way by all people at all times and in all cultures. Certainly, Hume's algebraic formulation of the problem fits well with our post-Enlightenment worldview. However, that does not make it true or definitive. It simply means that it fits well into our post-Enlightenment worldview! Approaches such as Hume's may appear timeless and universal, but in fact they are a relatively recent development.[5]

Take, for example, the perceived contradiction between the idea of a God who is all-powerful love and the existence of evil and suffering. Alasdair MacIntyre points to the fact that:

> the contradiction of a benevolent divine omnipotence and the existence of evil were not seen by the Christian thinkers of the Middle Ages as an obstacle to belief. Only after the seventeenth century did the problem of evil become the central challenge to the coherence and intelligibility of Christian belief per se. . . . *Why do the same intellectual difficulties at one time appear as difficulties but no more, an incentive to enquiry but not a ground for disbelief, while at other times they appear as a final and sufficient ground for scepticism and for the abandonment of Christianity?*[6]

MacIntyre's question is fascinating. Why does the focus of the problem of evil shift and change in significant ways across time and cultures? What is it about Western culture that makes aspects of the logical, algebraic formulation of the problem of evil so attractive and apparently normal, while at other times and in different contexts such formulations may be perceived as insignificant?

Stanley Hauerwas picks up and develops this point further. He notes, in particular, the way in which the early church responded to the presence of evil and suffering.

> For the early Christians, suffering and evil . . . did not have to be "explained." Rather, what was required was the means to go on even if the evil could not be "explained." Indeed it was crucial that such suffering

---

5. Kenneth Surin, *Theology and the Problem of Evil* (Oxford: Blackwell, 1986).

6. Alasdair MacIntyre, "Is Understanding Religion Compatible with Believing?" in *Rationality*, ed. Bryan R. Wilson (Oxford: Basil Blackwell, 1977), pp. 62-77 (italics added).

or evil not be "explained" — that is, it was important not to provide a theoretical account of why such evil needed to be in order that certain good results occur, since such an explanation would undercut the necessity of the community capable of absorbing the suffering.[7]

Hauerwas's point is important. Early Christians didn't seek to explain evil and suffering, at least not in the abstract, rationalistic way of theodicists. Instead, they chose to frame evil and suffering quite differently. Their response to the problem of evil and the existence of suffering was not to question God's goodness, love, and power, but rather to develop faithful forms of community within which the impact of evil and suffering could be absorbed, resisted, and transformed as they waited for God's return. The early Christians did not separate the question of suffering from their calling to be people of faith. As Hauerwas puts it:

> [H]istorically speaking, Christians have not had a "solution" to the problem of evil. Rather, they have had a community of care that has made it possible for them to absorb the destructive terror of evil that constantly threatens to destroy all human relations.[8]

Instead of developing abstracted philosophical theodicies, the early church responded to evil by building theodic communities. In other words, their response was profoundly *practical* rather than philosophical. "Suffering was not a metaphysical problem needing a solution but a practical challenge requiring a response."[9] The key response was to help individuals and communities persevere in the faith and endure their experiences until Christ returned. In 2 Thessalonians 1:4-11, the apostle Paul highlights this dimension of the early church communities:

> Therefore, among God's churches we boast about your perseverance and faith in all the persecutions and trials you are enduring. All this is evidence that God's judgment is right, and as a result you will be counted worthy of the kingdom of God, for which you are suffering. God is just: He will pay back trouble to those who trouble you and give relief to you who are troubled, and to us as well. This will happen when the Lord Jesus is revealed from heaven in blazing fire with his powerful

7. Stanley Hauerwas, *Naming the Silences* (Grand Rapids: Eerdmans, 1990), p. 49.
8. Hauerwas, *Naming the Silences,* p. 53.
9. Hauerwas, *Naming the Silences,* p. 51.

angels. He will punish those who do not know God and do not obey the gospel of our Lord Jesus. They will be punished with everlasting destruction and shut out from the presence of the Lord and from the majesty of his power on the day he comes to be glorified in his holy people and to be marveled at among all those who have believed. This includes you, because you believed our testimony to you. With this in mind, we constantly pray for you, that our God may count you worthy of his calling, and that by his power he may fulfill every good purpose of yours and every act prompted by your faith.

Paul does not try to explain why there is evil and suffering. He simply calls the church to persevere and hold on to the faith even in the midst of suffering. Paul's focus is not on this world (although this world does hold significance for Paul). All that the church experiences in the present must be understood in terms of the glory it will experience in the future. When Christ returns, he will redress the imbalance between good and evil. Until then, Christians must learn to persevere in faith, hope, and love.

The theodicist's image of God is focused on a generalized god-figure rather than on the intricate and specific history of the Trinitarian God who is revealed in the life, death, and resurrection of Jesus. In contrast to the theodicist's, the early church's response to evil was *christological* and *eschatological*.

Jewish Roots: Awaiting the Messiah

Telford Work points to the Jewish roots of the early church and their significance in the developing understanding of the early Christian church.[10] Work argues that, in first-century B.C.E. Judaism, a recognized response to the existence of evil lay in the way in which the Jewish people perceived the significance of the coming Messiah.[11] For many Jews, the eschatologi-

10. Telford Work, "Advent's Answer to the Problem of Evil," *International Journal of Systematic Theology* 2, no. 1 (March 2000): 100-111.

11. Work correctly highlights the fact that it is probably fair to say that there was no real uniformity or formal coherence to the various Jewish responses to evil and injustice. Nevertheless, "the figure(s) of the Messiah and the Son of Man figured prominently in many, and it was from these circles that Christianity seems to have emerged" ("Advent's Answer," p. 110).

cal promise of the coming Messiah was God's answer to whether God had abandoned Israel to a world of injustice. This tradition emphasized the figures of the Messiah and the Son of Man as "solutions" to the problem of evil. These figures would later come to be associated with the person of Christ. The "solution" lay in the belief that it was the Messiah who would bring about an end to evil and suffering when he ushered in the coming eschaton. Like Paul, the Jewish people saw evil and suffering as things that it was necessary to endure in the present, with the hope that relief would be provided by the coming eschaton. Evil and suffering would be defeated as the future eschaton was initiated and completed in the Christ figure.

Work suggests that it was from this context and with this set of theological presuppositions that the early Christian church emerged and engaged with the reality of evil and suffering:

> The first Christians shared this expectation (John 2:45), and associated Jesus' career with the coming of the age of justice (Luke 19:38). Even when Jesus died, rose, and ascended without apparently having brought the promised age to pass, so strong was the Christian belief that Messiah was the answer to the world's suffering and evil that Christians quickly associated Jesus' *second* coming with the full arrival of the age of justice. (italics added)

Within this eschatological perspective, early Christians saw life in the present as transient and not definitive of human fulfillment, hope, and expectation. The "solution" to the problem of evil was the return of Christ and the subsequent defeat of evil and suffering. In *response* to the problem of evil, the early church communities created a context within which such faith and hope could be nurtured and sustained even in the presence of evil and suffering, in the expectation that it would ultimately end with the return of Christ. As Paul puts it in Philippians 3:20, "Our citizenship is in heaven. And we eagerly await a Savior from there, the Lord Jesus Christ." The hope of ultimate redemption and liberation from evil and suffering was always on the horizon; it was this future hope that enabled people to tolerate and make sense of suffering in the present.

Contemporary Thinking

This early Christian way of understanding and responding to evil and suffering differs markedly from the response offered by contemporary theodicy. It stands in contrast to the assumptions that Enlightenment thought has taught us to adopt in response to the experience of evil and suffering. A key aspect of the Enlightenment was its turn towards the individual and the subsequent emphasis on personal happiness and self-fulfillment as an achievable human goal. Attaining and maintaining happiness has become a primary human goal and ultimately a human right. Evil and suffering are perceived first and foremost as a threat to our *personal* happiness and well-being. Those of us who share such assumptions about life's telos are not impressed with the suggestion that our present life is insignificant when compared with eternity, or that we may have to struggle *together* against evil and suffering. We assume that life should be pleasant and make sense in the present and that God should be judged, not by future promises, but by God's actions in the present world. This takes a significant turn away from the community-oriented christological and eschatological discourse of the early church. Interestingly, within such a context and worldview, the idea of theodicy becomes not only *possible* but absolutely *necessary*.

Why Theodicy Has Become "Necessary"

Reason, science, and technology have undoubtedly provided many benefits for humanity. Nevertheless, they have also had some interesting and often overlooked "side effects" that are important for understanding why we do theodicy as we do and why we think the questions asked by theodicy are natural and inevitable. Take, for example, advances in medicine. At one level, medicine has offered us the possibility of freedom from, or at least the alleviation of, many forms of horrific sickness. Medicine has taken tremendous steps to overcome disease, and many millions of people have reaped the benefits of this mode of practically-oriented human knowledge. However, as well as enhancing our lives, successes in medicine have significantly altered our expectations about the inevitability of suffering. Increasing successes in medicine bring with them increased expectations that suffering should no longer be a part of our experience. We no longer see suffering as inevitable. Within a context where, for example, a high rate of infant mortality is considered the "norm," the meaning of and approach to suffering and life-expectancy will be quite different from a context within which infant mortality is considered rare and avoidable. Within a context where there is gross, uncontrollable suffering, there is no need for theodicy. However, as Marquard points out, in a context where it is assumed that suffering is not inevitable, theodicy becomes necessary:

> Experience of life seems to me to show that when one is up against suffering, under its immediate pressure, the problem is never theodicy; for what is important then is simply the ability to hold up through one's suffering or one's sympathy. It is stamina in enduring, in helping, and in comforting. How can I reach the next year, the next day, the next hour? In the face of this question, theodicy is not an issue, because a mouthful of bread, a breathing space, a slight abbreviation, a moment of sleep are all more important in these circumstances than the accusation and the defense of God. Only when the direct pressure of suffering and compassion relents, under conditions of distance, do we arrive at theodicy. . . . [T]he modern age is the age of distance: the first epoch in which impotence and suffering are not the taken-for-granted and normal state of affairs for human beings.[12]

It is interesting that, while in previous times evil was perceived as the source of suffering, in today's context, where suffering is not assumed to be the norm, *suffering is perceived as evil*.[13]

As the experience of suffering begins to relent, questions one asks about evil and suffering and the responses one develops begin to change. The problem of evil, as it is presented within the type of philosophical theodicy examined thus far, emerges in an acute form within a relatively stable and affluent social context in which suffering no longer *appears* to be a necessary part of life.[14] The advances in science and technology from

12. Odo Marquard, "Unburdenings: Theodicy Motives in Modern Philosophy," in *In Defense of the Accidental: Philosophical Studies,* trans. Robert M. Wallace (New York: Oxford University Press, 1991), pp. 8-28.

13. The early church found itself involved in a situation of grinding, uncontrollable suffering, persecution, and affliction. Consequently, the mode of responding to evil and suffering mirrored, at least to some extent, the social context within which it was experienced.

14. I stress the word "appears," because in reality suffering is an inevitable part of life, and it is only partially eased by advances in technology and only for some.

which Western society has benefited have created a cultural psyche within which people assume, perhaps for the first time, that the inability to act decisively against evil and the necessity of suffering are not normal. This, combined with the Enlightenment mindset that assumes that all problems are solvable, meant that the idea of theodicy would inevitably emerge. Indeed, it became a *necessary* aspect of any form of rational belief in God.

While the cross-centered faith of the early church allowed them to accept suffering and evil as inevitable dimensions of living in a world that was, in some sense, fallen and broken, post-Enlightenment Western culture has different expectations of God, expectations that reflect the type of culture within which we reside and the particular worldview that guides it. Within such a culture it is easy, even for Christians, to accept the algebraic approach to theodicy as normal.

All of this provides the background for beginning to understand why theodicy has developed as it has within Western culture and why all of us who participate in or are influenced by that culture simply tend to assume that theodicy is a correct and indeed the only way to respond to the problem of evil and suffering.

The God of the Philosophers

Perhaps the most troubling thing about philosophical theodicy is how unclear it is about who their god is. Who is the god whose love, power, and goodness are being challenged by the theodicists? In his critique of traditional philosophical theodicies, Kenneth Surin points out that

> It is certainly no exaggeration to say that virtually every contemporary discussion of the theodicy-question is premised, implicitly or explicitly, on an understanding of "God" overwhelmingly constrained by the principles of *seventeenth and eighteenth century* philosophical theism.[15]

This important observation resonates with the discussion presented thus far. The god that is the object of traditional theodicy is what we will call, after Pascal, *the god of the philosophers,* a god who is a free-floating, ahistorical entity. Pascal describes the god of the philosophers in this way:

15. Surin, *Theology and the Problem of Evil*, pp. 4, 76, 106n12.

> I shall not undertake here to prove by reasons from nature either the existence of God, or the Trinity, or the immortality of the soul, or anything of that kind . . . because such knowledge without Christ is useless and sterile. Even if someone were convinced that the proportions between numbers are immaterial, eternal truths, depending on a first truth in which they subsist, called God, I should not consider that he had made much progress to his salvation. . . . The Christian's God does not consist merely of a God who is the author of mathematical proofs and the order of the elements. . . . But the God of Abraham, the God of Isaac, the God of Jacob, the God of the Christians is a God of love and consolation: he is a God who fills the soul and heart of those whom he possesses: he is a God who makes them inwardly aware of their wretchedness and his infinite mercy; who unites himself with them in the depths of their soul; who fills it with humility, joy, confidence and love; who makes them incapable of having any other end but him.[16]

Pascal distinguishes between the absolute, rational, acontextual god of the philosophers and the personal, engaged, and historically active God of the Christian scriptures who addresses the world in the person and work of Jesus Christ, a God who is deeply embedded in a very particular narrative that is peopled by real individuals: from Abraham through Moses to Christ, the one who lived, died, and rose again. A god that can be found without that specific narrative may make an interesting philosophical concept, but it bears little if any resemblance to the Christian God. The problem with theodicy is that it is precisely this type of faceless god that it chooses as the object of its philosophical reflection.

Philosophers perceive their god as an abstracted object of investigation that can be understood without any necessary reference to history, historical processes, particular instances of God's action, or people's lived experience of good or evil. They assume that such a god is impassible, universal, and timeless. They presume that the arguments they use to justify the existence, power, goodness, and love of this god are reasonable and logical to all humans, in all cultures, and throughout all periods of history. Theodicies based on the god of the philosophers perceive evil and suffering as dislocated ideas that enter into the theodicist's conversation as abstract concepts rather than as unique divine or human experiences.

16. Blaise Pascal, *Pensées,* trans. A. J. Krailsheimer (London: Penguin Books, 1966), p. 449.

Significantly, such philosophical proof of the goodness of God is explained without any necessary reference to the person of God, Jesus, or the Holy Spirit or to the triune God's particular salvific actions in history. This is an important point. The specific actions of God in response to evil, particularly as they are revealed in the life, death, and resurrection of Christ, are not part of the discourse of philosophical theodicists. By omitting the historical actions of God and narrowing the argument over the problem of evil solely to the question *Why does God allow evil?* rather than, for example, *What does God do in response to evil?*, vital epistemological dimensions of the problem of evil are omitted, dimensions critical for an understanding of God that is genuinely Christian.

By constructing the argument in this way, theodicists present the unusual possibility that God is *not* loving, *not* powerful, *not* good, *not omnipotent,* and so forth, *unless* this can be proved intellectually. Such a line of questioning cannot be sustained if one takes seriously the doctrines of grace, creation, redemption, and providence. If we are residents in God's creation, saved by grace through Christ, and if in Christ the whole of creation is being redeemed, then why would we feel the need to ask questions about God's love and power? Even though there is clearly evil and suffering in the world, it is being redeemed. Does not the important question relate to the redemption of creation rather than the existence of evil: "What is God doing in response to evil as he seeks to redeem the world?" Suffering is temporary. The question is not whether God is loving and powerful enough to destroy evil and suffering.[17] The incarnation and the resurrection of Jesus are living proof of God's love and power. The questions arise (or should arise) in relation to whether or not we can sustain our faith in a way that retains the eschatological hope of redemption even in the midst of evil and suffering. Viewed in this way, theodicy could be viewed as a mark of faithlessness. It asks questions about God that are simply inappropriate and perhaps even idolatrous.[18] It asks the wrong questions from the wrong

17. Assuming these are taken as true. Of course, because such beliefs appear as foolishness to those who base their faith in reason, they cannot authentically be considered part of the equation.

18. John Howard Yoder offers a useful argument on the idolatrous nature of theodicy. Theodicy in some way or another means "that someone holds that there exists a criterion whereby some kind of human process of adjudication (the root dikein or dikazein means to adjudge) will test whether God measures up. But then that other criterion, by which we measure God, is really (functionally) our God. Or the person doing the measuring has be-

starting point. It seeks to begin and end in human reason rather than accepting the apparent unreasonableness of divine revelation.[19]

If this is so, then we can see the theodical enterprise as, at least, questionable, and at worst, idolatrous. The god of the philosophers is *not* the triune God of Christian history. As Terrence Tilley puts it, "for better or for worse, [within traditional theodicies] the particularity of Christianity, in which the figure of Christ and the doctrine of the Trinity are essential, is ignored."[20] Karen Kilby makes a similar point:

> The God whose compatibility with evil they [philosophers of religion] discuss is presented as an abstract entity with a number of characteristics, a God who can be described without reference to any particular narratives, without any discussion of Incarnation, Christology, Trinity.[21]

In the discourse of theodicy, God becomes an argument; a free-floating concept that can be separated from the specifics of the narrative of God, Jesus, and concrete realities of the continuing practices of the Christian community. The christological dimensions of an understanding of evil and suffering, which we have seen were so important for the early church, are subsumed to an amorphous and undistinguished form of theism. Theodicy viewed within this frame is incompatible with Christian faith.

---

come functionally god. The concept itself (and not merely one answer or another to it) is, in other words, a buck-passing, question-begging, or petitionary move. The prior questions are (a) Where do you get the criteria by which you evaluate God? Why are the criteria you use the right ones? (b) Why do you think you are qualified for the business of accrediting God? (c) If you think you are qualified for that business, how does the adjudication proceed? What are the lexical rules?" Importantly, Yoder points out that "it would seem prima facie that 'theodicy's being an oxymoron might not have to be the case for all possible "gods." It suffices to be clear that it is the case for JHWH/Adonai of the Hebrew tradition and for Abba the Father of Jesus, and for Allah for whom Mohammed spoke. It is the case for any God conceived of as "true" and as "jealous."' Theodicy may then be appropriate for the god of the philosophers, but it has no place within thinking which is focused on the God of Christian scripture." In John Howard Yoder, "Trinity versus Theodicy: Hebraic Realism and the Temptation to Judge God," unpublished paper, 1996. See http://www.nd.edu/~theo/research/jhy_2/writings/philsystheo/THEODICY.htm.

19. "For the message of the cross is foolishness to those who are perishing, but to us who are being saved it is the power of God" (1 Cor. 1:18).

20. Terrence Tilley, *The Evils of Theodicy* (Washington, D.C.: Georgetown University Press, 1991), p. 223.

21. Kilby, "Evil and the Limits of Theology," *New Blackfriars* 84, no. 983 (2003): 13-29.

What Does Evil Do?

The observations on the problems with theodicy that have been offered in this chapter and the last have presented us with a quite different frame within which to view the problem of evil. They have opened up the possibility of a very different set of responses. If we assume that the proper starting point for understanding the problem of evil should be the human experience of evil and the specific actions of the triune God within these experiences, rather than the "concept of evil" and the "concept of a loving God," we begin to see the problem of evil differently. If we start with the human experience of evil, then the question *Why does evil exist?* is always held in critical tension with a second question that is, I would argue, more important: *What does evil do?* Answering the first question will not necessarily bring relief, release, or hope. Suppose that when my friend's daughter Gemma died on her way home from skating I had answered George's pained cry "Why me?" with the words, "Because you had an affair three years ago and God is angry with you. God had no compunction about taking the life of King David's son,[22] so you are really not in a position to complain!" (I hasten to add that George did not have an affair!) (This would not be a ridiculous theodicy and it is one for which I could gather some scriptural support.) Would George really have wanted that answer? What good would it do? Would it move George closer to or further from God?

The second question, "What does evil do," has much more potential for bringing healing, even if culturally we are more inclined to focus on the first question. In asking what evil *does,* we move the problem of evil away from abstract theory and speculation and begin to ground it in the human and divine encounter with evil. Evil has practical consequences, and these practical consequences have divine significance. Above all else, what evil does is to separate human beings from their primary source of hope: *God.* The problem of evil is its propensity to tear human beings asunder from their identity and purpose as creatures made in the image of God and loved by God beyond all things. In other words, the problem of evil is *practical* and *theological,* relating to evil's ability to prevent human beings from fulfilling their goal to love God in all things and above all

---

22. 2 Sam. 11.

things. This quite significantly reframes the nature and consequences of the problem of evil.

This central, theological dynamic means that any response to what evil does must aim not only to mend those who are broken by the effects of evil (although it does of course include this), but also and most importantly to enable and sustain faith even in the midst of evil and suffering. Upcoming chapters will make clear the significance of this point. Here it will be enough to recognize that the problem of evil relates to the impact of *what evil does,* rather than why it exists. To reframe the problem of evil in this way, from a theoretical question to a practical one, is not to "change the subject" of theodicy.[23] We are still working through what it means to sustain belief in a good, loving, all-powerful God in a world that is filled with evil and suffering. It *is,* however, to acknowledge that traditional ways of framing the problem of evil are deeply flawed and misguided both in content and purpose. We need a new approach to theodicy, one that recognizes the vital practical and theological aspects that have been hinted at thus far and that seeks to embody strands of theodical practice within particular forms of community that can absorb the pain and suffering that threatens to overpower our world.

---

23. That is, to move from one set of questions to another that is totally unconnected to the first.

CHAPTER THREE

Defining Evil

Before we move on, it is important to make clear the implications of the arguments presented in chapters one and two. I am *not* suggesting that there is no explanation for the way the world is and why there is so much evil contained within it. I am not arguing for unfathomable mystery as the key to the problem of evil. Scripture tells us that ultimately we will know and understand. As the apostle Paul puts it in his first letter to the Corinthians:

> Now we see but a poor reflection; then we shall see face to face. Now I know in part; then I shall know fully, even as I am fully known. (1 Cor. 13:12)

All will be revealed in the fullness of the eschaton. The point of the preceding chapters is that, because of the limited nature of our present understanding and the inevitable boundaries of our intellect when it comes to fathoming the ways of God,[1] we cannot reach a coherent understanding of the reasons for evil and suffering. While our cultural mindset and expectations may demand concrete answers to all of our questions, in reality, some questions simply have no answers. Indeed, attempting to answer them can be dangerous, meaningless, and offensive to those who are forced to live through the experience of evil and suffering. Over the past hundred years, more human beings have killed each other than at any

---

1. "Can you solve the mysteries of God? Can you discover everything there is to know about the Almighty?" (Job 11:7, New Living Translation).

other point in history. Chris Hedges reminds us of the horrors that have occurred even within the past fifteen years:

> Look just at the '90s: two million dead in Afghanistan; 1.5 million dead in the Sudan; some 800,000 butchered in ninety days in Rwanda; a half million dead in Angola; a quarter of a million dead in Bosnia; 200,000 dead in Guatemala; 150,000 dead in Liberia; a quarter of a million dead in Burundi; seventy-five thousand dead in Algeria; and untold tens of thousands lost in border conflict between Ethiopia and Eritrea, the fighting in Colombia, the Israeli-Palestine conflict, Chechnya, Sri Lanka, southeastern Turkey, Sierra Leone, Northern Ireland, Kosovo, and the [first] Persian Gulf war (where perhaps as many as thirty-five thousand Iraqi citizens were killed). In the wars of the twentieth century not less than sixty-two million civilians have perished, nearly twenty million more than the forty-three million military personnel killed.[2]

Combine this with the loss of life in two World Wars and the Holocaust, and the fact that every day thirty-four thousand children die from lack of adequate nutrition, and we find that the logic of theodicy begins to fade very quickly. Only a very few privileged elite have been fortunate enough not to be touched by evil and death on a massive scale. Trying logically to correlate God's love and power with such dreadful events in the form of some kind of philosophical, algebraic equation is insulting both to God and to the victims of such horrific evil.

The first two chapters have highlighted the fact that what we need is not an answer to the question of why God allows evil, but rather an ability to live with unanswered questions and still retain faith in the goodness of God and the hope of God's providential promises. We require, not clever arguments, but resistance practices that will enable people to persevere and sustain their faith in the midst of evil until the time comes when there will be no more suffering and tears.

The first two chapters have suggested that we have been framing the questions relating to evil and suffering in the wrong way. In this chapter we will continue this process of reframing as we examine a key question: *What is evil?* To answer this question, we will continue to reframe our un-

---

2. Chris Hedges, *War Is a Force That Gives Us Meaning* (New York: Anchor Books, 2002), p. 13.

derstanding of the nature of the problem of evil, which in turn will lead us to a different theodical and practical response. We will argue that the problem with evil is not so much its *existence,* as our *response* to its existence. In other words, it is not how we conceptualize and "solve" the problem of evil and suffering that is important, but how we respond faithfully to the problem. Developing this suggestion will help us see that the ways in which the Christian community should respond to the reality of evil and suffering are much deeper and more theologically rich and complex than simply finding answers to the problem of the relationship between a good God and the existence of evil. Only when we firmly grasp what evil *is* and what evil *does* can we truly begin to understand what the problem with it actually is and how we should respond to that problem.

Varying Definitions of Evil

So far, we have used the term "evil" as if it had a universal and instantly recognizable meaning. Deeper reflection informs us that this is clearly not the case. Similarly, like theodicists in general, we have used the term "suffering" as if it were synonymous with evil. In this chapter we will challenge both suggestions and argue that while suffering always accompanies evil, not all suffering is evil.

The concept of evil contains a multitude of diverse meanings that alter from person to person, context to context, and culture to culture. Some understand it in evolutionary terms of having survival benefits.[3] Others attribute evil directly to the specific actions of the Devil or his demons.[4] Evil can be used to rationalize actions that seem unexplainable. Some have noticed the gendered nature of assigning the label "evil": Women are more likely than men to be called evil in certain circumstances.[5] Others have observed the way in which people with certain forms of mental illness are labeled "evil," even within a therapeutic con-

3. P. Thompson, "The Evolutionary Biology of Evil," *The Monist* 85, no. 2 (2002): 239-59.

4. John Wimber and Kevin Springer, *Power Healing* (San Francisco: HarperSanFrancisco, 1991).

5. M. Barker, "The Evil That Men, Women, and Children Do," *The Psychologist* 15, no. 11 (2002): 568-71. For a theological exploration of gender issues as they relate to evil, see I. Gebara, *Out of the Depths: Women's Experience of Evil and Salvation* (Minneapolis: Fortress Press, 2002).

text that claims to be secular.[6] Clearly, there is no universally agreed-upon understanding of precisely what the term "evil" means or to whom or what it refers.

This becomes particularly interesting within the context of our discussion of theodicy. If there is no universally agreed-upon definition of evil, then how can we develop a universally applicable logical explanation as to why it exists? Philosophical inquiry requires a degree of clarity regarding the concepts it is working with. If such clarity is missing, the enterprise must surely become suspect. The lack of clarity over the definition of evil and over precisely what the problem with evil is poses significant difficulties for theodicy. If we can't definitively tie down what evil is, then how can we solve the problems that it brings?

Evil and Suffering

Intuitively we might assume that evil should primarily be equated with suffering. Framed in this way, the problem of evil is essentially the problem of human suffering and why God allows suffering to happen.[7] This idea, however, assumes that *all* human suffering is necessarily evil. David Morris notes this tendency and ties it to developments within postmodern culture:

> The advent of postmodern times have seen evil not so much transformed as turned inside out. Evil has long been understood by theologians and by popular audiences . . . as the *cause* of suffering. The postmodern era has redefined suffering *as* evil. Suffering becomes one of the few agreed-upon new shapes that evil assumes in the postmodern world.[8]

Our brief discussion above on the many definitions of evil illustrates how, within a fragmented postmodern context, evil has come to take on a vari-

---

6. J. Richman, D. Mercer, and Y. Mason, "The Social Construction of Evil in a Forensic Setting," *The Journal of Forensic Nursing* 10, no. 2 (1999): 300-308.

7. A good example of this merging of evil and suffering can be found in A. B. Pinn, *Why, Lord?: Suffering and Evil in Black Theology* (New York: Continuum, 1995).

8. David B. Morris, "The Plot of Suffering: AIDS and Evil," in Jennifer L. Geddes, ed., *Evil After Postmodernism: Histories, Narratives, Ethics* (New York: Routledge, 2001), p. 60.

ety of shapes, one of the most powerful being suffering. Suffering is not simply the product of evil, it *is* evil.

But must we tie suffering and evil so tightly together? Is suffering really evil, or could it be that only some forms of suffering are evil? Might there be a way in which we can take suffering seriously without giving it the status of evil and thereby raising the types of pastoral problems that we explored in chapter one? To answer these questions, we will find it helpful to change the frame a little and take the question of what evil *does* just as seriously as the question of what evil *is*.

A Theology of Evil: Two Perspectives

Here we will work out a distinctively *theological* prespective on evil. More specifically, this might be described as a practical, christological understanding of evil, an understanding of evil rooted in the nature and person of Christ and the practical implications of such knowledge for faithful living. By considering the vital theological dynamics present in the early church and by focusing on the person of Christ and the nature of his redemptive mission, we can develop an understanding of evil that will enable us to reframe the problem of evil in significant ways. This new frame will form the basis of the specific responses to evil that we will work out in the later chapters of this book.

Traditionally, evil has been divided into two primary types: *moral* and *natural*.

Moral Evil

Theologians consider moral evil to be the product of human action or the failure of humans to act in particular situations. If individuals did or did not act in particular ways, moral evil would not exist. Murder, rape, torture, and child abuse all come under the banner of moral evil. Moral evil also functions in a wider communal dimension. For example, evils such as mass starvation are often the product of complex political processes that work together to cause that particular form of evil. Given the political will, these situations could be mended, but often there is no such will. Moral evil, then, is evil that is perpetrated, directly or otherwise, by human beings. In other words, there is an element of moral responsibility to such evil. Suffering, and in particular innocent suffering, inevitably accompanies moral evil. Moral evil assumes both a *victim* who is the object of the experience of evil and a *perpetrator* who is in some way directly or indirectly morally responsible for the ways in which she acts towards the victim.

Natural Evil

The second theological perspective on evil comes under the heading of *natural* evil. Natural evil differs from moral evil in that it is *not* the direct product of human action or inaction. Natural evil is the product of the world being the way the world is. It comprises events that humans cannot control and do not inflict upon themselves. Natural evil includes such things as earthquakes, diseases, tornadoes, and hurricanes, occurrences that inflict suffering on humans in ways over which they have no power or control. Death, particularly the type of sudden, unexplained death of children like Gemma, on whose tragic death we reflected in chapter one, would come under this category. When Gemma's heart stopped beating, no one was to blame; she was the victim of a form of natural evil that is mysterious and unexplainable in this life. Human beings are not directly culpable for natural evil. It simply occurs because that is the type of world in which we live. For those of us who find ourselves victims of natural evil, there is no one to blame.

Is All Suffering Evil?

The framework of moral and natural evil helps us develop a general perspective on what evil is. Conceptually separating "natural" from "moral" evil allows us to focus in on that which human beings can take active responsibility for in the present, and that over which human beings have no control. The division between natural and moral evil fits well with the overall understanding of evil and suffering necessary for the philsophical practice of theodicy. Placing *all* of human suffering under the banner of "evil" presents, in neat form, the raw material for the philosophical exploration of God's character. All suffering is, by definition, evil and is therefore the legitimate subject of theodical reflection.

51

While the division between moral and natural evil is in some ways useful as a rough conceptual guide, in practice it is problematic. Few would argue that such things as murder and child abuse do not slip easily under the banner of "evil," according to most definitions of the term. However, identifying as distinctly evil such things as earthquakes, tornadoes, and bones broken in accidents does not sit quite so easily with our intuitive definition of evil. When people choose to carry out devastating actions on other human beings, defining evil seems relatively straightforward. However, whether it is appropriate to use the same term, "evil," to describe both the Holocaust (a case of moral evil) and the death of an elderly man from heart failure (a case of natural evil) is much less clear. That is not, as we shall see, to suggest that the death of an elderly man from heart failure *cannot* be an evil event, only that it need not be. Certainly, both modes of evil produce forms of suffering that are in some sense deprivations of God's goodness. Scripture indicates that such events were not part of the original goodness that God had planned for the world. "God saw all that he had made, and it was very good. And there was evening, and there was morning — the sixth day" (Gen. 1:31). In this sense, one might find some rationale for using the term "evil" in a blanket manner.

Nevertheless, to suggest that all forms of suffering are evil is to run the risk of defining the term so broadly that it loses its potency.[9] Equating all forms of suffering with the term "evil" dangerously widens and waters down the impact of the term in a way that can easily blind us to the crucial pastoral, eschatological, and relational dimensions of what we might describe as *real* evil. I will argue below that, while all forms of suffering have the potential to become evil, evil and suffering are not necessarily synonymous. Suffering is always tragic, but it need not be, nor become, evil.

A Theological Definition of Evil

In working towards an understanding of evil that will guide the remainder of the book, we should begin by noting certain key assumptions that Christians have about the world:

9. Seen from a pastoral perspective, framing all suffering as evil by definition risks instilling in sufferers the type of unhelpful guilt that was highlighted and argued against in chapter one.

1. We live within God's creation. The doctrine of creation informs us that we are residents in a world that we do not own.[10] Despite the presence of evil and suffering, Christians still believe that the place in which they reside belongs to God, is sustained by God, and ultimately will be redeemed by God through Christ.[11]

2. The world is not the way that it should be or the way that God planned it to be. Something very wrong has occurred that has caused creation to move from a position of goodness to one of suffering and tragedy.

3. But, we are not left alone to face the rigors of the world. In the person and work of Christ, we discover God gently and lovingly transforming and re-creating the world.[12]

4. Christians wait in hope for the day when that re-creating work will be completed. Despite the presence and reality of evil and suffering, the world is being shaped by a God whom we believe to be loving, just, and present in and for the world, who will, in God's providential time, "wipe every tear from their eyes. There will be no more death or mourning or crying or pain" (Rev. 21:4).

These four basic presuppositions form the necessary bedrock for an effective theological account of evil.

In the face of the magnitude of the world's suffering, this deceptively simple account of the way the world is and how it will be might not appear particularly logical; it cannot be captured within the limited boundaries of human reason and knowledge. (See 1 Corinthians 1.) This view of the world requires a different frame of understanding. While it does not ex-

---

10. This suggestion implies that any enterprise that thinks it can argue God out of existence is necessarily fundamentally flawed.

11. "I consider that our present sufferings are not worth comparing with the glory that will be revealed in us. The creation waits in eager expectation for the sons of God to be revealed. For the creation was subjected to frustration, not by its own choice, but by the will of the one who subjected it, in hope that the creation itself will be liberated from its bondage to decay and brought into the glorious freedom of the children of God" (Rom. 8:18-21).

12. "Since we have now been justified by his blood, how much more shall we be saved from God's wrath through him! For if, when we were God's enemies, we were reconciled to him through the death of his Son, how much more, having been reconciled, shall we be saved through his life! Not only is this so, but we also rejoice in God through our Lord Jesus Christ, through whom we have now received reconciliation" (Rom. 5:9-11).

clude reason, the Christian narrative must be seen through the eyes of *faith*. It is as we approach the problem of evil with the eyes of faith that our understanding of precisely what the problem is begins to shift. Luther describes faith in this way:

> Faith is God's work in us, that changes us and gives new birth from God (John 1:13). It kills the Old Adam and makes us completely different people. It changes our hearts, our spirits, our thoughts, and all our powers. It brings the Holy Spirit with it. Yes, it is a living, creative, active, and powerful thing, this faith.[13]

Faith offers us a profound way to reframe ourselves, the world around us, and the God who sustains both. It is not something that is achieved through human endeavor. Rather it is something that is received in intimate communion with the Holy Spirit and that is worked out in faithful lives of discipleship. Luther continues:

> Faith is a living, bold trust in God's grace, so certain of God's favor that it would risk death a thousand times trusting in it. Such confidence and knowledge of God's grace makes you happy, joyful, and bold in your relationship to God and all creatures. The Holy Spirit makes this happen through faith. Because of it, you freely, willingly, and joyfully do good to everyone, serve everyone, suffer all kinds of things, love and praise the God who has shown you such grace.[14]

Faith, then, is countercultural. It is not a work of reason; indeed, it is not something that, on their own, human beings can achieve at all. It is an act of God's grace wherein a person learns what it means to live in the power of the Holy Spirit and to love God in all things, even in suffering. Faithful Christians are called to look beyond our present sufferings and to live among them in the light of that which is to come. As Daniel Migliore puts it:

> [While] the inauguration of the reign of God has happened "once for all" (Rom. 6:10) in Jesus Christ, believers know that they must continue

13. Martin Luther, "An Introduction to St. Paul's Letter to the Romans," *Dr. Martin Luther's Vermischte Deutsche Schriften,* trans. Robert E. Smith, ed. Johann K. Irmischer (Erlangen: Heyder and Zimmer, 1854), vol. 63, pp. 124-25.

14. Luther, "An Introduction to St. Paul's Letter to the Romans," p. 125.

to watch, pray, and struggle for God's new world in the company of all who are afflicted and cry for deliverance.[15]

To adopt such a faithful stance within the world, we must develop an *eschatological imagination*. The term "eschatological imagination," as we will use it here, refers to a way of perceiving the world that is not bounded by assumptions about the way that things seem to be according to our present understanding. Eschatological imagination is inspired and sustained by God's promises in scripture of how things will be. Such a position presumes that knowledge of Christ and his redemptive movement within history has practical implications for the present and that the ways in which we live in the present have eschatological rhythms and echoes. The church's practices bring into the present, if only partially, the possibilities of the eschaton. When we view the present in the light of the future, we begin to perceive both differently.

This being so, we might offer an initial definition of evil in this way:

> *If God is the creator, and if in Christ God is working towards the redemption and re-creation of fallen creation, then evil is defined as everything that stands against God and his intentions for the well-being and transformation of human beings and God's creation.*

This definition is a helpful beginning point insofar as it implies that evil is not a necessary dimension of human suffering. Rather, suffering *becomes* evil when it interferes with or blocks the process of the re-creation of the good in Christ. Suffering in itself is, therefore, not inherently evil. Suffering may be tragic and inevitable because of the type of world in which we live, but it is not inherently evil. *It is forms of suffering that specifically impede the purpose of God for human beings that are truly evil.* In other words, evil only becomes real in the midst of suffering when it interacts negatively with the good purposes God desires for human beings. Things such as heart failure, cancer, and diabetes are not inherently evil *unless* they initiate a crisis of faith that draws people away from God. On the other hand, crushing suffering such as the Holocaust is inherently evil, partly because it is clearly a deliberate violation of human beings who are made in the image of God and loved by God beyond all things. But it is also evil

15. Daniel L. Migliore, *Faith Seeking Understanding: An Introduction to Christian Theology* (Grand Rapids: Eerdmans, 1991). p. 119.

because it draws people away from God or even the possibility that there is a God, thus actively blocking God's redemptive mission.[16]

If this is so, then evil is not defined by suffering *per se*. Likewise, the reframed problem of evil does not relate to suffering in general, but to particular forms of suffering that serve to block or impede the possibility of loving God and sharing in God's eschatological hope for the world. Understood in this way, the problem of evil is not simply why suffering exists, but *what evil does* in the midst of suffering, and in particular, what evil does to faith in the midst of suffering.

What Does Evil Do to Faith?

In Genesis 1:31a, we find this statement: "God saw everything that [God] had made, and indeed, it was very good." If we begin our exploration of what evil does at this point, rather than at the point of the fall, which is often the norm in defining the origins of evil, some interesting aspects emerge. Sam Wells observes that "The Christian story does not begin with sin but with God's decision to be in relationship with humanity and the whole creation."[17] God created the world and called it good. God created human beings and called them very good. God loved human beings and desired to relate with them. This relational dynamic was challenged but not altered in the fall. In a world so marred by evil and suffering, we can easily forget this aspect of the creation narratives. God's love for creation remains steadfast despite the way the world has become.[18]

To lose our sense of the original goodness of creation and God's parent-like delight in it is to miss out on a vital dynamic of human history. Susan Nelson points out that

> A central tenet of the Christian faith is that the world in which human creatures abide is a "creation," formed, ordered, and blessed by a Creator who has named it good. The earth, our bodies, and our passions,

16. Such evil draws not only its immediate victims away from God, but it also draws away those who inherit the cultural and psychological trauma of these events.

17. Sam Wells, *Improvisation: The Drama of Christian Ethics* (Grand Rapids: Brazos Press, 2004), p. 169.

18. "For God so loved the world that he gave his one and only Son, that whoever believes in him shall not perish but have eternal life" (John 3:16).

our dependency upon one another, our strengths, and our vulnerabilities, the complexities of life lived in community with all sorts of creatures — all of this is good.[19]

Certainly, sin must be introduced into our narrative of the created order. All was not well in the Garden of Eden. Not to introduce sin into our narrative is to create·a false world and a false consciousness within which grace is cheapened beyond recognition. Without sin the cross is meaningless. However, the way in which sin is introduced is important.

> The fact that a declaration of God's overarching purpose precedes it [sin] means that it does not have the first word — it is not a given, it is not something that must be accepted with resignation, as the tragedy of the human condition. It is a later, secondary interruption of an original, possibly restorable relationship.[20]

Sin, evil, and suffering are undoubtedly realities in the world, but they are secondary realities, intruders into the goodness of the world. As such they require, indeed demand, to be resisted in faith and hope rather than resigned to with stoicism and despair. Goodness is our original state, even if sin is an unavoidable part of our inheritance. The turn towards evil drags us into a state that is alien to the desired purposes of the creator. The presence of evil separates us not only from God, but also from our true selves. As such it needs to be strongly resisted. Resistance relates to the faithful participation in Christ's redemptive movement in the world now and in the future. Evil is that which blocks and fragments Christ's work of reclamation, restoration, and redemption and prevents human beings from experiencing the loving presence of God in and for the world.

Different Types of Suffering

Evil is always accompanied by suffering, but not all suffering is evil. The type of suffering that accompanies evil needs to be understood in a quite

---

19. Susan Nelson, "Facing Evil: Evil's Many Faces — Five Paradigms for Understanding Evil," *Interpretation* 5, no. 4 (October 1, 2003): 398.

20. Sam Wells, personal correspondence with the author, reproduced here with permission.

specific way. Nelson provides a helpful insight that will help us tease out the particular form of suffering that is the product of evil. Reflecting on the tension between the original goodness of creation and the reality of human suffering, she notes that the

> disjuncture between the pronouncement that "it is good," that life is God's good creation over which we also proclaim God continues to exercise providential care, and the knowledge that suffering and violence are real and threaten not only life and health but also a sense that there is meaning, order, and blessing is the awareness of evil. *Evil is that experience of suffering, misery, and death and the accompanying fear that such suffering undermines any hope that there is meaning and order in the world or a God who exercises providential care.*[21]

This perspective on evil captures some crucial dynamics of what evil *does* as well as what it *is*. Evil is present in experiences of suffering, misery, and death that strip a person of the possibility of finding meaning and hope and leave one facing the prospect of dealing with the experience without feeling the assurance of God's providential love, hope, and presence. To face a situation within which one encounters such hopelessness is to find oneself in the presence of evil. When individuals or systems implicitly or explicitly engender or even nurture such experiences in the lives of others, they are acting in an evil manner. To be able to face such experiences and retain a sense of meaning, hope, and the possibility of God's providential presence is to engage in a powerful mode of resistance to evil.

Karen's Story

An illustration will help make this point. Karen was twenty-four years old when she walked into the sea. She had taken an overdose of the pain-killer Paracetamol, and just to make sure that the job was done, she chose to wander into the freezing sea at midnight. When she was just four years old, she had begun to be abused, first by her father and then by her brother. There was no one whom she could tell, no one who could save her. Eventually, she began to believe that was just the way life was. Evil began to seem the norm in her life. The abuse did not stop until she left

21. Nelson, "Facing Evil," pp. 398-99.

home at age sixteen. But the darkness and inner death remained. "Something is dead inside of me," was how she described it. "There is a darkness in my soul that nothing can reach, a pain so deep that I cannot live with it at times.... They have destroyed my life and ... no one knows it ... just me and God ... and where was he? Where was God? Where was God!? They are evil ... pure evil."

In a certain sense, Karen was dead before she died. Her experience of evil had stripped her of a meaningful life and turned what should have been fullness into deep despair. Her suffering and hopelessness were beyond the abilities of most others to identify with, which in itself added to the disconnection and isolation that are primary marks of the experience of evil. The sense of being isolated and trapped, along with the endlessness of her suffering, dislocated her from God, from herself, and from others. Karen's suffering had a very particular meaning that moved it from tragic suffering to the experience of evil. Karen's experience of evil destroyed the possibility of her experiencing the goodness and providential care of God, and it evoked a crisis of meaning and hope, plus a deep sense of existential suffering, that ultimately took her life. Her experience was truly evil in a way that other forms of suffering clearly are not.

The *Real* Problem of Evil

Drawing on Nelson's insights, we are now in a position to offer a definition of evil that will guide the remainder of this book:

> *Evil occurs when human beings or systems created and controlled by human beings carry out actions that deliberately or consequentially engender forms of suffering, misery, and death which are marked by the absence of hope that there is meaning and order in the world or a God who exercises providential care.*

The *real* problem of evil is not simply that evil and suffering exist, but rather its ability to separate suffering human beings from the only true source of healing and hope: knowledge of the love of God and a sense of providential meaning and hope. Evil is that which destroys hope in and love for God. Events within the world that bring about suffering are not inherently evil; they can, however, *become* evil if they are given the power to separate the sufferer from the hope and meaning that emerges from faith and a providential understanding of and relationship with God. So the loss of a child like Gemma is not necessarily evil, but it is certainly tragic. It *becomes* evil when the suffering and misery that such a death evokes place a wedge between the grieving parents and their relationship with and faith and hope in God. If George's cry "Why, Lord!" tears him away from God and into a void of meaninglessness and alienation from God, then Gemma's death will have become a locus for evil. If, however, her parents can find a means of persevering in their faith and can discover ways of coping with her death that enable them to maintain hope in the love and providential goodness of God *despite* the pain of their suffering, then evil has been resisted and the possibility of a good and hopeful outcome becomes real. Systems and approaches to pastoral care, or indeed any other dimension of the church's formal or informal practice, that exclude a focus on developing ways of restoring such a relationship with God and creating a context for a hopeful outcome can easily find themselves functioning in ways that are implicitly or explicitly evil.

Note that one can become implicated in evil without noticing it. Through the simple act of not noticing or not bothering to think about what one is doing or what is going on around one, a person can find himself implicated in and, indeed, perpetrating evil. That we have not noticed our involvement in evil does not abrogate our responsibilities, as the parable of the sheep and the goats in Matthew 25 makes clear. Thinking about evil and noticing ways in which we may be implicated in it is a critical task with eternal consequences. We will explore this in some detail in chapter seven.

It follows, then, that *evil actions are not qualitatively different from other forms of human action.* We will look at this suggestion in some detail in chapter six. Here simply bear in mind that, while we might want to project our understandings of what evil is and what comprises evil actions onto particular individuals or systems that carry out high-profile evil actions, the understanding of evil developed in this chapter points to the fact that evil may be found in the most apparently mundane of situations. As we will argue later, even the most obscene forms of evil can stem from roots that are quite banal. If correct, this observation has at least two consequences.

First, as the book moves on we will see that evil actions, even those that we would consider extreme, are not perpetrated by monsters but by fellow human beings for whom the possibility of redemption is always real and available. We will argue that there is no category of "evil persons" or "sub-human beings" who carry out evil actions. To a degree, all human beings are capable of the most dreadful acts of evil. This raises significant questions as to how the Christian community should deal with the perpetrators of evil actions.

Second, *any* action that separates people from God has the potential to become evil. One would imagine that this is why Paul in 1 Timothy 1:8-11 places lying alongside murder and killing one's parents in his reflection on the sinfulness of human beings:

> We know that the law is good if one uses it properly. We also know that law is made not for the righteous but for lawbreakers and rebels, the ungodly and sinful, the unholy and irreligious; for those who kill their fathers or mothers, for murderers, for adulterers and perverts, for slave traders and liars and perjurers — and for whatever else is contrary to the sound doctrine that conforms to the glorious gospel of the blessed God, which he entrusted to me.

Small actions that, at one level, seem relatively innocuous can have longer-term consequences that are evil.

Tragedy and Evil Are Not Synonymous

The understanding of evil we have developed thus far in this chapter raises a number of important and contentious issues, chief among them being the tension between suffering that is evil and suffering that is not. By our understanding of evil, suffering, misery, and death are always tragic, but they need not in themselves be perceived as evil or even as direct products of particular acts of sinfulness. The key point is that, when we understand suffering, misery, and death within the context of the Christian narrative of creation, providence, and redemption, then we see them as dimensions of the *tragic* structure of a creation that is not as it should be, but which remains the subject of God's providential redemptive care, love, and action. Tragedy and evil are not synonymous.

The Tragic Structure of Creation

The suggestion that creation has "tragic structure" is evocative and helpful in some ways if we think it through properly. First, let us be clear about what this means. In discussions of theodicy, we find the term in its most developed form in Wendy Farley's critique of theodicy in her book *Tragic Vision and Divine Compassion*.[22] We use the expression here in a different sense from Farley, but it is important to begin by exploring her use of the term. Farley argues that while it is true that the world was created good, it is also true that the original goodness was always fragile. The potential for brokenness is woven into the very fabric of creation. She argues that

> created perfection is fragile, tragically structured. . . . The potential for suffering and evil lie in the tragic structure of finitude and cannot be overcome without destroying creation.[23]

In Farley's view, suffering is an inevitable dimension of living within the type of creation that has been given to us. To have a world that was not fragile and did not contain the possibility of tragedy would be to have a different creation from the one in which we reside.

In developing her position, Farley draws on process theism to work out an understanding of the relationship of God to creation. In her view, God is deeply and intrinsically involved with creation in a di-polar sense. The term "di-polar" indicates that in some respects God never changes and in others God always does; there is a sense of continuity in God and yet still an openness to change and surprise. Farley weaves her way through a difficult path that enables her to preserve the differentiation of God from creation, thus avoiding pantheism, while at the same time viewing God as working through creation as a redemptive power that enables creation itself to overcome its intrinsically tragic structure of finitude and evil. In this way, she establishes creation as "authentically other than God but at the same time, [as something that] evades complete determinism at the hands of divine power."[24] Farley's God is a God who is woven into the struggle of divine eros in order to evoke order out of chaos

22. Wendy Farley, *Tragic Vision and Divine Compassion: A Contemporary Theodicy* (Louisville: Westminster/John Knox Press, 1990).

23. Farley, *Tragic Vision and Divine Compassion,* p. 123.

24. Farley, *Tragic Vision and Divine Compassion,* p. 127.

and meaning out of suffering. Her God is a God of love and commitment to creation, but who has non-absolute power. The endpoint of God's endeavors to redeem the world remains tentative and uncertain.

Farley's position is helpful in a number of ways. It reminds us of God's deep involvement with creation and God's constant redemptive movement of creation towards redemption (or, in Farley's perspective, the *possibility* of redemption). She also highlights the importance of recognizing the fragility of creation and its intrinsically tragic dimensions due to its finite and temporal nature. In so doing, Farley moves us away from a viewpoint that would suggest that creation is in itself somehow evil. In her perspective creation is not inherently evil — fragile yes, but not evil. Creation may contain evil, but it is not in and of itself evil. Farley points out that while creation may not be inherently evil, it is most certainly tragic. This being so, human life within such a creation will inevitably contain aspects of tragedy. This is a helpful insight.

Nevertheless, Farley's theodicy, while it is more practical than most, remains problematic. It is difficult to equate her God of limited power working towards an outcome that is less than certain with the God of scripture and the certainties of the eschatological outcome that are recorded there:

> The wolf will live with the lamb, the leopard will lie down with the goat, the calf and the lion and the yearling together; and a little child will lead them. The cow will feed with the bear, their young will lie down together, and the lion will eat straw like the ox (Isa. 11:6-7).

Isaiah's statement about the end times gives no indication that the wolf *might* live with the lamb or that the lion *may* eat straw. Rather, with faith and the use of his eschatological imagination, Isaiah offers a certainty about the outcome that is missing from Farley's position. When the apostle Paul in his discussion of the Eucharist states, "For whenever you eat this bread and drink this cup, you proclaim the Lord's death until he comes" (1 Cor. 11:26), he gives no indication that the Lord may not come or that, if he does, his redemptive mission may be less than fully successful. Scripture claims a certainty that makes Farley's God of limited power problematic.

That Farley positions God in the midst of the struggles of creation is appropriate and important. One of the main problems with theodicy as it has been outlined in this book is the way in which it loses sight of the immanence of God by focusing almost solely on God's transcendent dimensions. Scripture is equally as concerned with the immanence of God as with God's transcendence. As Migliore correctly observes, "God is present with the creatures both as co-agent and as co-sufferer."[25] The immanent presence of God in the world, reconciling the world to God's self, reveals the important fact that

> The destructiveness of evil in creation can be overcome not by divine fiat but only by a costly history of divine love in which the suffering of the world is really experienced and overcome by God.[26]

At the center of this divine involvement is the cross of Christ, the ultimate sign of atonement. Yet, Farley argues that "tragic suffering cannot be atoned for; it must be defied."[27] Again, it is not clear how Farley squares such a position with the scriptural witness, which is clear that *all* suffering and death *has been* atoned for and indeed conquered in the sacrifice of Christ *in spite of* the continuing presence of evil and suffering.[28] Certainly, suffering should and indeed must be resisted and defied, but that resistance and defiance takes place within a world that has been offered, even if it has not yet fully appropriated, the atoning sacrifice of Christ. Without the knowledge of that atoning sacrifice, we would have no meaningful basis for resistance or defiance. It is true that Christ's atoning sacrifice does not "make up" for the suffering experienced by individuals. However, it does assure the victims of evil of God's solidarity with them and God's continuing presence in the midst of suffering, thus opening up the possibility of finding meaning in suffering and having hope in the providential goodness of God. The uncertainty surrounding God's providential actions that forms a center-point of Farley's argument seems to run contrary to the eschatological certainties revealed in the cross and the resurrection of Christ.

25. Migliore, *Faith Seeking Understanding,* p. 115.
26. Migliore, *Faith Seeking Understanding,* p. 115.
27. Farley, *Tragic Vision and Divine Compassion,* p. 29.
28. "The sting of death is sin, and the power of sin is the law. But thanks be to God! He gives us the victory through our Lord Jesus Christ. Therefore, my dear brothers, stand firm. Let nothing move you. Always give yourselves fully to the work of the Lord, because you know that your labor in the Lord is not in vain" (1 Cor. 15:56-58).

The Importance of Tragedy

Nevertheless, despite these difficulties and tensions, the fact that Farley highlights the importance of tragedy in understanding suffering remains significant, although we need to put the idea of tragedy into a particular frame. Ray Anderson offers some useful insights into the nature of tragedy as it relates to creation. In line with the arguments presented here, he suggests that tragedy is not by itself evil, though it can be the precondition of evil. In Anderson's perspective,

> the freedom of creation in its own authentic nature as differentiated ontologically from the Creator is only tragic from the perspective of human beings who are endowed with a spiritual nature (Imago Dei), which promises a destiny beyond that of its own creaturely nature. . . . For all creatures but the human, their nature determines their destiny. For the human creature, their destiny lies beyond the power of a creaturely nature, though humans "suffer" from the exigencies of a creaturely nature.[29]

Suffering is an inevitable, if tragic, consequence of living in the type of world we have and of being made in the image of a God who *is* suffering love. Anderson continues:

> In this way, love is "intrinsically tragic" for it is an investment of the self (the power of personal, spiritual being) in the face of the powers of nature, over which it is, at times, powerless. The power of love to risk itself in the course of a history over which it has no absolute power is a different kind of power. It is what I call a "third dimension" of power, which operates in our two dimensional world (physical and social) with spiritual intentionality, concrete commitments, and eschatological hope. This is the kind of suffering which is not due to evil, but rather due to the contingencies of the created order, which is only fragile because human beings are "fragile creatures" due to their spiritual nature.[30]

To love requires fragility and vulnerability. It requires an opening up to the other in a way that inevitably makes the lover vulnerable and open to being

29. Ray Anderson, personal correspondence with the author, reproduced here with permission.
30. Anderson, personal correspondence.

65

either loved or broken. The world was created out of love and for love. Creation is fragile because it is underpinned by divine love, which is both powerful and inevitably fragile. Human beings are fragile because they are made in the image of the triune God who *is* suffering love. Genuine love means opening oneself up to the possibility of rejection. The inevitable consequence of such a love and the process of loving is fragility. The fragility of love, even divine love, is embodied and enacted in the Christian narrative from the Garden of Eden right through to the New Jerusalem.

Perhaps, then, rather than talking about the fragility of creation, it might be better to speak of the fragility of humankind. The type of fragility that Anderson highlights is unique to human beings. It is true that we often use the term "tragic" to describe events that occur to nonhuman creatures, but perhaps this is nothing more than a projection of the human tragic sense onto and into the created order.[31] Evil, then, is the "intensification of the tragic measured by its power to attack and destroy the good that God intended."[32]

Grounding Resistance in Suffering Love

If this is so, then God is all-loving and does indeed have "absolute power"; but the nature and purpose of that power are radically different from our culturally bound expectations. It is a radical form of power grounded in suffering love, a form of love that suffers the fragility and fate of humanity under sentence of death and has overcome this tragic state through resurrection. The source and the revelation of this power are given to us in Christ. As Tom Torrance puts it:

> This movement of God's holy love into the heart of the world's evil and agony is not to be understood as a direct act of sheer almighty power, for it is not God's purpose to shatter and annihilate the agents and embodiments of evil in the world, but rather to pierce into the innermost center of evil power where it is entrenched in the piled-up and self-compounding guilt of humanity in order to vanquish it from within and below, by depriving it of the lying structures of half-truth on which it

31. Anderson, personal correspondence.
32. Anderson, personal correspondence.

thrives and of the twisted forms of legality behind which it embattles itself and from which it fraudulently gains its power. Here we have an entirely different kind of and quality of power, for which we have no analogies in our experience to help us understand it, since it transcends every kind of moral and material power we know.[33]

It is therefore only through the cross of Christ that we can see and understand how God deals with evil in this world and how the church, which follows and seeks to image such a God, should act in response. Torrance continues:

Yet this is only at the cost of an act, utterly incomprehensible to us, whereby God has taken the sorrow, pain, and agony of the universe into himself in order to resolve it all through his own eternal righteousness, tranquility, and peace. The center and heart of that incredible movement of God's love is located in the cross of Christ, for there we learn that God has refused to hold himself aloof from the violence and suffering of his creatures, but has absorbed and vanquished them in himself, while the resurrection tells us that the outcome of that is so completely successful in victory over decay, decomposition, and death, that all creation with which God allied himself so inextricably in the incarnation has been set on the entirely new basis of his saving grace.[34]

In Christ, the evil and suffering of the world are absorbed and transformed. In like manner, the community that seeks to image God and wait faithfully for the return of God's Messiah is called to develop modes of being and forms of action that will similarly absorb suffering and resist evil. Precisely how this task might faithfully be fulfilled will form the content of the remainder of this book.

The understanding we have developed thus far of evil, its separation from other forms of suffering, and God's response to its presence gives us a framework within which we can accept that (if not fully understand why) there are suffering, misery, and death in the world and begin to understand what it might mean to resist such evil. The presence of suffering, misery, and death reveals the tragic structure of God's creation, a form of tragic

33. Tom Torrance, *Divine and Contingent Order* (New York: Oxford University Press, 1981), p. 136.

34. Torrance, *Divine and Contingent Order*, pp. 13, 139.

brokenness that runs throughout scripture like a golden thread. Evil is always accompanied by suffering, but not all suffering is evil. Such a position is not a theodicy in the traditional sense of the word; it doesn't explain why there is evil, but it does help us to understand who God is, what evil does, and what it might mean to live with the reality of evil in a way that maintains our faith and hope in the providential goodness of God.

Learning to Live with Unanswered Questions

In this chapter we have developed a foundational understanding of what evil is and what it does that will guide the remainder of the book. The perspective offered here reframes "the problem of evil" from an intellectual dilemma that requires to be solved to an issue of faith, hope, and perseverance that needs to be embodied and lived out. In so doing, we have reframed the problem of evil from a philosophical dilemma to a relational task. That task has to do with discovering ways of enabling people to retain meaning and hope in the providential goodness of God *despite* the presence of evil. Such a reframing takes evil seriously, and in acknowledging the difference between the crushing, radical evil of the Holocaust and the accidental breaking of an arm, this reframing lets us begin to discern the presence of evil in a way that is honest, faithful, and ultimately, potentially transformative. The definition of evil developed in this chapter has also tentatively raised the important issue of our need to be vigilant concerning our own implication in various forms of evil. *Evil is not something that "others" do; it is something that each of us has the potential to become involved with.* We must, therefore, be both vigilant and resistant.[35]

The movement from philosophical theodicy to issues of lived faith, hope, and perseverance brings us closer to the ways of the early church and the scriptural witness that they left behind and opens the way for a return to a more practical, christological approach to the problem of evil. The question, then, is how we might begin to achieve such a goal.

---

35. "Be self-controlled and alert. Your enemy the devil prowls around like a roaring lion looking for someone to devour" (1 Pet. 5:8).

CHAPTER FOUR

From Theodicy to Resistance:
Developing the Practices of Redemption

Suffering yearns more for experiences of healing presence than for logical arguments. Theory can provide some meaning to suffering, but it is in compassionate relationship that suffering discovers redemption.

Wendy Farley

Removal of the effects of evil is the exorcism of evil wherever it occurs.

Ray Anderson,
Dancing with Wolves, Feeding the Sheep

The Philosophers have only interpreted the world, in various ways: the point, however, is to change it.

Karl Marx and Friedrich Engels, *On Religion*

In chapter two, we reflected on Stanley Hauerwas's suggestion that the early church did not attempt to develop theodicies but rather sought to create communities within which the impact of evil and suffering could be absorbed, resisted, and transformed as the people of God waited for Christ's return to earth. We saw how difficult it is for post-Enlightenment minds to accept such a suggestion. It makes no sense to view evil and suffering eschatologically if the culturally acceptable understanding of eschatology relates primarily to human progress. Offering rational arguments that try to make

69

sense of the apparent discrepancy between the existence of evil and the existence of an omnipotent, loving God appears to be a much more logical response to the problem of evil than developing patterns of faithful practice in the face of the unanswerable questions raised by the existence of evil. Nevertheless, as we have seen, philosophical theodicy is pastorally problematic and theologically questionable. If, as we have argued, the problem of evil is profoundly practical for most of the world's population, and if evil relates first and foremost to real experiences that threaten to separate human beings from sustaining hope in God's providential love, then theodicy is clearly a practical problem that requires a practical response.

To suggest that theodicy is a practical task is not to say that we reject intellectual activity for a form of atheoretical pragmatism. As Felderhof correctly points out:

> To look at a topic practically is not to concede that it is any the less intellectual, since practical problems can require considerable intellectual application. There is a difference, for example, between the thoughtful action of a skilled master and the blundering deed of an apprentice. It is the applied intellect and experience that make the difference. An overriding commitment to the intellect does not, therefore, necessitate the abstract approach of traditional theodicies. Use of the intellect can be the hallmark of both theory and practice.[1]

In working out a practical theodicy, we take seriously the contribution of intellectual activity in responding to the problem of evil but recognize that intellectual activity is not an end in itself, but rather a means for developing transformative perspectives and practices that will enable faithful living.

In this chapter, we will begin to develop a practical theodicy and to tease out some of the implications of what it might mean to create communities that absorb suffering and enable people to be sustained in their faith until the Sovereign God returns.

---

1. Marius C. Felderhof, "Evil: Theodicy or Resistance?" *Scottish Journal of Theology* 57, no. 4: 398.

Foolishness to the Greeks

At the heart of any Christian understanding of God's response to sin, evil, and suffering is the cross of Christ. It is in and through the cross of Christ that God has defeated evil and initiated an unstoppable movement towards the eschaton. In Christ's death on the cross, we discover the ultimate, practical solution to the problem of evil. Suffering is redeemed and healing is initiated in and through the wounds of Christ.

> He himself bore our sins in his body on the tree, so that we might die to sins and live for righteousness; by his wounds you have been healed (1 Pet. 2:24).

While suffering and evil are not immediately eradicated in the cross of Christ, they are ultimately defeated. On the cross Jesus "disarmed the powers and authorities, he made a public spectacle of them, triumphing over them by the cross" (Col. 2:15). The suggestion that evil was defeated on the cross makes little logical sense. The world is still wracked with pain and suffering; evil frequently appears to triumph over good. The suggestion that the victory is won seems bizarre and illogical. As Paul puts it, "For the message of the cross is foolishness to those who are perishing, but to us who are being saved it is the power of God. For it is written: 'I will destroy the wisdom of the wise; the intelligence of the intelligent I will frustrate'" (1 Cor. 1:18). The solution to the problem of evil can be grasped only by faith and can then be embodied in practices that witness to the truth of Jesus' victory over death and evil.

The strangeness of the cross is important. If God's response to evil is strange, unexpected, and counterintuitive, then it may well be that the responses of those who follow God and await the return of the Messiah will be equally as strange, unexpected, and counterintuitive. If the cross offers a theodicy that is embodied and practical, so also should the church.

The message of the cross is also important insofar as it locates God firmly within the realm of human suffering. The solution to the problem of evil that God offers on the cross is not abstract condolence but costly solidarity. God's response to evil is practical, embodied, costly, and painful. Theodicists move away from engagement with creation into abstract reflection. As God seeks to redeem creation and to put an end to evil and suffering, God moves *towards* creation through radical gestures of redemption. These gestures, ultimately exemplified on the cross, are powerful blows to the darkness of this age; but the power of these blows is not earthly or human power that crushes or annihilates evil. Rather, God demonstrates power in gestures of redemption that appear foolish and pointless in the eyes of the world. But, scripture informs us, it is through these gestures that God is transforming the world.[2] In the cross of Christ, we discover victory and redemption, even when all that we can see is defeat and suffering. In the cross of Christ, we see one man behaving strangely: forgiving his torturers, crying out to God in lament, handing over the welfare of his mother to his best friend. These strange gestures seem small and weak in the eyes of the world. And yet, it is precisely through these gestures that we discover the possibility of redemption, providential hope, and the certainty that evil will not have the ultimate victory. In this chapter, we will argue that by practicing gestures of redemption that reflect the gestures of God in the face of evil, the church can live faithfully in the midst of evil and suffering until Christ returns.

Gestures of Redemption

In her reflections on the horrors of Auschwitz, Susan Nelson notes how the threat of random cruelty from which one could find no protection added to the terrifying hopelessness of the prisoner's experience. The conditions of the camp and the treatment of prisoners emptied their lives of meaning and hope and forced them to focus almost exclusively on issues of survival. However, survival and hopelessness were not always the final words.

> [P]risoners at Auschwitz *practiced acts of resistance* to the evil of that place. Some destroyed a crematorium (and were executed for their act); others resisted evil by *practicing* simple acts of justice and kindness that bore witness to a world order different than the terror and cruelty imposed by the Nazis.[3] (italics added)

---

2. "God was reconciling the world to himself in Christ, not counting men's sins against them. And he has committed to us the message of reconciliation" (2 Cor. 5:19).

3. Susan Nelson, "Facing Evil: Evil's Many Faces — Five Paradigms for Understanding Evil," *Interpretation* 5, no. 4 (October 1, 2003): 410.

She goes on to give one prisoner's account:

> The loaf of camp bread, always the same shape, was supposed to be cut into four pieces, one for each prisoner. It never was that way. We never got more than one slice. All the rest vanished on the way to us. Many hands grabbed their share as the bread rations were distributed to us: the kitchen kapo and company, the barrack kapo with his court, the room supervisor and his pals. Only at the end of the line, we, the prisoners, with our primitive scales made with a stick, weighed those slices, and even then we divided up the bread crumbs so that every thing was equal. That was our internal justice.[4]

Here, in a most startling way, in the context of the darkest form of evil, the simple act of sharing crumbs of bread with equity became a witness to an order of justice that challenged the dominant order. Victor Frankl, in his reflections on his experiences in Auschwitz, makes a similar observation:

> We who lived in concentration camps can remember the men who walked through the huts comforting others, giving away their last piece of bread. They may have been few in number, but they offer sufficient proof that everything can be taken from a man but one thing: the last of the human freedoms — to choose one's attitude in any given set of circumstances, to choose one's own way.[5]

Both Frankl's story and the narratives related by Nelson highlight the possibility that through simple gestures of redemption, even the most profound modes of evil can be challenged and resisted. Even in the midst of the deepest darkness, small gestures can bear powerful witness to the possibility that the way that things are is not the way they should be or indeed will be. Simple gestures such as these — sharing bread; offering comfort, friendship, and consolation — broke through the evil and offered hope and humanness within a context quite consciously designed to destroy both. These gestures did not prevent the evil or bring it to an end. Nor did they offer an explanation for it. They did, however, make a profound statement that evil does not need to have the final word. The expe-

4. Nelson, "Facing Evil," p. 410.
5. Viktor E. Frankl, *Man's Search for Meaning: An Introduction to Logotherapy* (New York: Washington Square Books, 1984), p. 86.

rience of evil in the camps drove some, the Kapos, to participate in acts of evil.[6] But others resisted the evil through simple gestures of redemption that provided hope in the face of extreme hopelessness. It seems that such apparently futile gestures have hidden powers.

Responding Strangely in the Face of Evil

Consider another example from quite a different context. In October, 2002, Robert Stewart Flores Jr., a nursing student at the University of Arizona, entered the nursing school and shot three of his nursing professors. His reasons? He had received failing examination marks, which raised the possibility of him failing to make the grade as a nurse. The story is, to say the least, sobering. Flores entered the classrooms of the professors and shot them in cold blood in front of their students and his classmates. He approached his task coldly and calmly, executing each professor with clinical efficiency. Before killing one of the women, Barbara S. Monroe, Flores asked, "Are you ready to meet your maker?" According to witnesses, "She choked out a 'yes,' and then he shot her." After shooting her, he told the other students to leave. Later, police officers searching the school found him dead.[7]

This incident is clearly horrific and evil. On the surface of it we see nothing but chaos, evil, and innocent suffering. Our temptation is to launch into the standard questions of theodicy: "How could a God of love and power allow this to happen, particularly to people who seemed to be God's followers?" However, if we reframe the story and look at it from a slightly different angle, we will discover a spiritual dynamic.

The Power of Faith to Resist Evil

There is something strangely hopeful and resistant in Monroe's final word in response to Flores' taunting question, "Are you ready to meet your

6. A Kapo was a prisoner who, in an attempt to save her or his own life, betrayed comrades and worked with those who ran the concentration camps.

7. CBSNEWS.COM, http://www.cbsnews.com/stories/2002/10/30/national/main52755.shtml.

maker?" While most of us would be pleading for our lives at this point, Monroe replied simply, "Yes." The word "yes" radically reframed the situation. Monroe's last word was very small, but its spiritual impact was enormous. As soon as she replied "yes" to Flores' question, the power of evil that had dominated up to that point was instantly dissipated; in that instant, the mocker became the mocked, the powerful one became powerless, despite appearances to the contrary. As soon as the word "yes" passed from Monroe's lips, the evil that Flores was about to do lost its power, if not its immediate impact. Instead of evil and hopelessness winning out, suddenly hope and meaning appeared, even in the midst of the reality of evil, suffering, and tragedy. Monroe's answer placed her in a position where evil could touch and torture her but could not destroy her soul:

> Do not be afraid of those who kill the body but cannot kill the soul. Rather, be afraid of the One who can destroy both soul and body in hell (Matt. 10:28).

The word "yes" brought both the evildoer and his victim to the foot of the cross, a place of vulnerability, where Flores' apparent strength was revealed as eternal weakness. By bringing this tragedy to the foot of the cross in faith, we have reframed the situation.

Despite this crucial, hidden spiritual dynamic, we still feel broken and saddened as we reflect on the fear, pain, and suffering that Monroe and the other professors were forced to endure. The suffering remains, but the evil is, nonetheless, faithfully resisted. Loving God does not take away the pain that evil inflicts, but it *does* transform it. The pain remains, but our eschatological imagination enables us to discover that the sting of pointless death has been removed. When we reframe such pain, we recall the cross, a place of apparently meaningless radical and innocent suffering, a place where the apparent victory of evil over good turned out, in fact, to be the crucial moment in history at which evil is defeated. The ultimate defeat of evil occurred in and through the cross of Christ, but it was also embodied in Monroe's faith-filled response to Flores. In Monroe's story, we discover that perfect love drives out fear, not by eliminating it, but by transforming it.[8]

8. A second tragedy that it is easy to overlook relates to Flores' taking of his own life. At one level, we feel relief that in some sense "justice has been done." However, as Christians we need to think carefully about such responses. The tragedy of this situation, from

Loving God at All Times:
Reframing the Problem of Evil

Munroe's faith-filled response to Flores offered a powerful mode of resistance to evil, and it reminds us of the nature of the *real* problem of evil. If the definition of evil presented in chapter three is correct, then the real problem of evil is its ability to separate human beings from God, who is their only true source of providential hope. That being so, the "solution" to the problem of evil lies in helping people respond to the experience of evil and suffering in ways that are faith-enhancing rather than faith-destroying. Put slightly differently, *a primary mode of resistance to evil is the ability to love God and to find ways of continuing to love God even in the midst of evil.*

Developing such a faith and a way of being in the face of evil are not easy tasks. To love God when things are going well is not always easy. So, to continue to love God when we are faced with evil and suffering can be incredibly difficult. Yet, that is the central calling of the gospel. In Matthew 22:37-40 Jesus says:

> "Love the Lord your God with all your heart and with all your soul and with all your mind." This is the first and greatest commandment. And the second is like it: "Love your neighbor as yourself." All the Law and the Prophets hang on these two commandments.

Jesus teaches clearly that *nothing* is more important than loving God; we are made in God's image, created to love God. Loving God is the

---

Flores' point of view, is that by taking his own life, he moved himself to a place where he was no longer actively able to seek redemption. To suggest that his suicide should evoke sadness is a difficult perspective to adopt in the midst of the pain and confusion that Flores' actions caused. Nevertheless, as Christians we are called to think differently, to move beyond thoughts of revenge and punishment, and to look at what Flores' life looks like when it is seen from the perspective of the open arms of Christ, who died for all and offers the possibility of forgiveness and redemption to *all* people. Flores' taking of the lives of the nursing professors was evil. His taking of his own life was equally evil. While we may struggle to sympathize with him, we are called to recognize the tragedy and loss of this situation in all of its dimensions. Redemption was always an option for Flores. The tragedy is that he placed himself in a position where he could not or would not accept it. What it might mean for a person who has acted in the way Flores did to find redemption and salvation is the subject of chapter five. Suffice it here to say that Flores' situation contains an eternal tragedy. The implications of this way of thinking will become clear as we move on.

linchpin of the Christian life and a key to resisting evil and enduring suffering. Loving God is not simply something that we do; it constitutes what we are and why we are here; it is what we are created to do. If we are unable to love God, then something deep is missing from our lives. This is why evil is such a serious problem. The experience of evil poses a significant threat to maintaining our primary reason for living: loving God. In isolating us from God and leaving us to face our sufferings alone, evil both depersonalizes and dehumanizes us. If a person does not have the resources to resist evil, then he or she moves from the natural state of a person-in-relation with God, self, and one another to a state of isolation, hopelessness, alienation, and death. Thus, learning to practice gestures of redemption that will enable faith in the face of evil and tragedy is imperative.

Loving God in All Things: Contemplation in Job

The importance of loving God in the midst of suffering is a central dimension of the book of Job. Frequently, Job is held up as an example of biblical theodicy.[9] However, reflecting more deeply on God indicates that this may not strictly be the case. In Job 1:1 we find this statement about Job's character:

> In the land of Uz there lived a man whose name was Job. This man was blameless and upright; he feared God and shunned evil.

Job loved God and sought to avoid evil. The evil things that happened to Job were not the consequences of his sinfulness or lack of faith. His was truly innocent suffering. Satan's attack on Job revolved around Satan's proposition that Job was religious only because it brought him particular rewards, that his love for God was based on utility rather than commitment and affection. Satan tried to persuade God that Job had a "barter conception of religion"[10] driven by a self-centered quest for rewards and

9. However, Terrence Tilley, in *The Evils of Theodicy* (Washington, D.C.: Georgetown University Press, 1991), offers a counterargument suggesting that the book of Job is actually more of a warning *against* theodicies than an advocacy of one.

10. Gustavo Gutiérrez, *On Job: God Talk and the Suffering of the Innocent* (New York: Orbis Books, 1987), p. 1.

the fear of punishment. In other words, Job only loved God for what he could get out of God.

> "Does Job fear God for nothing?" Satan replied. "Have you not put a hedge around him and his household and everything he has? You have blessed the work of his hands, so that his flocks and herds are spread throughout the land. But stretch out your hand and strike everything he has, and he will surely curse you to your face" (Job 1:9-15).

However, the book reveals a different vision and motivation as the innocent Job continues to love God even in the midst of horrendous, unmerited suffering. Job's experience offers a serious challenge to retributive theodicies that assume a causal connection between sin and suffering. Job is clearly an innocent sufferer. His suffering was not caused by disobedience or a lack of faith. If anything, it was caused by his faithfulness and his refusal to let go of his faith. In the end, we see that Job did not love God for reward but for the sake of love.

> Then Job replied to the LORD:
> "I know that you can do all things;
> no plan of yours can be thwarted.
> You asked, 'Who is this that obscures my counsel
>   without knowledge?'
> Surely I spoke of things I did not understand,
> things too wonderful for me to know.
> You said, 'Listen now, and I will speak;
> I will question you,
> and you shall answer me.'
> My ears had heard of you
> but now my eyes have seen you.
> Therefore I despise myself
> and repent in dust and ashes."
>
> (Job 42:1-6)

Job let go of his anger and his questioning of God and returned to God in trust and repentance. The primary message that emerges from the book of Job is not "How can a loving God allow this to happen to an innocent sufferer?" The main question posed by Job's experience is "How can human beings continue to love God in the midst of evil?"

Interestingly, the first two chapters of Job suggest that there may be an answer to the origin of evil, although one would hope that it didn't relate to God's gambling habits! Nevertheless, Job never knew what that answer was. He had to work out his understanding of what it means to love God in the face of unmerited suffering without knowing any of the reasons behind his suffering. In learning how to live with that unanswered question, Job's greatest challenge emerged. In wrestling seriously with what it means that life is a gift, Job began to come to terms with his own suffering and did not let himself move from suffering to evil:

> At this, Job got up and tore his robe and shaved his head. Then he fell to the ground in worship and said: "Naked I came from my mother's womb, and naked I will depart. The LORD gave, the LORD has taken away; may the name of the LORD be praised." In all this Job sinned not, nor charged God foolishly (Job 1:20-22).

The model of resistance outlined in the remainder of this book finds its roots and goal in enabling people to live with Job's questions and to learn what it means to offer Job's response of faith and love.

Practicing Theodicy

How, then, can people carry out such an awesome task? How can they possibly continue to love God when they are battered by storms of evil and suffering? At such times, anger towards God often comes much more easily than love. The answer this book offers is that the task begins by practicing particular gestures of redemption. As we learn these gestures through the power of the Holy Spirit, we are enabled to build up resistance to evil. These gestures are embedded in specific forms of Christian practice that are embodied in a particular way of life. Taken together, such practices form the basis for what we will describe as a *practical theodicy*.[11] Practical

---

11. Another good example of practical theodicy is M. M. Adams, *Horrendous Evils and the Goodness of God* (Ithaca, N.Y.: Cornell University Press, 1999), which develops a philosophical perspective on the problem of evil that is clearly intended to be practical. Our practical theodicy differs from Adams's insofar as ours, based in practical theology, develops specific forms of pastoral practice that respond to the experience of evil and suffering in the world.

theodicy takes seriously both the impact of what evil does and the embodied and practical ways in which God has responded to and continues to respond to the problem of evil and suffering. Practical theodicy is pastoral because it seeks to develop forms of practice that resist evil and to initiate actions that are saturated with compassion, mercy, and healing. It is a theodicy because it seeks to explore and respond to the problem of evil as it has been reframed here. Practical theodicy begins its examination of the problem of evil with reflection on the cross of Christ, which places it in a position of embodiedness, solidarity, and involvement, rather than in intellectual abstraction and objectivity. For practical theodicy, the reframed understanding of the problem of evil relates primarily to the ways in which evil interferes with and seeks to destroy our relationships with God. Practical theodicy, of course, seeks to offer compassionate responses to those who are injured and broken by their encounters with evil and suffering. However, those responses are always aimed first and foremost at restoring a person to right relationship with God, self, and others.[12]

Understanding Christian Practices

At the heart of a practical theodicy lies a cluster of Christian practices that have great promise in terms of resisting and transforming evil and in preventing suffering from becoming evil. However, first we need to be clear as to precisely what is meant by the term "practice." Christian practices are particular forms of Christian action. At a basic level, Christian practices are meaning-filled actions that are informed by scripture and tradition, inspired by the Holy Spirit, and learned through participation within particular forms of community. Craig Dykstra and Dorothy Bass describe Christian practices as the

> things Christian people do together over time to address fundamental human needs in response to and in the light of God's active presence for the life of the world.[13]

12. This starting point moves pastoral care away from the therapeutic/pragmatic paradigm towards a way of caring that treats God and theology with the utmost seriousness.

13. Craig Dykstra and Dorothy C. Bass, "A Theological Understanding of Christian Practices," in Miroslav Volf and Dorothy Bass, eds., *Practicing Theology: Beliefs and Practices in Christian Life* (Grand Rapids: Eerdmans, 2002), p. 18.

Practices are divinely inspired gestures of cooperation through which human beings seek to participate faithfully in the redemptive mission of Jesus. Dykstra and Bass are correct in stating that such practices seek to meet human needs. However, they do more than that. Indeed, they actually create *new* needs. When understood and practiced faithfully, they draw attention to dimensions of reality and aspects of God that people are often unaware of. That knowledge, in turn, produces fresh challenges and new needs. For example, the practice of preaching, at one level, meets a deep human need by offering comfort, hope, and the promise of the gospel. At another level, it challenges us to rethink the way we understand the world and to re-imagine the possibilities for our lives.[14] In this way, the practice of preaching not only meets needs, but it also creates new needs. Practices are not simply pastoral responses to human need; they are challenging, embodied modes of transformative revelation.

Importantly, practices are forms of purposeful, *communal* action that contain personal, social, and historical dimensions. For example, when we engage in the practice of individual, silent prayer, at one level we do this alone. However, a deeper reflection on the practice of prayer reveals that we carry it out because we have learned to do so from others. The content of our prayers is always shared with others in the past and in the present. When we pray, we engage in a practice that has continuity with those individuals and communities who have similarly practiced prayer in the past and who continue to do it throughout the world today.[15]

Practices are skills learned in particular communities that are formed and shaped by specific traditions and that contain implicit and explicit social and theological histories. While the theological essence of the practice remains constant down through the ages — for instance, prayer is always offered to the same God — practices are constantly being modified, reconstituted, and shaped by the particular social and historical contexts within which they are experienced and carried out.

Practices are individual and communal enactments of God's redemptive movements within creation. They are forms of embodied theology that communicate and reveal meaningful theological truth. "[P]ractices are essentially belief-shaped and beliefs are essentially

14. Walter Brueggemann, *Texts Under Negotiation* (Minneapolis: Fortress Press, 1993).
15. Dykstra and Bass, "A Theological Understanding of Christian Practices" in Volf and Bass, *Practicing Theology,* p. 13.

practice-shaping."[16] They emerge from reflection on and responses to the actions of God and the historical and social implications of God's desire to reach out and attend to human need. This need is wide and diverse, but it is first and foremost a need for reconciliation with God and the patterning of lives that are lived faithfully according to God's purposes. Such reconciliation inevitably results in the development of new, compassionate rhythms of life that seek to meet human need in all of its dimensions through initiating forms of action that mirror and are shaped by our experiences and memories of God's redemptive actions in history. Miroslav Volf puts this point well:

> Christian practices have what we may call an "as-so" structure (or correspondence structure): *as* God has received us in Christ, *so* we too are to receive our fellow human beings. True, the way in which Christ's life is exemplary has to be carefully specified. Above all, the important difference between Christ and other human beings should counter both the temptation to supplant Christ and the presumption that human beings can simply "repeat" Christ's work. But in an appropriately qualified way . . . we must say "As Christ, so we."[17]

Practices, then, enable people, in a limited sense, to mirror the practices of God and to develop ways of living that reflect God's graceful movement towards creation.

The Significance of Grace

The significance of grace cannot be underplayed in our understanding of Christian practices. Practices are not simply the actions of determined human beings. It is not enough for Christians simply to attempt to copy the practices of God in their own strength: "If I practice this and try harder eventually I will be like God!" Practices result from participating in and receiving grace, and as such they find their dynamism not in the human will, but in the vitalizing power of the Holy Spirit. Such an emphasis on God's grace reminds us that the Christian life and faith are not primar-

16. Miroslav Volf, "Theology for a Way of Life," in Volf and Bass, *Practicing Theology,* p. 254.

17. Volf, "Theology for a Way of Life," in Volf and Bass, *Practicing Theology,* p. 250.

ily about *doing* but about receiving.[18] That is why *prayer* is foundational. As we wait on God in prayer and allow ourselves to be touched and changed by the Holy Spirit, the possibility of developing strange practices that gesture towards redemption begins. Practices are more than endless repetition; they are the product of a continuing relationship with God.

Nevertheless, such an emphasis on receiving and waiting on God does not annul the significance of humans practicing in ways that seek to respond faithfully to God's gracious actions. As Volf again puts it:

> Inscribed in the very heart of God's grace is the rule that we can be its recipients only if we do not resist being made into its agents. In a precisely defined way that guards the distinction between God and human beings, human beings themselves are made participants in the divine activity and therefore are inspired, empowered, and obliged to imitate it. Which is where practices come in. Christian practices may be construed as human "resonances," under a variety of circumstances, of the divine engagement with the world through which human beings are sustained and redeemed.[19]

We might describe Christian practices as *resonances of grace* that occur in response to the human experience of divine grace. Such practices are designed to enable and sustain faith and hope in the midst of a world that often appears hopeless and less than grace-filled. Importantly, participating in such practices enables people to be shaped in particular ways; it develops habits and virtues that will enable them to move towards a deeper form of Christ-likeness and holiness.

Continuity and Complementarity

It is important to note the continuity and complementarity of Christian practices. Taken together, Christian practices form "the constituent elements in a way of life that becomes incarnate when human beings live in the light of and in response to God's gift of life abundant."[20] If Jesus came

18. Volf, "Theology for a Way of Life," in Volf and Bass, *Practicing Theology,* p. 254.
19. Volf, "Theology for a Way of Life," in Volf and Bass, *Practicing Theology,* p. 255.
20. Dykstra and Bass, "A Theological Understanding of Christian Practices," in Volf and Bass, *Practicing Theology,* p. 21.

to bring life in all of its fullness, and if evil destroys life and liveliness,[21] then practices that enable people to continue to experience God's abundant life even in the midst of evil and suffering will be crucial for a practical theodicy. A practical theodicy will enable people to learn and participate in certain vital Christian practices that will help them to retain their hope in and love for God's providential love despite the reality of evil.

The key thing about practices is that they must be *practiced*. It is not enough to know about and understand a practice theoretically. In the same way as one works at riding a bike or learning to walk on a tightrope, so also one needs to work at practices if the skill that is implicit within them is to be actualized. By constantly employing them in our day-to-day experiences, by picking ourselves up when we fail to achieve them, and by persevering when they appear pointless, practices become habits. When a practice becomes a habit, it then defines the natural way that a person will respond to a particular situation. When engaged in regularly, Christian practices cease to become things that we simply do; instead, they become vital aspects of *who we are*. As we practice compassion, so we become compassionate people; as we practice forgiveness, we become forgiving people; as we practice lament, we become the type of people who know what it means to bring our sadness faithfully before God. When we practice theodicy, we become the type of people who know what evil is and understand how to resist it.

Developing a Practical Theodicy

With this understanding of Christian practices in mind, we can now begin to work through in more detail what a practical theodicy looks like. As we have seen, intellectual theodicy is the defense of God's goodness, love, and power in the face of the existence of evil. We have argued that this theodicy tends not to relate to any particular God and that it has no necessary telos beyond solving the generalized problem of evil and suffering. Practical theodicy is aimed at the same experience — evil — but its mode of interaction with it is quite different. Practical theodicy does not seek to explain why there is evil, primarily because, as we have suggested, it is inexplicable. Rather, practical theodicy attempts to reframe the problem of

21. M. Scott Peck, *People of the Lie: The Hope for Healing Human Evil* (London: Arrow Books, 1990).

evil in light of the specifics of the Christian God by *revealing* ways in which the all-loving, all-powerful (in the sense outlined in chapter two), triune God responds to the presence of evil and suffering in the world. The response offered by practical theodicy is not intended to be logical or reasonable (although it does not exclude such things); it is intended to be *faithful*. The goal and endpoint of practical theodicy is the enabling of the Christian community to live faithfully *despite* the presence of evil.

Practical theodicy is a mode of resistance that addresses issues of evil and human suffering through engagement in particular forms of specifically Christian practices that are carried individually and corporately. Such a theodicy is not simply a generalized, compassionate response to the suffering of the world, a practical equivalent of the philosophical theodicist's general statements about *a* god of love. Rather, the "practical" response referred to in practical theodicy is theological and eschatological in shape and intention, seeking to mirror, embody, and participate faithfully in God's providential actions in, to, and for the world. Its goal is not simply the alleviation of suffering (although clearly it includes this), but the restoration of divine-human relationships, that is, deliverance from the effects of what evil *does*.

We might then describe practical theodicy in this way:

> Practical theodicy is the process wherein the church community, in and through its practices, offers subversive modes of resistance to the evil and suffering experienced by the world. The goal of practical theodicy is, by practicing these gestures of redemption, to enable people to continue to love God in the face of evil and suffering and in so doing to prevent tragic suffering from becoming evil.

The tools of practical theodicy are the particular forms of communal, ecclesial practices that are inspired by the Holy Spirit and intended to reflect and embody aspects of and responses to the redemptive actions of God in, to, and for the world. These practices exist to enable healing and to bring comfort, hope, and transformation to both church and world. In so doing, they point towards eschatological hope and new possibilities in the present.

Practical Theodicy and the Church

Practical theodicy has a particular relationship with the church community. It assumes that the church, formed in response to and in relationship with Jesus, continues to reveal his ministry of reconciliation and redemption through its life and practices. As Dietrich Bonhoeffer put it:

> The space of the church is the place where witness is given to the foundation of all reality in Jesus Christ. The church is the place where it is proclaimed and taken seriously that God has reconciled the world to himself in Christ, that God so loved the world that God gave his Son for it. The space of the church is not there in order to fight with the world for a piece of its territory, but precisely to testify to the world that it is still the world, namely, the world that is loved and reconciled by God.[22]

Encountering suffering without the knowledge of Christ emerges from a false understanding of reality. To begin to understand what it means to suffer with Christ in the recognition that "[the] world is not divided between Christ and the devil; it is completely the world of Christ, whether it recognizes this or not,"[23] is the starting point for practical theodicy's task of reframing suffering and indeed reframing the world. The task of practical theodicy, then, is to find ways and modes of practice that will enable the church to recognize and witness to the reality of Christ's providential, redemptive action for the whole of creation, even in the midst of evil.

Practical theodicy assumes that God is in and for the world, not in abstract reasoning, but in compassionate actions of resistance and transformation. It does not view the problem of evil as a dislocated philosophical argument but rather as a grounded context for practical, faithful engagement with the reality of evil and human suffering. Such an approach calls not for *explanation,* but for the learning of faithful practices of *resistance* that open up the possibility of transformation and redemption. As Farley puts it, "Suffering yearns more for experiences of healing presence than for logical arguments. Theory can provide some meaning to suffering, but it is in compassionate relationship that suffering discovers redemption."[24]

22. Dietrich Bonhoeffer, *Ethics* (Minneapolis: Fortress Press, 2005), p. 63.
23. Bonhoeffer, *Ethics,* p. 65.
24. Wendy Farley, "The Practice of Theodicy," in Margaret E. Mohrmann and Mark J.

Such an approach to theodicy fully recognizes the reality of evil and suffering and seeks to enable people to continue to love God and to live faithfully *despite* the presence of evil and in the hope of the coming eschaton. Such an approach to theodicy assumes that the "incarnation, the crucifixion, and eschatological hopes are not theses to be believed or not, but *signatures of the way in which God relates to suffering*"[25] and by extension to evil.

God's Responsibility towards Evil

Practical theodicy understands God's relation to evil and suffering in a very particular way. It assumes that God stands in solidarity with the world and takes *responsibility* for the evil and suffering in the world. We need to be clear about what is meant by such a suggestion. Taking responsibility does not necessarily imply culpability. It does, however, acknowledge God's commitment to be with the world in its struggles as it awaits transformation and redemption. As Ray Anderson correctly observes,

> God does not duck and dodge the reality of evil, attributing it to human sin and blaming it on the Devil. God is the author of the drama, in which pain and pleasure, suffering and joy, good and evil are part of the plot. Faith means that we as human participants in that drama know there is an author and that the drama is being constructed even as we live it out. The righteous do not live by their righteousness, God reminded Habakkuk, but by faith. God takes full responsibility. This, at least, is a start. The theological question with regard to suffering is: What does it mean to say that God takes responsibility for evil and that we can have faith in him to do this? The biblical tradition has no view of evil as a problem outside of the concept of God's providence. God's providence is expressed through his partnership with human persons in suffering, which is the divine power to be present as our advocate in the context of suffering and for the purpose of redeeming those who suffer. The providence of God is bound to his promise. This promise is

---

Hanson, *Pain Seeking Understanding: Suffering, Medicine, and Faith* (Cleveland: The Pilgrim Press, 1999), p. 103.

25. Farley, "The Practice of Theodicy," in Mohrmann and Hanson, *Pain Seeking Understanding*, p. 110. Italics added.

a miracle and mystery of divine love. Suffering and injustice can produce a crisis of faith, leading us directly to God as the one who must ultimately take responsibility. In his taking responsibility through participation in the dilemma of evil, *God provides redemption from evil, not a solution to it as a problem.*[26] (italics added)

God's taking responsibility for evil and suffering relates to the nature of the incarnation, cross, and resurrection and God's promised continuing presence in the midst of the suffering of the world. By entering into human suffering and offering the possibility of hope, healing, and redemption *despite* the presence of evil, God opens up new vistas of hope for a world which often appears to be hopeless. Through the Holy Spirit the church is empowered to stand in solidarity with God in God's resistance to evil and in so doing it is enabled to develop forms of practice which mirror God's redemptive actions. In striving to remain faithful to the redemptive practices of God in history through the development of faithful human practices within the church, practical theodicy seeks to reveal the goodness and power of God and the nature and reality of God's continuing response to evil and suffering. When viewed in this way, the "solution" or perhaps better the response to the problem of evil lies within forms of communal practice which actively engage with, resist, and seek to transform evil and suffering and struggle in solidarity to reveal love and hope to victims, survivors, and perpetrators of evil.

Practicing Resistance

The remainder of this book will examine four Christian practices that can form the basis of the practical theodicy that has been outlined thus far. Each practice offers a different but intricately connected mode of resistance to the type of evil that has been discussed thus far. Each one approaches evil from a different perspective, but taken together they offer a cluster of core practices that form the basis of a practical theodicy. The four practices that we will look at are *lament, forgiveness, thoughtfulness, and hospitality.* We will argue that, taken together, these four Christian

26. Ray Anderson, *Dancing with Wolves, Feeding the Sheep: Musings of a Maverick Theologian* (Eugene, Ore.: Wipf & Stock Publishers, 2002), p. 105.

practices provide the basis for resisting evil and faithfully responding to suffering; they form a practical theodicy that reveals something of the way in which an all-loving, all-powerful God responds to the presence of evil and suffering in the world. By exploring the theoretical and practical implications of these four practices, we can develop an embodied, practical theodicy that will create communities of resistance that can absorb evil and suffering and help us to persevere until Christ returns.

CHAPTER FIVE

Why Me, Lord . . . Why Me?
The Practice of Lament as Resistance and Deliverance

The Lament Psalms offer important resources for Christian faith and ministry, even though they have been largely purged from the life and liturgy of the church. Such purging attests to the alienation between the Bible and the church.

Walter Brueggemann

For I am convinced that neither death nor life, neither angels nor demons, neither the present nor the future, nor any powers, neither height nor depth, nor anything else in all creation, will be able to separate us from the love of God that is in Christ Jesus our Lord.

Romans 8:38-39

I must admit I cry easily.

Desmond Tutu

On 15 August 1998, an event took place that shook, changed, and destroyed the lives of many people. Although I wasn't directly involved, this event became a turning point in my understanding of the nature and practice of faith in the midst of a world wracked with evil and suffering. On that day, in the town of Omagh in County Tyrone, Northern Ireland, the "Real IRA" detonated a car bomb in the packed town center, killing twenty-eight people and injuring and maiming 220 others. They claimed that their target was not civilians but a courthouse. However, the evidence and personal testimonies surrounding the event suggested otherwise. Nine children were among the dead, one of them only eighteen months old. The attack was the worst violence since the troubles had begun in Northern Ireland thirty years earlier. Ironically, the bomb was indiscriminate in its religious targets; Protestants and Catholics alike were killed and maimed.

People who saw the bombing described scenes of utter carnage. The bodies of the dead and the dying were strewn across the street. Other wounded victims were screaming for help. The bomb was particularly devastating because it went off just as police, responding to a telephone warning, were clearing people away from an area of the town center. It is not clear whether the warning was simply unclear or whether it was deliberately misleading. Either way, it led the police to usher people into the area where the bomb went off.

The bomb exploded outside one of the town's busiest shops, completely flattening it and the shop that stood next to it. The blast came on the final day of the town's week-long annual carnival. A trail of blood leading up the steps of Tyrone County Hospital illustrated the destruction. "As dozens of worried relatives gathered outside, porters cleaned blood from the gurneys used to ferry the injured and dying. Patrick McCormick of Northern Ireland's Ambulance Service, said, 'The injuries are horrific, from amputees, to severe head injuries, to serious burns, and among them are women and children.'"[1]

It was the type of attack at which even those involved in terrorism balked. Sinn Féin, the political wing of the IRA, issued an unprecedented attack on the bombers. Martin McGuiness, the party's chief negotiator, gave his own statement of contempt for the perpetrators: "This appalling act was carried out by those opposed to the peace process." Prime Minister Tony Blair described the bombing as "an appalling act of savagery and evil."[2] And it was.

Intense television coverage gave viewers disturbing, unrelenting images of the tragedy and the human misery that accompanied it. This, com-

1. BBC News online, http://news.bbc.co.uk/1/hi/events/northern_ireland/latest_news/152156.stm.

2. BBC News online, http://news.bbc.co.uk/1/hi/events/northern_ireland/latest_news/152156.stm, accessed Sunday 16 August 1998, 10:26 GMT 11:26 UK.

bined with the bloodstained testimonies of the injured and those searching for their loved ones, made me, even as a distanced onlooker who was
not directly involved with the situation, feel shattered and traumatized. I
felt my faith shudder as I imagined the pain of the relatives, the injured,
and the maimed. I tried to imagine what it would be like if I lost one of my
sons or daughters in such circumstances. One of my daughters was, at the
time, around the same age as the murdered toddler. "How would I cope?
Would I cope?" I wondered. Then, as I moved on from projecting the horror and suffering experienced by the victims onto my own family, my
thoughts began to move towards God and God's involvement in such an
event. "How could this happen? God! How could you let this happen!?
Was this really a planned part of divine providence?" My Calvinist roots
rebelled in the face of the sheer horror of the situation. Deep and pene-
trating questions about the goodness and fairness of God raged within
me, and I am certain, within all who called upon God for comfort, guidance, and hope on that day. This truly was an act of evil.

On the next day, a Sunday, I went to worship in our local church. All
of these questions were still racing around in my mind, but I was a bit
calmer now, and I just wanted to join with the people of God and receive
some guidance as to how, together, we might deal with our confusion, disorientation, and anxiety. The first hymns went by; nothing was said. We
were told to worship, to praise the Lord, to lift our hearts and our hands
heavenwards and appreciate the wonderful things that God had done for
us. We did. And still nothing was said. The prayers went by and we
thanked God for his great mercy towards us; nothing was said about the
bombing. The sermon was narrated. We were instructed to have faith and
be thankful that God was God and had reached down to love us despite
our sinfulness . . . still nothing was said. The prayers of intercession came
. . . and went . . . silence. The entire service came and went with no recognition of the tragedy that had happened in our country to our own people.
The service ended. I left without saying much to anyone.

Something was seriously wrong with our church, and despite the fact
that I had been attending there for ten years, I had never noticed it. It
seemed that we had no capacity for dealing with sadness. As I reflected on
the way in which my church worshipped, its emphasis, its tone, its expectations, its expressed hopes, I suddenly understood clearly that there was
no room in our liturgy and worship for sadness, brokenness, and questioning. We had much space for love, joy, praise, and supplication, but it

seemed that we viewed the acknowledgement of sadness and the tragic brokenness of our world as almost tantamount to faithlessness. As a result, when tragedy hit, either directly at home or at a slight distance as in the Omagh bombing, we had no idea what to do with it or how to formulate our concerns. Because we had not consistently practiced the art of recognizing, accepting, and expressing sadness, we had not developed the capacity to deal with tragedy. In the wake of the tragedy of Omagh, our failure to publicly and communally acknowledge such a major act of evil within our liturgical space demonstrated our implicit tendency towards denial and avoidance. Evil was not resisted by our community, it was simply sidelined. In the face of evil and suffering, we sang cheerful songs and expressed happy thoughts rather than weeping with the wounded and lamenting with the Sovereign God. It was clear that we had few resources to enable us to resist the evil caused by such outrageous suffering as was inflicted on the people of Omagh on that terrible day. So we closed our eyes and worshipped God, or at least those aspects of God that brought us most comfort and relief.

Silencing Evil

In a sense, the silence of my church community in the face of horrendous evil reflects something of the imposed silence that emerges more generally in response to the experience of evil and suffering. The picture reproduced on page 94, *The Scream,* is the work of the Norwegian painter Edvard Munch, who was highly influential in the development of German Expressionism in the early twentieth century. In *The Scream,* Munch captures something of the disturbing and disorienting experience of suffering. The picture is highly evocative. It stimulates extreme emotions and receives many interpretations. The distorted nature of both background and figure indicate confusion and disorientation, a collapse of the world within which all of the participants' assumed boundaries and "edges" begin to wobble and shake, a disturbing merger of collapsing horizons and disintegrating worlds. As our gaze is drawn to the central figure, questions begin to emerge. Why is the person screaming? Is it a male or a female? How does the scream relate to the two approaching figures? Who are they and what have they done, or what does the figure think that they will do that causes him or her to utter what looks like such a gut-rending

Edvard Munch, *The Scream* (1893)

© 2006 The Munch Museum / The Munch-Ellingsen Group / Artists Rights Society (ARS), NY
Photo credit: Erich Lessing / Art Resource, NY

scream? Are they coming to bring solace or to inflict pain? Is the scream expressed or simply felt within? If the former, then to whom is it expressed and why?

Munch's painting evokes but refuses to answer questions such as these. As I "read" this painting, the power of the scream comes from the possibility that it was not expressed, that it was an internal, silent scream. Seen this way, the scream reflects the depth of pain that suffering evokes in sufferers. The silent scream reflects the voicelessness imposed by suffering, a silent, disorienting entrapment that defies language but remains, nonetheless, meaningful. The two figures in the background indicate the way in which normalcy continues and surrounds the one who is suffering. All three are in the world, but the sufferer is, in a very real sense, no longer of it. The surrounding normalcy means nothing to the sufferer, who sees and feels nothing but distortion, confusion, pain, and chaos. She screams and screams . . . yet nothing is heard. She has no language to express what she is feeling. Her lips move, her eyes widen, straining to articulate the scream; she covers her ears in anticipation of its impending volume . . . but, . . . only silence reigns. Where can she find a language that will enable her to articulate her pain and sadness?

The Silence of the Cross: Solidarity-in-Suffering

Reflecting on the significance of such painful silence in the face of evil and suffering draws our minds towards an aspect of the cross that often goes unnoticed: *the silence of Christ.* Those of us brought up in the Christian tradition are most familiar with the *words* of Jesus. We have encountered and been touched by the teachings of Jesus, and we have experienced the transforming power that these words can have for us and others. The words of Jesus give us insight into strange new worlds and a kingdom of God that are very different from the world in which we currently reside. His words help us, in Walter Brueggemann's words, to re-imagine the world[3] in new ways that allow us to recreate our universe and to recognize that the way things seem to be is not necessarily the way that they are or the way that they will be in the future. The words of Jesus fund

3. Walter Brueggemann, *Texts under Negotiation: The Bible and Postmodern Imagination* (Minneapolis: Fortress Press, 1993).

the type of eschatological imagination that we have previously suggested is vital for our understanding of and response to evil and suffering. However, as important as Jesus' words are, his silence in the face of evil and suffering raises some vital issues.

The Silence of Jesus and the Voicelessness of Pain

Something that often goes unnoticed about Jesus' experience on the cross is his silence. Mark's gospel suggests that Jesus' ordeal lasted about six hours, yet during that time, according to the biblical record, he utters only seven sentences.[4] When Jesus does speak, his words are both powerful and compassionate. He forgives his oppressors; laments to God; shows care and compassion for his mother, his best friend, and the criminal at his side; and finally shouts in victory that his work is finished. These are strong words that have changed millions of lives. But, for most of his time on the cross, Jesus remains silent. What might this silence mean?

Jesus' experience on the cross was a profound encounter with evil and suffering. As Paul puts it, "And having disarmed the powers and authorities, he made a public spectacle of them, triumphing over them by the cross" (Col. 2:15). Jesus' cry "It is finished!" marks the end of evil and suffering, even though they remain realities that have to be faced with perseverance and hope until he returns. His words inaugurate a great victory. But what was going on within Jesus' silence?

Dorothy Soelle notes,

> There are forms of suffering that reduce one to a silence in which no discourse is possible any longer.... The kind of grinding, relentless suffering of the holocaust or the horrendous hopelessness of thousands of people caught up in a famine over which they have absolutely no control leaves people stunned and without words.[5]

Robert Lifton calls this kind of silence "psychic numbing," a protection of the self against the destructive forces to which it has been exposed. Those caught in its grip feel isolated, cut off from the rest of humankind,

---

4. For a fascinating reflection on Jesus' last words, see Stanley Hauerwas, *Cross-Shattered Christ: Meditations on the Seven Last Words* (Grand Rapids: Brazos Press, 2005).

5. Dorothy Soelle, *Suffering* (London: Darton, Longman & Todd, 1975), p. 68.

including their own history.[6] Those of us who have experienced or been with others who have experienced sudden, unexpected trauma know well the numbing silence of the moment of revelation; the shock, horror, and disbelief of what has happened at the dreadful moment when one encounters suffering are inexpressible. When we encounter suffering, we are silenced. Whether that suffering is present in the diagnosis of cancer in a child or in the trauma of a rape victim, the initial response is silence. There is nothing to say, only overwhelming pain, loss, and disorientation to be felt. In an instant, we discover that the world is not the way we thought it was. All of the old road maps that guided our lives and the ways in which we understood the world now make no sense. Suddenly, our horizons narrow to the level of this one aspect of our experience. The experience of suffering either expands to fill the whole of our universe or contracts our universe and confines it within the boundaries of our immediate experience.

Elaine Scarry in her reflections on the effects of pain notes that:

> Pain comes unsharably into our midst as at once that which cannot be denied and that which cannot be confirmed . . . whatever pain achieves it achieves in part through unsharability, and it ensures this unsharability through resistance to language.[7]

The experience of suffering and evil functions in a similar way. Billman and Migliore helpfully develop this suggestion:

> Survivors of abuse, torture, and the terrors of death camps testify to the veil of silence that falls over the eruption of massive evil and suffering. The flames of Auschwitz, writes Elie Wiesel, drive speech to silence.[8] Wiesel's writings bear witness to the almost unbearable burden of speaking of the horrors of the holocaust. The same is true of other people's histories of experienced brutality such as that of native Americans and African slaves in America. It is far easier to suppress the mem-

6. Charles B. Strozier and Michael Flynn, eds., *Trauma and Self: Essays by Robert J. Lifton* (Oxford: Rowman & Littlefield, 1996).

7. Elaine Scarry, *The Body in Pain: The Making and Unmaking of the World* (London: Oxford University Press, 1985), p. 4.

8. Elie Wiesel, "Jenseits des Schweigens," in *Das Gegenteil von Gleichgultigeit Ist Erinnerung,* ed. Dagmar Mensink and Reinhold Boschki (Mainz: Matthias-Grunewald Verlag, 1995), p. 12.

ory of such events or to entomb them in silence than to bring them to memory and speech with all the pain this entails.[9]

As the avoidance and denial of my own church demonstrated, the experience of evil can immobilize individuals and communities and prevent them from engaging in effective resistance. The silence evoked by the experience of evil and suffering not only imposes itself on individuals, but it also often "destroys the memory" of societies and cultures who may find themselves, implicitly or explicitly, co-conspirators in the processes of evil that underlie the various manifestations of suffering.[10]

The Pastoral Significance of Jesus' Silence

This kind of imposed silence in the face of evil and suffering formed the heart of Jesus' experience on the cross. The extent of Jesus' abandonment, pain, isolation, and loneliness is encapsulated in his silence. The intensity of his pain and spiritual alienation becomes clear when his silence turns to lament. "Eloi, Eloi, lama sabachthani?" "My God, my God, why have you forsaken me?" Jesus' cry of lament from the cross reveals something significant about his experience. Jesus' movement from silence into speech startles us not just with its bold and unrelenting challenge to God, but also with the particular form of language he uses to address God. Earlier in the gospels, Jesus found God close, nurturing, and protecting. He referred to God in familiar terms as "Abba, Father," a term that expresses intimacy, trust, and security. The God whom Jesus addresses in his lament from the cross is different in a subtle but profound way. No longer does Jesus address God in the language of "Father," for now the Father appears distant, absent in perception if not in reality. Jesus no longer addresses him as Father but as "God." The God who "forsakes" Jesus on the cross is distant, and the experience of evil creates that distance.[11]

It is clear then that Jesus' suffering on the cross was not romantic or

9. K. D. Billman and Daniel L. Migliore, *Rachel's Cry* (Cleveland: United Church Press, 1999), p. 106.

10. Billman and Migliore, *Rachel's Cry*, p. 106.

11. Note that this movement from "Abba, Father" to "God" does not reflect a movement to the distant generic god of theodicy. God remains the same Trinitarian God of history. What has changed is Jesus' perception of the relationship between him and that God.

heroic but real and terrible. In *The Cost of Discipleship,* Bonhoeffer highlights the totality of Jesus' suffering. Not only did Jesus suffer, but he also was *rejected.* Bonhoeffer suggests that if Jesus' suffering is simply framed as tragic, it could "convey its own value, its own honor and dignity. But Jesus is the Christ who was *rejected* in his suffering."[12] That Christ not only suffered but was also rejected is important for Bonhoeffer's theology of suffering. The rejection and humiliation of Jesus makes his suffering *dishonorable.* "Suffering and rejection express in summary form the cross of Jesus. Death on the cross means to suffer and die as one rejected and cast out."[13] Jesus' suffering was not the suffering of one of Hollywood's wounded heroes. His suffering had no earthly merit; he was rejected, humiliated, and scorned. There was no honor.

At one level, Jesus' suffering was qualitatively different from human suffering. It was not simply human suffering on a grand scale. His suffering on the cross had divine implications. It was to bear the sins of the world, a task to which no human being could aspire. At this level, Jesus' suffering was radically different from any form of human suffering. Nevertheless, Jesus was divine *and* fully human. While there is discontinuity between Jesus' suffering and human suffering, there is also continuity, for at another level, Jesus identifies with the sufferer, and the sufferer finds solidarity in the co-suffering of Christ. While we must recognize that which is radically different about Jesus' suffering, it is important that we do not try to separate or idolize Jesus' suffering in a way that distances it completely from other experiences of evil and suffering. As Dorothee Soelle points out, the fact that

> a world of immeasurable suffering that wants to isolate Jesus' suffering and make it something that outweighs the rest in order to be able to understand it as unique, is rather macabre. It is not in Jesus' interest to have suffered "the most." On the contrary, the truth of the symbol lies precisely in its repeatability. Jesus' experience as it stands . . . can befall anyone. Wherever a person is conscious of dying, wherever pain is experienced, there too one's earlier certainty about God is destroyed. People have given testimonies that demonstrate that the symbol can be repeated, that is that it can be appropriated. They have experienced

---

12. Dietrich Bonhoeffer, *The Cost of Discipleship* (Minneapolis: Fortress Press, 2003), p. 85.

13. Dietrich Bonhoeffer, *Ethics* (Minneapolis: Fortress Press, 2005), p. 85.

Gethsemane, the fear of death, but also the conquest of all fears in the place in which the cup of suffering is drunk to the bitter dregs.[14]

Jesus' suffering does not have to be "the worst of all human suffering" in order to prove to us that God loves us and is with us in our sufferings.

Jesus' silence in the presence of evil acknowledges the full numbing horror of suffering and legitimizes every sufferer's experience. Jesus' sense of alienation from God, which paradoxically was a mark of his experience on the cross, echoes the sense of alienation and disconnection that many people go through when they experience evil and suffering. The silence of Jesus is a statement that God not only empathizes with suffering "from a distance," but also actually experiences it in all of its horror. The cross of Jesus reveals that God is with us and for us in the midst of the most horrendous and undeserved suffering.

We may, of course, not want a God like this. The disciples clearly did not want such a God:

> From that time on, Jesus began to explain to his disciples that he must go to Jerusalem and suffer many things at the hands of the elders, chief priests and teachers of the law, and that he must be killed and on the third day be raised to life. Peter took him aside and began to rebuke him. "Never, Lord!" he said. "This shall never happen to you!" Jesus turned and said to Peter, "Out of my sight, Satan! You are a stumbling block to me; you do not have in mind the things of God, but the things of men" (Matt. 16:21-23).

We may demand a God who reaches into history and frees us from our pain and suffering, but the nature of the cross and the silence of Jesus in the face of evil and suffering would indicate that such a God is not the God of scripture. That is not the God who was nailed to the cross and who continues to inhabit the history of the Christian church.

Listening to the Silence of Jesus

We can understand the words of Jesus only in the light of his silence. If we are to transform and resist evil, we must understand the imposed silence

14. Soelle, *Suffering,* pp. 81-82.

that accompanies evil and suffering before we can break that silence. We can understand the experience of suffering only when we learn how to listen to the silence, when we learn to interpret and understand the meaning of silence and the dangers of breaking that silence with words that can be harmful even when intended to be healing. Suffering is a meaningful experience, but the meaning of silence is not always accessible through language. In solidarity and awkward presence with the sufferer, we must learn the practice of listening to silences. Reflection on the cross of Christ moves us to become sensitive to the subtle nuances of the experience of pain, desolation, brokenness, and suffering.

As we listen to the silence of Jesus, we recognize that the sufferer's experience of distance from God is not necessarily a mark of faithlessness. Rather, it is an experience closely identified with the experience of Christ on the cross. If the Holy One of Israel can experience such suffering and alienation, then it is not surprising that many sufferers have similar experiences. If this is so, then Jesus' silence and alienation legitimate the experience of suffering. The cross speaks loudly to the experience of suffering: "It's okay to feel this way; God remains with you and for you despite what you are experiencing at this moment." The silence of Jesus on the cross is a liberating force that reveals God's solidarity with the sufferer, not in unrealistic platitudes or false expectations, but in total identification and solidarity. Only when we learn to listen to the silences can we prevent suffering, which is often tragic, from moving into suffering that is evil.

Practicing Friendship in Silence

But how do we learn to listen to the silence? Where can we turn to receive schooling in such listening? Henri Nouwen's observation will help us answer these questions:

> . . . when we honestly ask ourselves which persons in our lives mean the most to us we often find that it is those who, instead of giving much advice, solutions, or cures, have chosen rather to share our pain and touch our wounds with a gentle and tender hand. The friend who can be silent with us in a moment of despair or confusion, who can stay with us in an hour of grief and bereavement, who can tolerate not-knowing, not-

curing, not-healing and face with us the reality of our powerlessness, that is the friend who cares.[15]

Nouwen's point is vital. We learn to listen to the silences and to stand in solidarity with the silence of suffering in and through our *friendships.* In practicing friendship, we gain the depth of character that will allow us to sit with others in suffering and strive to understand their words and their silences. As a mode of embodied compassion, friendship provides a way of *being with* (both physically and psychologically) that enables us to sit with others in the darkness of the abyss and model hope in the midst of hopelessness. More than that, friendship is where we learn the true meaning of the cross. At the cross, we discover the meaning of God's offer of friendship to the world. In the broken body of Christ, we discover something of the depth of God's love for humanity. In the wounds of Christ, we discover the cost of God's offer of friendship and humanity's rejection of that offer.

Christian friendship is based on the friendship that is offered to the world in and through Christ. Christians are called to offer themselves as friends to one another and to God in a way that mirrors God's friendship towards us in Christ. Such mirroring may be partial and flawed, but it is nonetheless a vital dimension of Christ-like living. Friends are comfortable with silence, uncertainty, and, at times, rejection. Friends sometimes wound one another with their words and with their silences, but they always remain bound together and seek reconciliation and new beginnings. Friends maintain solidarity and commitment. Job's comforters are a good example of such friendship. By sitting with Job in silence and solidarity, they offered him comfort, solace, and hope in the midst of his suffering. Sadly, they refused to listen to Job's silences, or at best they listened wrongly. Their solidarity was healing until they began to speak. Their silence was healing, but their theodicy was devastating.

The friendship of others gives us dignity, value, meaning, and hope in our suffering. In the midst of the silences, friends hope on our behalf, even when we cannot hope for ourselves. Friends help us to believe in the possibility of knowing a God who loves us even when the pain makes it too much for us to love God. Friends help us to see the world a little differently . . . even when we may not want to. The practice of friendship and

15. Henri Nouwen, *Out of Solitude* (Notre Dame, Ind.: Ave Maria Press, 1974), p. 34.

the practice of listening to silence are inextricably interlinked. We will return to the importance of the practice of friendship in the final chapter of this book.

Recovering the Practice of Lament

Powerful as the experience of silence is in the face of evil, and vital as the practice of listening to that silence is in the process of healing and resistance, silence is not a state that we should be forced to endure forever. The silence of the sufferer needs to be "heard into speech." But how can we enable the movement from silence into speech?

It strikes me, looking back, that my church community was stuck in a position of psychic numbing and stunned silence in the face of evil. It was not that people did not care about what had happened in Northern Ireland on that dreadful day. We simply lacked the confidence to ask legitimate questions of God and had no language that might express the reality and pain of such evil and suffering. This problem is not unique to this particular congregation. The lack of such language is common in many western churches. This being so, the question is: Where can we find a language that will enable us to express these experiences and also to resist the evil that is inherent within them?

One of my colleagues, a young pastor, tells of a time when he was called to the scene of a devastating accident. Mary Anne Skinner was driving home with one of her four children. It was midday and her journey was a short one, about two miles, from the local superstore to home. Four hundred yards from her house, her car was hit head-on by another car driven by a young man who was drunk. He lost control of his car, veered off the road, skidded as he attempted to regain control of the car, and swerved back onto the road and into the path of Mary Anne's car. Her husband heard the noise and ran out of the house, accompanied by their other three children. He called for an ambulance on his mobile phone and ran towards the car. It was not until he got up close that he realized that the tangled mass of metal was his wife's car. Both Mary Anne and the child with her were killed instantly. The young man emerged from the crash unhurt. As the ambulance drove off, the youngest son moved closer and lay over his father, who was sitting on the curb, shocked. One by one, the other two children lay across their father and began to cry out. At first it was simply sobbing, but eventually words began to formulate from the huddle of bodies: "Why?" "Why did you take her, Lord!" "Why her? Why now?" "I want my mum back — now!" "Why did he not get killed!?" "Where were the angels?" My colleague, who had arrived at the scene, sat down beside the huddled pile of broken people. In silence he prayed . . . and wept.

Finding a Language: Raging with Compassion

This narrative resonates with the movement from silence to lament that was so powerfully expressed in Jesus' experience on the cross. And here we discover a clue about a language that might help us express and deal with the experiences of evil and suffering that we encounter. In what follows, we will examine the suggestion that by rediscovering the "forgotten" language and practice of lament we can develop a mode of resistance that can help us overcome the hopelessness and voicelessness that result from evil and suffering.

Lament is an important and frequently overlooked aspect of contemporary pastoral practice. Put simply, a lament is a repeated cry of pain, rage, sorrow, and grief that emerges in the midst of suffering and alienation. Lamentation is, however, much more than mere catharsis. Paul Ricoeur points out that lament "occurs as the opposite of blame; whereas blame makes culprits of us, lament reveals us as victims."[16] This is an interesting observation. Lament suggests that the person who is lamenting has a genuine grievance; he or she has been done wrong. Lament, and in particular psalm-like lament, is the cry of the innocent, the one who feels treated unfairly, who feels that God has somehow not lived up to the sufferer's covenant-inspired expectations. Most importantly, lament is prayer. It is, however, a very particular form of prayer that is not content with soothing platitudes or images of a God who will listen only to voices that appease and compliment. Lament takes the brokenness of human experience into the heart of God and demands that God answer.

> Relent, O LORD! How long will it be? Have compassion on your servants. (Ps. 90:13)

16. Paul Ricoeur, "Evil, A Challenge to Philosophy and Theology," *Journal of the American Academy of Religion* 53, no. 4 (2001): 636.

How long will the wicked, O LORD, how long will the wicked be jubilant? (Ps. 94:3)

How long must your servant wait? When will you punish my persecutors? (Ps. 119:84)

Lament allows us honestly to express rage to God for the injustices that constantly befall us but helps us at the same time to hold onto the compassion of God in the midst of human suffering. Lament enables us to recognize that we are not alone and that, ultimately, God has covenant responsibility for the consequences of evil. As Billman and Migliore put it:

> Those who lament and protest call upon God to exercise redeeming power to overcome the evil and suffering that is being experienced. They trust that God has the power to save them even as they ask why God has not yet so acted. What would the prayer of lament mean if the one who prayed did not believe that God had the power to rescue and redeem?[17]

Lament provides us with a language of outrage that speaks against the way that things are, but always in the hope that the way things are just now is not the way they will always be. Lament is thus profoundly hopeful.

> How long, O LORD? Will you forget me forever? How long will you hide your face from me? How long must I wrestle with my thoughts and every day have sorrow in my heart? How long will my enemy triumph over me? Look on me and answer, O LORD my God. Give light to my eyes, or I will sleep in death; my enemy will say, "I have overcome him," and my foes will rejoice when I fall. But I trust in your unfailing love; my heart rejoices in your salvation. I will sing to the LORD, for he has been good to me. (Ps. 13)

Lament gives a voice to suffering and releases rage in a context of faith and compassion. In so doing, it opens up the possibility of life and liveliness in the face of those forms of evil that would seek to destroy both. Engagement in such a process of lamentation is a pastoral practice that enables one to hang onto one's humanity in the midst of apparent dehu-

---

17. Billman and Migliore, *Rachel's Cry,* p. 114.

manization and to emerge from the silence that is forced upon us through our encounters with evil. As Hauerwas puts it, the psalms of lament

> are meant to *name the silences* that our suffering has created. They bring us into communion with God and one another, communion that makes it possible to acknowledge our pain and suffering, to rage that we see no point to it, and yet our very acknowledgment of that fact makes us a people capable of living life faithfully.[18]

Practicing Lament: The Form and Function of the Psalms

Later in the chapter, I will argue for reclaiming the practice of lament and for the importance of this particular form of Christian practice for practical theodicy. In order to do this, we need to reflect in some detail on what the lament psalms are and what they are intended to do. Walter Brueggemann suggests that these psalms have a very specific form, which moves from "*articulation* of the hurt and anger, to *submission* of them to God, and finally to *relinquishment*."[19] In the psalms, articulation of the pain and the submission of it to God are prerequisites for the third phase, relinquishment. Without this third phase of the lament, there is no possibility of moving towards praise and, ultimately, a healing of wounds. In this way, "the relational dynamic vis-à-vis God corresponds to the move of the formal elements."[20] The form and the function of the laments are thus intricately connected. But what exactly is it that the lament psalms are meant to do?

The Function of Lament: Rehabilitation

Study of the psalms includes much discussion about the original context and function of each psalm. One particularly fruitful approach is offered by Erhard Gerstenberger who argues that

> the individual complaints belonged to the realm of special offices for suffering people, who, probably assisted by their kinsfolk, participated

---

18. Stanley Hauerwas, *Naming the Silences* (Grand Rapids: Eerdmans, 1990), p. 82. Italics added.

19. Walter Brueggemann, *The Psalms and the Life of Faith* (Minneapolis: Fortress, 1995), p. 100.

20. Brueggemann, *The Psalms and the Life of Faith,* p. 100.

in a service of supplication and curing (probably rehabilitation) under the guidance of a ritual expert. The liturgies of such offices very likely would vary a good deal from place to place and throughout the centuries. It is important to note that individual petition rituals were apparently independent of local shrines.[21]

In taking this localized approach, Gerstenberger challenges those who would argue that the lament psalms belonged primarily to the larger liturgical context of the worship of the Jerusalem temple. Instead, he argues that their primary area of use was at a local level, their main function being the *rehabilitation* of an individual within the context of the tribe, clan, or family setting. In other words, the original setting of the lament psalms was within the worship of *small groups,* their primary purpose being the *restoration* and *rehabilitation* of those experiencing evil and suffering.

Patrick Miller, reflecting on the work of Gerstenberger, makes an interesting observation:

> If all this sounds more like the family or group therapy than prayer and worship in the church, that is neither surprising nor accidental. In his concluding remarks, Gerstenberger, noting the increasing isolation of individuals in a modern technological society, compares the rehabilitation of the sufferer in the Old Testament with contemporary group therapy movements that seek to reintegrate a distressed person into the primary group in a process of words and actions under the group leader who is an expert in the process or "ritual," (Gerstenberger, pp. 67-69). . . . The lament psalms are an indication of the fact that individuals live their lives "above all in the small world of the primary group" . . . rather than in the larger . . . sphere of community or people. It is in the small group that meaning is found and religion experienced.[22]

We will return to the significance of small groups for the practice of lament later in this chapter. But first we will focus on the idea of "rehabilitation." Precisely how might the lament psalms function in the process of rehabilitation and ultimate healing following traumatic events?

21. Erhard S. Gerstenberger, *Psalms, Part One, with an Introduction to Cultic Poetry,* The Forms of the Old Testament Literature (Grand Rapids: Eerdmans, 1988), p. 135.

22. Patrick D. Miller, "Current Issues in Psalms Studies," *World and Word* 5, no. 2 (1985): 135-36.

The "Formfulness" of Suffering

Medical anthropologists have taught us that suffering and pain are not experienced in a vacuum.[23] The way in which we experience suffering and the coping strategies that we use to deal with it are learned from family environment, cultural expectations, the media, and our religious values and beliefs. That is not to suggest that pain doesn't exist or that one suffers less simply by thinking more positively about it. The point is that suffering is shaped by external as well as internal forces. In other words, it is, to use Brueggemann's term, *formful*.[24] It tends to take its shape and form according to particular contexts, perceptions, and experiences. If this is so, the practice of lament may have the ability to form our suffering in quite specific ways.

Brueggemann, drawing on the work of the sociologists Peter L. Berger and Thomas Luckmann, highlights the way in which regularized use of language by a community creates, forms, and sustains the contours of their life-worlds:

> [R]egularized speech activity serves both to *enhance* and to *limit* the experience so that dimensions of it are not lost and to *limit* the experience so that some dimensions are denied their legitimacy. This suggests, applied to the lament form, that its regularized use intends to enable and require "sufferers" in the community to experience their suffering so that it can be received and coped with according to the perspectives, perceptions, and resources of the community. Thus the function of the form is definitional. It tells the experiencer the shape of the experience that is legitimate to be experienced.[25]

If this is so, then it becomes clear that the psalms of lament are not designed simply to *express* human pain and suffering. They are also designed to *form* human pain and suffering in quite specific ways. The

---

23. See, for example, the following, which discuss the cultural construction of illness and illness experience in some detail: Arthur Kleinman and Byron Good, eds., *Culture and Depression: Studies in the Anthropology and Cross-Cultural Psychiatry of Affect and Disorder* (Berkeley: University of California Press, 1985) and Z. J. Lipowski, "Physical Illness, the Individual, and the Coping Process," *Psychiatry in Medicine* 1 (1979): 91-102.

24. Walter Brueggemann, "The Formfulness of Grief," in Patrick D. Miller, ed., *The Psalms and the Life of Faith* (Minneapolis: Fortress Press, 1995), pp. 84-98.

25. Brueggemann, "The Formfulness of Grief," p. 86.

psalms of lament provide a language and a structure within which pain, suffering, grief, and despair can be ritualized and worshippers moved from one way of seeing their situation to a radically different way of see-ing. The form of the lament psalm is:

> a) to give a new definition of the situation, and (b) to get some action that is hoped for because of this peculiar definitional world. The form not only describes what is but articulates what is expected and insisted upon.[26]

Thus, the lament psalm is an important liturgical source and means of reframing suffering in the light of the hope and promises of God. The reframing enables, or at least initiates, movement from hurt and broken-ness to joy and praise.[27] This movement does not necessarily include physical deliverance from the situation, although such deliverance is often anticipated. The reframe is a spiritual one that opens up new possibilities that were not previously available.

The context of the psalms of lament is speech to and about God with the purpose of forming and re-forming our sadness and anger in particu-lar ways. To engage in the practice of lament is to enter into a process of *protest* within which one rages against the injustice of the way that things are in the *hope* that the way things are is not the way they should be or will be. When the psalmist agonizes, "My soul is in anguish. How long, O LORD, how long?" his question is not raged at a vague, unnamed God, but specifically at Yahweh, whose covenant promise has apparently been rup-tured by the horrors of the psalmist's experience. Lament is therefore not a mark of faith*less*ness but an act of faith*ful*ness in situations where faith and hope are challenged.

Lament as Practical Theodicy

While some psalms of lament are penitential, most appear to relate to in-nocent suffering. Brueggemann suggests that the experience of innocent suffering brings about a *theodic crisis,* that is, a crisis in the way that evil

26. Brueggemann, "The Formfulness of Grief," p. 88.
27. Claus Westermann, *Praise and Lament in the Psalms* (Atlanta: John Knox Press, 1981).

and good are understood.[28] For the psalmist, God's covenant with the Hebrews should mean that the good will prosper and the wicked will suffer. The reality of Israel's history frequently challenged this perspective, calling the Hebrews to rethink their worldview and their theodicies in the midst of their experience. However, Israel's theodicy differs from contemporary theodicy, for it is *profoundly practical.*

> Israel's theodicy is intensely *interpersonal, interactive, and covenantal.* Theodicy is not a riddle to be solved, but a troubled relationship to be restored. Israel is not preoccupied with a philosophical question but with the reality of life and communion with Yahweh. In the end the pain and suffering are not "explained" in this practice; rather Israel and Yahweh *work through* to a new depth of relationship in which, in the face of pain, serious healing and hope-filled communion are made possible and are embraced in praise, confidence, and joy.[29]

Thus, just as we saw in chapter two that the early church's response to evil was practical, we discover here that the theodicy of ancient Israel is similarly practical at its very core.

> Ancient Israel knows no "resolution" to the "problem" of theodicy. Such a pursuit is futile. But what Israel does know and practice is a candid relationship with Yahweh that permits communion in more intense and intimate dimensions of life. In that practice, Israel is determined that suffering is not finally a *barrier* to communion, but it is at least an *arena* for communion and at best a *resource and instrument* for communion. In the end, Israel finds covenantal communion adequate for its life, even in the midst of unbearable, inexplicable suffering. But that communion is only possible if and when Israel abrasively and relentlessly summons Yahweh back into its life.[30]

It is precisely such a theodic crisis that we encounter time and again within a pastoral context when people experience evil and suffering. "This is not the way the world should be!" "Why did you take her, Lord?"

---

28. Walter Brueggemann, *The Message of the Psalms: A Theological Commentary* (Minneapolis: Augsburg Publishing House, 1984), pp. 168-77.

29. Walter Brueggemann, "Some Aspects of Theodicy in Old Testament Faith," *Perspectives in Religious Studies* 26, no. 3 (1999): 265.

30. Brueggemann, "Some Aspects of Theodicy in Old Testament Faith," p. 267.

"Why her? Why now?" "My soul is in anguish. How long, O LORD, how long?" "How could God allow this to happen?" "Why do the guilty survive?" "How long must I wrestle with my thoughts and every day have sorrow in my heart? How long will my enemy triumph over me?" "Why me . . . why me?"[31]

However, for Christians, as for the psalmist, this crisis of theodicy should not be framed as a crisis of faith, but rather *a crisis of understanding.* Lamentation is first and foremost a mode of communication with God; it is a form of prayer. It is not "mere rage" or "therapeutic catharsis." Lament has a purpose and an endpoint beyond the simple expression of pain: reconciliation with and a deeper love of God. As a form of prayer, lament is both transformative and subversive. It is a profound statement against the world and the assumptions that drive the world. In putting into words their desires and expectations about the way things should be and the injustice of the way things are and by directing these words to a God who, they assume, exists, those who practice lament deal with their suffering in a radically countercultural way. Lament expresses rage, anger, hurt, and disappointment about situations and about God, but it does so within a context that is bounded by trust and a hope that, despite the apparent lack of any evidence, God is active in the world. Lament, then, points to the possibility that we are not trapped in situations over which we have no control and no power with which to grasp hold of our future. Lament asserts that the way the world is cannot be legitimated by blind triumphalism and false hope in human progress and that the pain of God's creation needs also to be embraced alongside the joy.

Suffering Differently

In this way Christians suffer differently from the way society expects. The New Testament claims that in the cross and resurrection of Jesus the power of evil and death is finally overcome. At one level, the New Testament does not appear to allow for the "ragged, raging unfinished business

31. Note that the question "Why me?" as it is expressed within the context of lament is deeply personal. The practice of lament pays little attention to the bigger question of why evil . . . the questions are why me, why now, why at this moment in time? The two sets of questions are quite different and indicate different starting points, one from a position of faith, the other from a position of doubt.

of protest that so characterizes the rhetoric of Israel in suffering."[32] Yet, lament continued to be practiced in the New Testament church.[33] Startling in this respect is, as we have seen, Jesus' use of Psalm 22 to lament from the cross. In its original context, this psalm accuses Yahweh of abandoning the people of Israel. Jesus uses it to express his sense of abandonment and alienation from God. Psalm 22 ends with praise and thanksgiving, which asserts the faith that God is in control and worthy of being praised. Such a return to God in faith and hope is really the only resolution that scripture gives to the problem of evil.

As noted, the psalms of lament not only reflect our experiences of suffering but they also *form* our experiences of despair in significant ways. We do not suffer in a vacuum. Our suffering is always mediated by our social context and our beliefs about ourselves, others, God, and the nature of reality. As Christians, we locate and interpret our suffering within the narrative of the life, death, and resurrection of Jesus. That story as it is revealed throughout scripture shapes and gives texture to our suffering and our experiences of evil. Put slightly differently, *Christians suffer, but they suffer differently.* They suffer differently because the narrative that guides the meaning of their suffering is different. The hopefulness of the gospel narrative enables Christians to take pain, confusion, and disorientation very seriously as awful human realities; yet at the same time, the gospel narrative places them within a framework of hope and new possibilities. The psalms of lament give us a certain perspective on the meaning of our suffering, one that takes seriously the real suffering of the cross and its implications for human suffering and the release and transformation of resurrection hope. As we release and sometimes vent our hurt and anger to God, we are freed to accept that even though this may not be the way we want life to be or indeed the way we want God to be, we are still safe to love God and to find hope in being loved by God in the midst of the pains of this world. In this sense, "the catharsis of the lament is to discover that the reasons for believing in God have nothing in common with the need to explain the origin of suffering."[34] The catharsis of lament occurs when we recognize the depths

32. Brueggemann, "Some Aspects of Theodicy in Old Testament Faith," p. 266.

33. For a deeper analysis of the use of lament in the New Testament, see Billman and Migliore, *Rachel's Cry,* chapter 2. For a useful recent exploration of the role of the Psalms in Christian life, see Sally A. Brown and Patrick D. Miller, eds., *Lament: Reclaiming Practices in Pulpit, Pew, and Public Square* (Louisville: Westminster/John Knox, 2005).

34. Ricoeur, "Evil: A Challenge to Philosophy and Theology," p. 647.

and reality of suffering and evil in all of their fullness and cry out against them from the our deepest hearts, while at the same time always remembering that God remains in control and is moving us towards a hopeful outcome. The task of the practice of lament is to produce a form of character that can live with unanswered questions, not through repression or denial, but by expression and active acceptance of the reality of evil and suffering and the love of God in the midst of it. By learning the practice of lament, we become the type of people who take seriously the pain and sadness of the world but refuse to be crushed by it. The "we" here is important. Pain and suffering do have the ability to crush even Christians. The importance of "we" is that even when an individual is struggling, the community to which the individual belongs carries and sustains him. When the sufferer "cannot reach Jesus," her friends open the roof of heaven and drop her down at the feet of Jesus in prayer, worship, and friendship (Luke 5:17-26). Lament requires a context of friendship and community that will sustain and enable an individual to move from lament to joy.

Lamenting as an Act of Faith

Thus, lament is not what it often appears to be. It is true that, as Brueggemann points out, the use of the "psalms of darkness" may be judged by those who do not understand their purpose as acts of unfaith or failure.

> [B]ut for the trusting community, their use is an act of bold faith, albeit a transformed faith. It is an act of bold faith on the one hand, because it insists that the world must be experienced as it really is and not in some pretended way. On the other hand, it is bold because it insists that all such experiences of disorder are a proper subject for discourse with God. There is nothing out of bounds, nothing precluded or inappropriate. Everything properly belongs in this conversation of the heart. To withhold parts of life from that conversation is in fact to withhold part of life from the sovereignty of God. Thus these psalms make the important connection: everything must be brought to speech, and everything brought to speech must be addressed to God, who is the final reference for all of life.[35]

35. Brueggemann, *The Message of the Psalms,* p. 52.

So lament is a public protest against the way things are. It enables victims of evil to express anger and disappointment with God and the ways things are. Lament breaks the silence and provides a hopeful voice that cries towards the future. Yet it does so in the context of the crucified and risen Christ, knowing that God has not only promised to answer those who lament, but has promised to journey with them until the promise reaches its ultimate fulfillment. Thus, lamentation is a process of spiritual catharsis, affirmation, and empowerment. As such it is a gesture of resistance in the face of evil.

> In the public utterance of such pain, both parties emerge with freshness. Obedience turns out to be not blind, *submissiveness* required by common theology. It is rather a bold *protest* against a legitimacy that has grown illegitimate because it does not seriously take into account the suffering reality of the partner. Where the reality of suffering is not dealt with, legitimate structure is made illegitimate when the voice of pain assumes enough authority to be heard.[36]

Lament gives a voice to suffering and provides a faithful language through which we can bring our pain before God. Lament spurs movement towards God at a time when our natural instinct is to move away from God. Lament gives a voice to rage and releases us to experience God's compassion. In so doing, it opens up the possibility of life and liveliness in the face of that which would seek to destroy both.

The Loss of Lament

Yet, despite their potential to give voice to suffering, transform evil, and enable healing, the psalms of lament are noticeably missing from contemporary liturgical practices. There is little doubt that the tradition of lament has been downgraded and often omitted from the liturgical and pastoral practices of contemporary western churches. Instead, much modern worship remains in denial, excluding the reality of pain and evil. Brueggemann suggests that "such a denial and cover-up, which I take it to be, is an odd inclination for passionate Bible users, given the large number of

36. Walter Brueggemann, *Old Testament Theology: Essays on Structure, Theme, and Text* (Minneapolis: Fortress Press, 1992), pp. 18-19, 21.

psalms that are songs of lament, protest, and complaint about the incoherence that is experienced in the world. At least it is clear that a church that goes on singing 'happy songs' in the face of raw reality is doing something very different from what the Bible itself does."[37]

While the psalms in general are used frequently within the worship and devotion of the church, they tend to be used selectively, with the psalms of lament often omitted. Denise Ackermann makes a similar observation from within a South African context: "Sadly, western Christianity has lost its ability to lament. Acts of lamentation have disappeared from our liturgies in our churches. Keening bodies addressing God directly, calling God to account for the intractability of suffering, are deemed to be liturgically inappropriate in mainline Christianity in my country."[38]

It is indeed odd that Christians claiming to be faithful to the Bible should choose to exclude such a significant dimension of the Bible's teaching. There seems to be an assumption that faith should not embrace negativity, that to acknowledge the reality of pain and sadness somehow diminishes God and threatens God's control over things. In an attempt to "defend God" we have excluded a vital dimension of human experience from God. It appears that we have overlooked the tradition of lament in an attempt to "protect" God or perhaps to protect ourselves from the possibility that the God we actually have is very different from the God we may want to have. As Hauerwas puts it:

> The God who calls us to service through worship is not a God who insures that our lives will not be disturbed; indeed, if we are faithful, we had better expect to experience a great deal of unrest. . . . The lament is the cry of protest schooled by our faith in a God who would have us serve the world by exposing its false comforts and deceptions. From such a perspective one of the profoundest forms of faithlessness is the unwillingness to acknowledge our inexplicable suffering and pain.[39]

Such a liturgical denial of the reality of sadness and suffering means that we can never effectively grieve over the way that life really is, nor can we

---

37. Brueggemann, *The Message of the Psalms,* pp. 51-52.

38. Denise M. Ackermann, "'A Voice Was Heard in Ramah': A Feminist Theology of Praxis for Healing in South Africa," in Denise M. Ackermann and M. Bons-Storm, eds., *Liberating Faith Practices: Feminist Practical Theologies in Context* (Leuven: Peeters, 1998), p. 96.

39. Hauerwas, *Naming the Silences,* p. 82.

develop strategies of resistance that are unfazed by negativity. Reclaiming the tradition of lament as a pastoral practice of resistance not only gives a voice to sufferers who are experiencing the effects of evil, but it also begins to mend the rift that evil tears between human beings and God.

Lamenting in Silence: Lament as Protest and Resistance

Before we move on to look at some strategies for practicing lament within Christian communities, one final dimension of lament requires attention. At the beginning of this chapter we reflected on the power of silence to express the experience of evil. But not only can silence express the personal pain of suffering; it can also be a radical vehicle of protest against evil in the public realm. We normally assume that lament is verbal. However, it can also silently resist evil.

The Politics of Silent Lament

Ackermann, reflecting on the political significance of lament during the years of apartheid, highlights the work of a South African organization called the Black Sash. She says:

> My interest in lament was originally aroused by the praxis of a women's human rights organization called the Black Sash. For well nigh forty years the women of the Black Sash engaged in the work of justice, in advice offices in different parts of our country, in acts of civil disobedience, in propagating and monitoring human rights, and in protesting waves of racist laws and repressive political actions. Their name was derived from the public wearing of black sashes as a sign of mourning for injustice. The sight of white women standing with their sashes, eyes downcast, at times holding punchy placards, became a familiar sight during the years of the struggle for democracy. This public lament for injustice haunted the lives of the apartheid politicians, a visible demonstration of (one of a few) pockets of white resistance to racist policies. The activities of the Black Sash earned them a generous accolade from Nelson Mandela who, in his first speech after his release from prison, called them "the conscience of white South Africans."[40]

40. Denise M. Ackermann, "Lamenting from the Other Side," http://www.crvp.org/

Such silence in the face of evil can be a symbol of resistance and hope.

Another example of silent lament as a powerful, public gesture of redemption is given by my colleague John Drane. He notes that

> in the last days of the communist regime in Poland, for several weeks thousands of people went onto the streets each night dressed as clowns. Demonstrations and meetings were officially banned, but it was the silent witness of this community of tragedy and comedy that eventually broke down the authorities' resistance: the message was all the more powerful because of the medium, because what the crowds were saying was obvious, but what kind of state could plausibly lock people up just for walking round the streets in silence dressed as clowns?[41]

Dancing Silently in Sadness

Many of us remember the horrors that took place in Chile during the Pinochet regime. It was a time of killings, tortures, and rapes; families were torn apart in the middle of the night; men, young and old, simply disappeared, never to be heard of again. At the height of the regime, groups of bereaved women, the mothers and wives of "the disappeared," would gather together and simply dance in front of the police stations. In gestures of lament and protest, they would pin photographs of their loved ones to their clothes and dance with invisible partners. It was a spiritual and symbolic act, dancing with the spirits of their lost ones and refusing to lie down before the evil forces that caused their grief. Their dance powerfully bound them together in the midst of their sorrows. An apparently intimate, personal spiritual act of lament reached beyond the individual and challenged evil at its very roots. When we in the West began to understand the meaning of those silent expressions of lament and spiritual pain, we also were moved to compassion, action, and protest, a protest that helped to overthrow that regime and curtail evil. Thus the personal

---

book/Serieso2/II-6/chapter_viii.htm. Another good example of how lament can be used within a political context is found in K. Jesurathnam, "Towards a Dalit Liberative Hermeneutics: Re-reading the Psalms of Lament," *Bangalore Theological Forum* 34, no. 1 (2002): 1-34. Here the psychological, theological, and liberating dynamics of lament are worked through in a challenging and transformative way.

41. John Drane, *The McDonaldization of the Church* (London: Darton, Longman & Todd, 2000), pp. 121-22.

and the political, the individual and the wider community, were bound together in the outreach of the spiritual dance of lament.

Significantly, each of these examples of political lamentation shows a *peaceful* way to counter and resist evil without embarking on violent actions, which can easily become evil in themselves. Evil is resisted, transformed, and ultimately defeated through the peaceful gestures of lament. As rock star Sting insightfully noted in his reflections on the Chilean women who danced for the disappeared:

> Its power is that it's ostensibly a peaceful gesture. It's innocent in a way: Security forces can't arrest you for dancing, although I'm sure they'd like to. But this is such a moving image, of women dancing with pictures of their loved ones pinned on their arms and clothes instead of going out there with Molotov cocktails, which only elicits another kind of violence. This is something that has to win — it's so powerful that it actually has to succeed. Whereas terrorism, no matter how justified by previous violence, will never work.[42]

Practicing Lament

Clearly, lament holds great significance for practical theodicy. It gives sufferers a hopeful language in which they can wrestle with God, self, and others as they attempt to make sense of the confusion that the experience of evil brings. Lament enables individuals and communities to move from silence into transformative speech that rages to God, but that ultimately has the capacity to reconcile people with God and help them learn to love God in spite of the presence of evil. Lament draws the sting of bitterness and opens up the possibility of reconciliation with God, with one another, and with one's self. Lament also provides a peaceful mode for challenging evil and presents a way of transformation that avoids the possibility of evil inspiring more evil. As such, it is a powerful pastoral tool.

All of this indicates that the church needs to reclaim the practice of lament in both its communal and interpersonal dimensions. We need to build our communities, structure our liturgies, and develop our relation-

42. Vic Garbarini, "Death, Rebirth, and the Business of Music: Sting on the Ties That Bind," *Spin*, November/December 1987, http://www.sting.com/news/interview.php?uid =1541.

ships so that the experience of evil, grief, and suffering need not be avoided or condemned as faithlessness, but so that, through the practice of lament, these things can be transformed into modes of resistance. So how might we achieve such a task?

Dealing with Hurt: Turning from Anger to Lament

There is little doubt that when the practice of lament currently has partic-ular poignancy. While I have been writing this chapter, the United King-dom has once again become a victim of terrorist activity. On 7 July 2005, fifty-two people were killed and many others seriously injured in London by Muslim suicide bombers. This attack comes in the wake of similar atrocities perpetrated against the United States on 11 September 2001 and in Spain on 11 March 2004. Such pointless destruction of life not only frightens us, but it also challenges some of our basic assumptions about individuals, society, and the world. How should we as individuals and as church communities respond? How we respond will determine whether such acts of wanton evil become the stimulus for further evil or whether we can discover, through the practice of lament, a different and more faithful way to respond and resist.

In his book *Grieving for Change,* theologian and social anthropologist Gerald Arbuckle notes the way in which religious communities (and soci-eties in general) develop unique cultures and psychological positions that influence the ways in which they respond to crisis, trauma, and change.[43] Such cultures contain the myths, assumptions, ideas, values, and plausi-bility structures that provide the community with a sense of identity and place in the world. Such a culture also determines how the community will respond in times of change and uncertainty. This culture develops in community members what might be described as a communal psyche, a tendency to think, act, and respond in similar ways by using similar psy-chological processes. Applying this to change in the church, Arbuckle applies the structure of the bereavement process to the question of why church communities find it so hard to accept and adapt to change. He takes as his framework the various stages of the grief process:

43. Gerald Arbuckle, *Grieving for Change: A Spirituality for Refounding Gospel Com-munities* (New York: Continuum, 1991).

- shock/denial
- inner and outer anger
- bargaining
- depression
- resolution/acceptance

Arbuckle argues that communities, like individuals, need to move through these stages when coping with change and loss. Unfortunately, many religious communities fail to adequately work through this process and find themselves stuck, often in the denial phase, failing to admit any sense of loss or need to change, and consequently finding themselves unable to move on to constructive resolution. Arbuckle suggests that a highly significant way to move communities from one stage to the next is through the use of ritual. Rituals can mark transitions for congregations that need to change and move on; they can help people accept the finality of the loss of the old and employ a transforming movement into the new.

Arbuckle's idea shows how church communities in particular should deal with the aftermath of events like 11 September or 7 July. Encountering such events, we face a real danger that our communal psyche will respond pathologically to the deep fear, grief, and loss that we suffer. Rather than working together through the complete grieving process, we can easily get stuck in one or other of the phases of grief. The political responses of the United States and the United Kingdom to these atrocities show the danger of getting stuck in outward anger. We find it easy to move from shock to anger, but moving towards acceptance is more complex. If we have no mechanism to move us from anger to acceptance, we are all in big trouble. Here the psalms of lament, especially the communal psalms of lament, have an important role to play. In his reflection on the events of 11 September, Brueggemann develops this suggestion:

> There is currently great attention to "Lament Psalms" as they function in "pastoral care," an immense gain in church practice. Not so much noticed, however, are "communal laments" (such as Pss. 74, 79) that bespeak the shattering of the most elemental public symbols of coherence and meaning, in the Old Testament embodied in the Jerusalem temple. This public dimension of grief is deep underneath personal loss, and for the most part, not easily articulated among us. But grief will not be worked well or adequately until attention goes underneath the personal

to the public and communal. My expectation is that pastors, liturgically and pastorally, most need to provide opportunity and script for lament and complaint and grief for a long time. No second maneuver after grief shall be permitted to crowd in upon this raw, elemental requirement.[44]

If we allow the gift of communal lament to free us from our corporate anger (if not our hurt, pain, and fear), then resolution becomes a reality and the danger of unfettered, unresolved anger is at least minimized. The question is how can we reach such a goal?

Remembering How to Lament

Changing the culture within our churches that denies sadness and anger at world events will not be easy. But if we are to resist and transform evil, then it is vital to find ways to reclaim the practice of lament. The work of Gerstenberger mentioned earlier and his use of the psalms of lament within a small group structure offer a way forward. A starting point for relearning how to lament can be with small groups within the church.[45] Small groups are a natural and time-tested way of doing church.[46] Indeed, small groups have been a dynamic factor in every major surge of new spiritual vitality in the church from Wesley to the Alpha course. I have written elsewhere about the significance of small groups for the pastoral ministry of the church:

> The creation of small pastoral care communities within the larger life of the church enables the church to provide a level of care and develop a depth of community which would not be possible within the traditional

44. Walter Brueggemann, "Truth-Telling Comfort," http://www.sermonmall.com/WTC/wtc22.html.

45. Paul Goodliff has noticed that, "One of the most significant changes to have affected the churches in the English speaking world over the past thirty years, and throughout the developing world for a longer period, has been the growth in importance of small groups in the church. From the base communities of Latin American Catholicism to the charismatic house groups of the New Church movement, new contexts for worship, learning, prayer, fellowship, and pastoral care have sprung up everywhere." Paul Goodliff, *Care in a Confused Climate: Pastoral Care and Postmodern Culture* (London: Darton Longman & Todd, 1998), p. 159.

46. See, for example, the model of church outlined in Acts 1.

pastor centered model of pastoral care. . . . The goal of small groups is to respond to the felt needs of a particular group of persons in the congregation, and to enable people to experience community in a real and tangible way. In so doing, people are enabled to develop a deeper understanding of themselves and of what it means to live within a caring community which *hears, listens, understands,* and *notices.*[47]

Such groups provide an ideal context within which the practice of lament can begin to find a central place within the life of the worshipping community.

Practicing Lament in Community

Groups like these provide a context within which both the personal and the political dimensions of lament can be reflected on and worked out. Ackermann highlights the significance and efficacy of such an approach within South Africa, a nation that has been broken and damaged by the many years of the evils of apartheid. Ackermann reflects on the need for both oppressors and oppressed within that context to find ways of lamenting that will bring healing and reconciliation:

> The hope is that communal lament of people in small groups in which lamentation of the afflicted is heard and responded to, will make for healing and the restoration of well-being. Although lament is expressed communally, it comes from individual hearts which are weeping and raging, seeking a response from God. The very nature of lament is profoundly spiritual and political. Remorse, anger, the need for accountability and justice combine as we contend with God.[48]

Such groups hold the potential to become places of honest rage and compassionate listening, places where an individual's pain and hurt can be "heard into speech" in the presence of God and within the fellowship of God's people.

The idea of being heard into speech resonates with the movement from silence into faithful speech that I reflected on at the beginning of

---

47. John Swinton, *From Bedlam to Shalom* (New York: Peter Lang, 2000), p. 120.
48. Ackermann, "'A Voice Was Heard in Ramah,'" p. 96.

this chapter. The expression "hearing into speech" comes from the thinking of Nelle Morton. While not focusing directly on lamentation, the following extended quotation from Morton helps illustrate the significance of the mode of lamenting that I am suggesting here:

It was in 1971 that I received a totally new understanding of hearing. It came from the lips of a most ordinary woman in a workshop I was conducting in Illinois. I remember well how this woman seemed a loner at first — quiet and almost frightened. Perhaps the idea of women needing to be free was new to her and she did not know what to make of it. Perhaps she was resisting and her silence reflected a subtle hostility or hesitance. As was my custom in such groups I was careful not to push her but wait until her time came and only she could judge that moment. I knew the easy talkers would in time run down and a more realistic, deeper level would emerge. The last day of the workshop, the woman, whose name I do not know, wandered off alone. As we gathered sometime later in small groups she started to talk in a hesitant, almost awkward manner.

"I hurt," she began. "I hurt all over."

She touched herself in various places before she added, "But I don't know where to begin to cry. I don't know how to cry."

Hesitatingly she began to talk. Then she talked more and more. Her story took on fantastic coherence. When she reached a point of the most excruciating pain, no one moved.

No one interrupted her.

No one rushed to comfort her.

No one cut her experience short.

We simply sat. We sat in a powerful silence.

The women clustered about the weeping one went with her to the deepest part of her life as if something so sacred was taking place they did not withdraw their presence or mar its visibility. Finally the woman, whose name I do not know, finished speaking. Tears flowed from her eyes in all directions. She spoke again: "You heard me. You heard me all the way." Her eyes narrowed then moved around the group again slowly as she said: "I have a strange feeling you heard me before I started. You heard me to my own story. You heard me to my own speech." I filed this story away as a unique experience. But it happened again and again in other such small groups when we allowed the pain to reach its own depth, or as another woman told me later: "You went down all the way with me. Then you didn't smother me. You gave it space to shape itself. You gave it time to come full circle."

It happened to me. Then I knew I had been experiencing something I have never experienced before. A complete reversal of the going logic. The woman was saying, and I had experienced, a depth of hearing that takes place before speaking — a hearing that is more than acute listening. A hearing that is a direct transitive verb that evokes speech — new speech that has never been spoken before. The woman who gave me those words had indeed been heard to her own speech.[49]

Reflecting on Morton's experience, we see how small groups that take seriously human pain and the need for understanding silence, listening, and lament could begin to enable the practice of lament-as-resistance. It is certainly true that to achieve such a trusting and open environment will take hard work and involves risk, patience, and perseverance. Nevertheless, the risk is one worth taking if evil is truly to be resisted and faithfully transformed.

Healing and Re-membering

Such groups take us back to the community of the early church where small groups of people met, often in the midst of extreme tribulation, to share fellowship, joy, pain, and hope, and to look forward to the coming time when evil would be no more. These communities shared their grief, pain, and alienation and sought to absorb it in ways that were faithful and sustaining. Developing small groups that can do the same will enable people to recognize their pain, express their lament and dis-memberment (the experience of being torn asunder), and begin the process of re-membering (the act of being drawn back together). To re-member something is to take that which was broken (dismembered) and make it whole again. In lamenting together, people take that which has been fragmented by the experience of evil and draw together the broken pieces, welding them into wholeness with the tears of God's people in the power of the Holy Spirit.

Understood in this way, the Eucharist has the potential to provide a

49. Nelle Morton, *The Journey Is Home* (Boston: Beacon Press, 1985), p. 75.

significant dimension of this process of re-membering. Sharing the Eucharist, with its symbolism of brokenness and unity embodied in the bread and the wine, mingles naturally with the cries of lament, the need for reconciliation, and the demand for a hopeful future. Within the theological movement of the Eucharist, the shift from despair to hope is cemented through the passionate meaning of the bread and the wine. Ackermann views the Eucharist as crucial for the healing process in the aftermath of personal and political suffering and fundamental to the process of lamenting in the face of evil:

> I imagine small, vital groups of people who, after lamenting together, give thanks for memories of God's loving power in the past and thereby affirm this power in the present. And, most importantly, faith in God's present desire to love, equips us to resist future evil. In particular God's dealings with women, children, the poor and the vulnerable, are remembered through recalling shared stories. This combination of memory and thanksgiving forges a new solidarity which is focused on Jesus, the one who was anointed to bring good news to the poor, to proclaim release to the captives, recovery of sight to the blind and freedom for the captives.[50]

Radical small groups, which recognize the importance of practicing lament and the personal and political dimensions of such practices, open up one way of re-introducing the tradition of lament to the worshipping practices of the church. As such they provide a crucial mode for the resistance of evil and are central to the practice of theodicy.

Friendship and Lament in Small Groups

As such groups form and develop, so also do the forms of friendship that it has been suggested are crucial for the resistance of evil. Friendship is a place where we practice lament. It is within the intimacy of our friendships that we can find a vital context to express the pain, the hurt, the agony, and the yearning for closeness to God that the lament psalms desire to instill in those who seek to love God and resist evil. Friendships shaped by Christ offer a secure and safe place where we can practice lament and resist the types of evil we have explored thus far.

50. Ackermann, "'A Voice Was Heard in Ramah,'" p. 99.

Creating New Laments

Within such small groups and friendships it is possible for people to learn how to use the psalms as a language to express their sadness and anger. It is also a place where people can learn how to create new lament psalms that reflect their own personal or communal pain and experiences of suffering and evil. A particularly good example of creating new psalms of lament is found in the work of Ann Weems. Weems writes out of her own experience of the tragedy of losing her son an hour after his twenty-first birthday. Weems expresses her pain in a series of moving personal psalms of lament:

> O God, have you forgotten my name?
> How long will you leave me
> In this pit?
> I sang hosannas
> All the days of my life
> And waved palm branches
> Greened in the new spring world.
> Rich only in promises
> From you
> I followed
> Believing
> And then they killed him
> Whom I loved
> More than my own life
> (even that you taught me)
> They killed him
> Whom you gave to me.
> They killed him
> Without a thought
> For justice or mercy,
> And I sit now in darkness
> Hosannas stuck in my throat. . . .
>
> Why should I wave palm branches
> Or look for Easter mornings?
> O God, why did you name me Rachel?
> A cry goes up out of Ramah,
> And it is my cry!

Rachel will not be comforted!
Don't you hear me,
You whose name is Emmanuel?
Won't you come to me?
How long must I wait
On this bed of pain
Without a candle
To ward off the night?

Come, Holy One,
Feed to me a taste of your shalom.
Come, lift to my lips
A cup of cold water
That I might find my voice
To praise you
Here in the pit.
Pull forth the hosannas
From my parched lips
And I will sing to all
Of your everlasting goodness,
For then the world will know that
My God is a God of promise
Who comes to me
In my darkness. (Psalm 1)[51]

Weems uses the structure and shape of the lament psalm to express the pain that she is experiencing in her encounter with suffering. The lament form offers her a genre that captures the reality of her pain and anger, but yet does so in a way that enables her to return to God in praise and with hope. Weems's approach offers much possibility for the type of rehabilitative group lament that has been highlighted here.

Within small groups it would be possible to create new lament songs in a similar way to Weems's approach and begin to practice lamenting in ways that are rich and appropriate. We might structure such an endeavor in the following way:[52]

51. Ann Weems, *Psalms of Lament* (Louisville: Westminster/John Knox, 1995), pp. 1-2.

52. I am grateful to my colleague Bill Gaventa, Coordinator, Community and Congregational Supports at The Boggs Center-UAP, New Brunswick, N.J., for providing me with this structure. It is reproduced here with his permission.

Instructions for Writing Lament Psalms

1. They are addressed to God. The community calls God by name, through a title, a phrase, or a metaphor reflecting an image of God. This section can call on God by many names.
2. They contain a complaint. This is what brings the one praying to prayer. The psalmist relates the undesirable situation. Again, several complaints can be mentioned.
3. There is an expression of trust. This flows from the first part and is an expression of faith in spite of the complaints. This is usually a simple one-sentence statement.
4. There is an appeal or petition. This is a cry that God intervene and is often accompanied by a reason for needing that intervention. "I am worn out with my groaning" (Ps. 6:6). Again, several petitions may be set forth.
5. There is an expression of certainty. The community assures God that it does not doubt even in the midst of its doubt. In everyday life we may follow a request with "I know you will do this for me."
6. The conclusion is a vow of praise. The community assures God of its love.

In these ways we can begin to initiate the movement from anger and denial towards the development of a position that is hopeful and faithful. Lament enables a movement from death and loss into hopeful new possibilities that encourage a vision of a meaningful and providential future.

The preceding suggestions for revised practice offer practical ways in which lament can be introduced to the worship of the church. There are, of course, many other ways that lament can be enabled. We need to reflect, for example, on how we preach about sadness, how we teach our young people to understand it, and how we might incorporate lament into our counseling practices. Nevertheless, in terms of developing communities of resistance that can begin to absorb pain and enable perseverance, learning the practice of lamenting in community may well be an appropriate place to begin.

Reclaiming Lament

In this chapter I have argued that practical theodicy needs to reclaim the practice of lament in its personal, communal, and political dimensions. Lament provides a peaceful mode for challenging evil and presents a practice for the transformation of suffering. Lament provides sufferers with a hopeful language in which they can wrestle with God, self, and others as they attempt to make sense of the confusion that the experience of evil brings. It draws the sting of bitterness and opens up the possibility of reconciliation with God, with one another, and with one's self. Lament enables individuals and communities to move from silence into transformative speech, speech that rages at God, but which ultimately has the capacity for and the goal of reconciling the suffering community with God and enabling both individual and community to find healing, hope, and the ability to love of God in spite of the presence of evil. As such, it is a pastoral practice that is crucial for practical theodicy.

As we have explored lament, we have also discovered its intimate connection with other forms of practice, namely listening to the silences and friendship. The interconnection of Christian practices was highlighted earlier. In this chapter the intimate connection between the practices of theodicy has become clear as we have explored one way in which evil can not only be resisted, but can also be transformed.

However, the movement from silence into lament is only a beginning. Indeed, taking lament seriously draws us into the presence of God in a way that is challenging, demands of us other steps, and requires us to learn other practices. In this chapter we have focused solely on the impact of evil on its victims. In the next chapter, we will shift the frame and consider how we deal with those who perpetrate evil and suffering. This brings us to the issue of forgiveness and repentance, justice and retribution. In the next chapter we will explore these issues by focusing on the practice of forgiveness as a mode of resistance to evil.

CHAPTER SIX

Battling Monsters and Resurrecting Persons: Practicing Forgiveness in the Face of Radical Evil

Jesus said, "Father, forgive them, for they do not know what they are doing."

Luke 23:34

Do not repay anyone evil for evil. Be careful to do what is right in the eyes of everybody.

Romans 12:17

Do not be overcome by evil, but overcome evil with good.

Romans 12:21

In the light of the discussion thus far, we might consider lament to be a foundational element of practical theodicy. It gives us a language that helps sufferers express and transform the pain and dislocation that accompany the experience of evil. By taking the pain and anger directly to God, we can reframe our experience in a context where the hope of God's providential goodness remains a practical and accessible option. Lament does not provide an explanation of evil or a reason for the existence of suffering. Quite the opposite, often it expresses human beings' total inability to comprehend why God would allow terrible things to occur. Rather than seeking to explain the presence of evil, it offers a language and a faithful response to its reality. Lament is a beginning point on the road to healing insofar as it enables us to move from silence into a mode of speech that is potentially healing and transformative. The act of lament is radical because it refuses to acknowledge the hopelessness and nihilism through which western culture views evil, suffering, and death.

From Lament to Forgiveness

But what do we do once we have brought our anger, hurt, and pain before God? Previously, I mentioned the dangers in becoming stuck in denial or anger. The act of lamentation hands over the experience of evil to God and trusts in God's judgment, mercy, and justice. It lets go of the desire for personal vengeance and moves towards trusting God to do what is right. This is not an easy thing to do. It is much easier to hold onto the hurts of the present and the memories of the past, thinking about how we might avenge the injustice that has been forced upon us. It is easier to hold onto our anger and bitterness and to look for revenge than it is to think about offering forgiveness to the perpetrators of evil and, perhaps, reconciling with them. And yet, Jesus' first words from the cross were words of forgiveness: "Father, forgive them, for they do not know what they are doing." A central challenge of the gospel and a primary response to the experience of evil that is modeled clearly in the life and death of Jesus is offering to forgive the perpetrators of evil. In Matthew 5:43-48, Jesus makes a disturbing statement:

> You have heard that it was said, "Love your neighbor and hate your enemy." But I tell you: Love your enemies and pray for those who persecute you, that you may be sons of your Father in heaven. He causes his sun to rise on the evil and the good, and sends rain on the righteous and the unrighteous. If you love those who love you, what reward will you get? Are not even the tax collectors doing that? And if you greet only your brothers, what are you doing more than others? Do not even pagans do that? Be perfect, therefore, as your heavenly Father is perfect.

These words are quite shocking and outrageous. Jesus calls his followers to discard the way of violence and revenge and to become known by their practices of peacemaking. He *commands* them not only to tolerate their enemies, but also in some sense actually to *love* them and to forgive them for their actions. The call to forgive and to love one's enemies runs coun-ter to our intuitive response to evil, which is often to hate and distance ourselves from the perpetrators. For many of us, revenge rather than for-giveness immediately springs to mind when we experience or witness acts of evil. We want to hit back at the perpetrator, often through mental or physical violence and force. To seek to forgive the one who offends against us or who commits violence against us or our families is not a "natural" way of dealing with evil. And yet, Jesus' words from the cross calling on God to forgive the perpetrators of his suffering initiates a radi-cal reframe of the "natural" responses of those who claim to be his follow-ers. Forgiveness sits at the heart of the gospel, and for Jesus it was clearly a powerful response to the experience of evil.

Such a radical practice of forgiveness raises important questions about the love and the justice of God. Does not the demand for forgive-ness place the victims of evil in an impossible situation? Is it fair to ask people who have gone through horrendous experiences to forgive those who caused those experiences? Is there not a danger, in taking Jesus' words seriously and in making such forgiveness central to practical theodicy and, indeed, to faithful discipleship, that we will create *victims of grace* — people who have already been wounded by the experience of evil and who now find themselves forced to forgive the very people who have done this to them? How can that be just and fair? Indeed, how can that be possible? How can we hold Jesus' command to forgive in critical tension with the understandable reality that many of us simply cannot forgive the things that have been done to us?

In this chapter we will explore the practice of forgiveness as a second element of practical theodicy. The key question that we will explore here is this: *How can we faithfully hold onto the tensions among the command to forgive, the desire for revenge, and the need to ensure that justice and hope are available for both the victims and the perpetrators of evil?* Failure to ade-quately resolve any aspect of these tensions will open up the very real pos-sibility that acts of evil end up begetting further acts of evil. In other words, without an adequate resolution of the tensions among forgiveness, revenge, and justice and hope for both victims *and* perpetrators, there is a real possibility that those of us who seek to battle evil may find ourselves becoming the agents of it instead.

Is There Such a Thing as Unforgivable Evil?

In working through these issues, we will find it helpful to begin by exploring a connected question: *Is there such a thing as unforgivable evil?* This key question runs throughout this chapter. Our answer will determine the way in which we understand forgiveness and our obligation (or otherwise) to learn how to practice it.

An Unforgivable Crime?

> In January 2000 a Pakistani man gave himself up to police, introducing himself by saying, "I am Javed Iqbal, killer of one hundred boys." He had lured the boys to his apartment in Lahore, given them food and entertained them, taken snapshots, and then suffocated them, dissolving the bodies in large vats of acid, which he poured into an alleyway sewer. Iqbal was proud that he had committed these killings after having made a pledge to himself that he would take the lives of one hundred children as an act of "revenge against the police." He had two young servants who had beaten him badly. When he took a complaint to the police, they ignored him and instead accused him of sodomy, something he had been charged with before. . . . He decided that the killing of children would be his means of retribution. "In this way I would take revenge from the world I hated," he said of his six-month homicidal binge. "My mother cried for me. I wanted one hundred mothers to cry for their children."[1]

On 16 March 2000, Iqbal was sentenced to death by Judge Allah Baksh Ranja, on one hundred counts of murder. In the verdict, the judge said that Iqbal and his co-accused, Sajid, should be strangled with the same iron chain that they had used as a weapon of offense and their bodies be cut into pieces and put into a drum containing acid as they had done with those of the dead children. All of this should be done in the presence of the families of their victims. The sentence was deferred and in October, 2002, Iqbal and his accomplice were found dead in their cells, apparently the victims of suicide. However, strangulation marks around the necks of

---

1. Trudy Govier, *Forgiveness and Revenge* (London: Routledge, 2002), p. 1.

the two prisoners combined with numerous injury marks on their bodies, some healed, some new, indicated that suicide may not have been the cause of death. The case is now closed.

Creating Monsters and Seeking Vengeance

Iqbal's actions are disturbing, monstrous, and unimaginably cruel. His murderous acts are undoubtedly evil and clearly challenge our providential hope in the goodness of God. We can begin to reflect on the implications of this situation by exploring our initial, intuitive responses. How we react at a pre-reflective level reveals much about the way we have been encouraged to deal with this type of trauma and distress.

Iqbal's actions evoke a mixture of responses. At one level, we are overwhelmed with outrage and disgust. Behavior such as Iqbal's makes us feel unsafe. Our outrage and disgust are saturated with a fear of the unknown that emerges from a situation that challenges the structures of our moral universe and which, if we allow it to, eats away at our existential sense of security and safety. If we are to be safe, then we have to find a way to distance ourselves from such behavior. *We* could not behave in such a way, so therefore Iqbal cannot be like us. One way of moving Iqbal from "us" to "it" is through the language of monsters and demons. "To act in this way is truly *demonic.*" "What kind of *monster* must this man have been to commit such evil?" "He is a *beast* who deserves all that is coming to him." "He is truly *evil.*" We feel comfortable and safe in the knowledge that he was "restrained" and "locked up." The world is now a better place, so we assume, because the ultimate sentence has been passed on him. We grieve for the parents, relatives, and friends of the dead children and identify easily with them, but Iqbal is something radically other than us. He is a *monster,* a *madman,* a *beast.* He is clearly "not like us." Ironically, when we think like this, we engage in a process of distancing and depersonalizing similar to that Iqbal probably used to justify his abuse of the children he killed.

At another level, the fear and loathing that we feel towards Iqbal can very quickly translate into thoughts of revenge. We are tempted to feel a sense of satisfaction, implicit or explicit, at the "natural justice" of Iqbal's demise. We may intuitively struggle with the nature and severity of the legal sentence passed on him — doing unto others what they have done to others is not always the best way to create a humane society and stands in stark contrast to Jesus' command to love one's enemies. We may also feel uneasy about his murder . . . and yet, there remains something primordially satisfying and apparently natural about the bad guy getting his comeuppance. We may not be willing to say so, but we take satisfaction in the fact that Iqbal met such an unpleasant and untimely end. The fact that we feel this way raises the awkward question of what it means for us to take pleasure or derive satisfaction from the demise of another human being, irrespective of what they may have done. Nevertheless, revenge and vengeful actions have a certain appeal, much as we may wish that it were otherwise.

Is Revenge an Appropriate Response to Evil?

If we reflect a bit more on these intuitive responses, how we should respond to Iqbal becomes even more complex. An initial problem with our intuitive responses relates to the question of revenge. Miroslav Volf highlights the problem thus:

> Deep within the heart of every victim, anger swells up against the perpetrator, rage inflamed by unredeemed suffering. The imprecatory psalms seem to come upon victims' lips much more easily than the prayer of Jesus on the cross. If anything they would rather pray, "Forgive them not, Father, for they knew what they did!" The powerful emotional pull of revenge is not the only reason we resist forgiving, however. Our cool sense of justice sends the same message: the perpetrator deserves unforgiveness; it would be unjust to forgive. As Lewis Smedes puts it in *Forgive and Forget,* forgiveness is an outrage "against straight-line dues-paying morality."[2]

We will return to the possible pastoral significance of the imprecatory psalms later. Here, we focus on the difficult tension between the command to forgive and the desire for revenge.

---

2. Miroslav Volf, *Exclusion and Embrace: A Theological Exploration of Identity, Otherness, and Reconciliation* (Nashville: Abingdon Press, 1996), p. 120.

What Is Revenge?

Often our first instinct, when we are faced with the consequences of evil, is to seek revenge. Not content to leave judgment in God's hands, as the practice of lament would urge us to do, we seek personal or corporate retribution on the evil-doers. But what is revenge? To take revenge on others is to deliberately inflict harm on them in response to some form of injury or insult, the object being to get personal or communal satisfaction. The idea of revenge as an appropriate response is ingrained within our culture and often appears to be a natural and morally acceptable response to hurt. "Classic" revenge films, such as *Death Wish, Rambo,* and *Die Hard,* propagate a culturally acceptable perception that vengeance is permissible, a perception that plays on culture's "natural" desire and expectation that the good guys will win and the bad guys will get what is coming to them.

But the problem with revenge is that it makes all of us evil. Irrespective of how intuitively and culturally "normal" revenge often appears to be, the act of revenge is morally and theologically highly problematic and has an inherent tendency to *create* rather than resist or deal satisfactorily with evil. Canadian philosopher Trudy Govier puts the problem with revenge thus:

> From a moral point of view, the desire to bring harm to another so that one may contemplate with satisfaction that harm and one's role in bringing it about is an *evil desire.* When we seek revenge, we do so in order to take pleasure in the fact that *the offender has been made to suffer* and *it is we who have brought this about,* as a response to the fact that this person has wronged us. What is wrong with revenge is that *to act as agents of revenge, we have to indulge and cultivate something evil in ourselves,* the wish to deliberately bring suffering to another human being and contemplate that suffering for our own satisfaction and enjoyment.[3]

Revenge takes us to a place where we find ourselves behaving in a similar manner to the way that the evil-doer behaved towards us. Govier puts it well when she states that "hatred that goes so far as to include joy at the evil meted out to another person is a morally unworthy emotion."[4] The problem with revenge is that it tends to turn innocent victims of evil actions into the perpetrators of more evil actions, which in turn precipitates

---

3. Govier, *Forgiveness and Revenge,* p. 13.
4. Govier, *Forgiveness and Revenge,* p. 13.

further evil actions. Revenge inevitably breeds revenge; vengeful actions are the precursors of vengeful actions. The desire for vengeance provides a rich context for the development of evil.

This is not to suggest that the perpetrators of evil should "get away with it." The issue of justice and the need for perpetrators to repent of their actions are vital and will be explored in more detail below. Perpetrators of evil should be held to account morally and legally for their actions. The point here is that rage without God enslaves us. It traps us in an endless spiral of revenge and counter-revenge. It forces us to turn persons into monsters and to act accordingly. When we act in this way, we easily become monsters ourselves. We simply need to look at the politics of Northern Ireland or the continuing tensions between Israel and Palestine to see the devastating impact of such a spiral of hatred and revenge. The problem with revenge is that it doesn't really make amends for the hurts that have been inflicted. Nothing could. It is a poor and unproductive attempt to solve what Hannah Arendt has described as "the predicament of irreversibility." This predicament is "an inability to undo what one has done though one did not, or could not, have known what he was doing."[5] If our deeds and their consequences could be undone, then revenge would not be necessary. The undoing, if there were a will for it, would suffice. But our actions are irreversible. Even God cannot alter them. And so the urge for vengeance seems irrepressible.[6]

The predicament of irreversibility informs us that we can never change what has happened, and worse, without forgiveness we run the risk of it happening again. In the absence of forgiveness violence becomes unending, and evil finds a permanent residence in the hearts of human beings and human communities. To take revenge is to take upon one's self a task that God has promised that God alone can and will fulfill. As the apostle Paul puts it: "Do not take revenge, my friends, but leave room for God's wrath, for it is written: 'It is mine to avenge, I will repay,' says the Lord" (Rom. 12:19; Deut. 32:35). Judgment and outrage belong to the victim, but vengeance belongs to God.

In talking about handing over the issue of revenge to God, we need to be careful about what is being said. We are not to let all our bitterness and

---

5. Hannah Arendt, *The Human Condition* (Chicago: University of Chicago Press, 1998), p. 212.

6. Volf, *Exclusion and Embrace*, p. 121.

hatred be placated by our fantasy that Iqbal will "rot in hell" or that God will "punish him eternally for his crimes." These things may be true. That is for God to decide. However, if the hope that God will reap revenge is the only motivation for not embarking on personal revenge, then we are simply being vengeful by proxy. Shults and Sandage, in their exploration of the theology and practice of forgiveness, recall the case of their work with a man who had been threatening to kill his former wife "and was daily praying the imprecatory psalms that call for God to wipe out his enemies. This was not the kind of lament that results in forgiveness."[7]

Handing over the issue of revenge to God's grace means letting go of it. When we let go we must be open to the possibility that God will not act in the ways that we might hope or desire God to. Giving the issue of revenge to God opens up the possibility that Iqbal may repent and that God, in mercy, may forgive him. We will need to examine this controversial suggestion very carefully.

Is Iqbal Forgivable?

Let us begin by examining the question: *Is it possible for someone to be unforgivable?* Intuitively, we might assume that Iqbal's crimes were too massive to be forgiven. Indeed, we may even argue that to forgive Iqbal would be to do an injustice to the children he murdered. However, the suggestion that those who commit evil acts are inevitably and irrevocably unforgivable actually does no favors to either the victims or the perpetrators of evil. Let us begin by thinking what it means to suggest that a person is unforgivable. Govier puts the point thus:

> To say that an act is from a moral point of view *absolutely unforgivable* is to say that it should forever be condemned and that the rage and resentment victims feel in its wake should never be overcome. To say that the person who has committed such an act is absolutely unforgivable is to say that he should never be forgiven for it, under any conditions. Absolute unforgivability in this sense is unqualified unforgivability, unforgivability *no matter what.*[8]

---

7. F. Shults and J. Sandage, *The Faces of Forgiveness: Searching for Wholeness and Salvation* (Grand Rapids: Baker Academic Books, 2003), p. 95.

8. Govier, *Forgiveness and Revenge,* p. 102.

For the person who is unforgivable, there is absolutely no possibility of redemption. If this is so, then the person who has suffered evil cannot find any sort of resolution or comfort by granting forgiveness. Even if the victim wanted to, she could not forgive that which is unforgivable. The victim has no recourse to anything other than hopelessness, unending bitterness, rage, or/and the desire for revenge. There is no hope that an offender will experience remorse or be able to repent for what has been done. It is also impossible for the victim to reframe his experience more positively, for example in the light of the cross, as even the atoning sacrifice of Jesus appears to have its limits.

Such a position raises some very challenging theological questions. At what stage does a person become unforgivable; that is, after what quantity of sin can we say that a person is unforgivable? Is it the quality or the quantity of the sin that counts? For example, does the accumulation of the average person's sins over a lifetime eventually add up to the equivalent of a murder or a rape, or do such acts of evil have a quality that lifts their perpetrators' guilt above that of the average sinner? If so, what is that quality and what is it that makes it unforgivable even for God? Most importantly, if a person *is* unforgivable, then is Christ's atoning sacrifice limited and can it bring atonement only for certain forms of sin? Such a position is theologically questionable and practically very difficult.[9]

---

9. All of this raises the interesting question of what Jesus meant by the unforgivable sin: "He who is not with me is against me, and he who does not gather with me scatters. And so I tell you, every sin and blasphemy will be forgiven men, but the blasphemy against the Spirit will not be forgiven. Anyone who speaks a word against the Son of Man will be forgiven, but anyone who speaks against the Holy Spirit will not be forgiven, either in this age or in the age to come" (Matthew 12:30-32). It is not possible to explore this in depth here. However, it is worth noting that this sin relates to the attribution of evil to the actions of the Holy Spirit. "But when the Pharisees heard this, they said, 'It is only by Beelzebub, the prince of demons, that this fellow drives out demons'" (Matthew 12:24). If one assumes that that which is profoundly good and revealing of the good is in fact evil, then one will never be able to turn to the source of forgiveness, God, and receive forgiveness. It may be that the point of Jesus' words is not so much that the sin is unforgivable, that is, qualitatively different from other sins. It is the fact that the sin makes repentance impossible which makes it unforgivable.

For God So Loved the World

In John 3:16 Jesus makes a statement that is clearly counter to our normal responses to acts of evil that appear to be "unforgivable":

> For God so loved the world that he gave his one and only Son, that whoever believes in him shall not perish but have eternal life.

This statement, which in many senses forms the essence of the gospel, implies that Jesus died, not for the good alone, but for *all* human beings; not only for the repentant, but also for those who *remain in their sin*. Paul emphasizes the challenging magnitude of this statement when he states in Romans 5:8 that "God demonstrates his own love for us in this: While we were still sinners, Christ died for us." Paul does not indicate that it is only certain sinners or certain forms of sin that Jesus died for. Jesus died for *all* human beings *while they were still sinners*. If this is so, then it would appear that Jesus' sacrifice was for Iqbal as well as all other sinners. More than that, *God loves Iqbal* in spite of his awful actions. A major challenge for Christians is the suggestion that God loves sinners as much as God loves those who have been redeemed. The difference between sinners and the redeemed is that the redeemed have realized how much God loves them and sinners have not yet come to such knowledge. The key point here is that *repentance, forgiveness, and, ultimately, salvation remain possibilities for even the worst sinner.* The idea of unforgivability is difficult to sustain in the light of the cross.

Understood within this frame, Jesus' words from the cross to those who inflicted evil upon him take on a strange new meaning. We come to realize that our own desire to be accepted and loved by God "just as we are," for who we are rather than for what we do, has radical implications, some of which may make us most uncomfortable. Yet, uncomfortable as we may feel, forgiveness of sinners remains the heart of the gospel. As we accept the forgiveness of God in faith, hope, and trust, we need to learn to be content with the fact that God can forgive whoever God in grace desires to forgive.

> Whether we are aggressors or victims, genuine repentance demands that we take ourselves, so to say, out of the mesh of small and big evil deeds that characterize so much of our social intercourse, refuse to explain our behavior and accuse others, and simply take our wrongdoing

upon ourselves: "*I* have sinned in my thoughts, in my words, and in my deeds," as the Book of Common Prayer puts it.[10]

There is no bipolar separation between the evil-doer and the innocent victim. Both need forgiveness and redemption, and, even though we may find it difficult, Jesus died for both. Repentance, as we shall see, demands a radical turning away from what was and a trusting in the unknown journey of faith. It means acknowledging one's implication in the sin of the world and beginning to live as if God were real. Repentance means giving up control and learning to trust God enough to feel certain that whatever God decides will be just and fair.

Forgiving and Excusing

To argue that all things are forgivable is not to suggest that all things are *excusable*. To suggest that something is excusable is to indicate that the perpetrators of a particular action may have an excuse for what they did. No excuse could meaningfully absolve Iqbal from culpability for his crimes. No matter what his upbringing, no matter what psychological or physical abuse he may have had to endure, his actions were totally inexcusable. Forgiving does not mean excusing. C. S. Lewis describes excusing in this way:

> Excusing says, I see that you couldn't help it, or didn't mean it, you weren't really to blame. If one was not really to blame then there is nothing to forgive. In that sense forgiveness and excusing are almost opposite.[11]

Forgiveness doesn't mean that everything is acceptable or excusable, simply that everything is forgivable. To forgive someone does not imply that his behavior is acceptable. Forgiveness assumes wrongdoing. Indeed, in recognizing wrongdoing and choosing not to be drawn into the circle of evil that wrongdoing creates, the victim sustains her dignity and redresses the power dynamic.

---

10. Volf, *Exclusion and Embrace*, p. 119.

11. C. S. Lewis, "On Forgiveness," in *The Weight of Glory and Other Addresses* (New York: Collier Books, [1949] 1980), p. 179.

Importantly, suggesting that there is no such thing as an unforgivable person draws attention to the often-overlooked fact that it is *people* whom we forgive, not acts. Very often person and act become inextricably intertwined in the ways in which we respond to evil. Such a conflation of acts and person is both understandable and dangerous.

> There is a sense, based on obvious logic, in which a person who has murdered is a murderer, one who has raped is a rapist, and one who has tortured is a torturer. But there is another sense, a human and existential one, in which such people are not *only* murderers, rapists, or torturers. They are human beings whose past lives have included evil, but whose future lives are open to new choices.[12]

What people like Iqbal or any other perpetrators of evil do is inexcusable. Nevertheless, particular actions, no matter how evil they may be, do not necessarily define the person who commits them. The actions may be monstrous, but that does not necessarily make the person who commits the acts a monster. Theologically, this line of discussion relates closely to the Christian imperative to love the sinner and hate the sin. Of course, the issue of repentance is of great importance, particularly in relation to receiving divine forgiveness. We will explore this later. Here the key point to have in mind is that all people can repent and gain forgiveness. No one is unforgivable.

This discussion of the possibility of unforgivability is important because to fail to recognize that perpetrators of evil can be forgiven and to refuse, implicitly or explicitly, to acknowledge their continuing humanity makes forgiveness impossible and makes further acts of evil possible. Failure to recognize this can draw victims into becoming participants in evil actions. When we write people off as unforgivable, we initiate a process that turns people into monsters. The consequences are dangerous: *We don't treat monsters in the same way as we treat people.* People we respect, monsters we fear and often seek to destroy.

12. Govier, *Forgiveness and Revenge*, p. 112.

"Evil Monsters"

Earlier, when we reflected on Iqbal's evil actions, I suggested that one response to the experience of evil was to distance ourselves from it, to pretend that the evil person was "not like us." Our discussion of unforgivability has challenged the reality of such a position. Nevertheless, the process of distancing is important to understand. When we encounter evil on a personal or a social level, a common response is to *objectivize* and *distance* ourselves from the evil act, evil person, or evil process. When this happens we set up strategies to battle against the evil or to exclude it from our presence either physically via prisons or special hospitals or psychologically through the processes of labeling, distancing, and scapegoating. We find it comforting to assume that evil is somehow external, a *thing* out there committed by the "other." The murderer, the rapist, the terrorist, the child-abuser cannot be "one of *us*" because *we* would not be capable of such horrendous acts. Thus, we keep evil on the margins of our worldview, framed as something that is radically different from us. When this happens we turn *people* into *monsters* and act accordingly.

An interesting example of how this process occurs is found in the work of Dave Mercer, Tom Mason, and Joel Richman on the discourse of evil in a forensic nursing context.[13] These researchers (themselves psychologists and mental health nurses) carried out a fascinating piece of research at Ashworth High Security Hospital in Liverpool in the United Kingdom.[14] They explored the significance of the language of evil used by forensic nurses in their relationships with people who were deemed to be "criminally insane," that is, people who had carried out extreme crimes of violence, abuse, and murder and who had been judged by the courts to be in some sense mentally disordered. Mercer and his colleagues uncovered evidence that, within a forensic nursing context, the allocation of the label

---

13. Tom Mason, Joel Richman, and Dave Mercer, "The Influence of Evil on Forensic Clinical Practice," *International Journal of Mental Health Nursing* 11 (2002): 80-93; Dave Mercer, Tom Mason, and Joel Richman, "Good and Evil in the Crusade of Care: Social Construction of Mental Disorders," *Journal of Psychosocial Nursing* 37, no. 9 (1999): 13-17; Dave Mercer, Joel Richman, and Tom Mason, "Out of the Mouths of Forensic Nurses: A 'Pathology of the Monstrous' Revisited," *Mental Health Care* 3, no. 6 (2000): 197-200.

14. Ashworth High Security Hospital is a highly secure psychiatric hospital in the United Kingdom that provides care and treatment for mentally disordered individuals who are considered dangerous or violent or who have criminal tendencies.

"evil" could have significant implications for nurse-patient relationships and might have been an underlying cause for previous abuses perpetrated by nurses on patients within that context.

In their research, Mercer and his colleagues noted that the term "evil" is quite regularly used within "lay" nursing discourse (that is, the day-to-day language used by nurses, as opposed to the professional language of psychiatry or law). However, they did not apply the term to all patients. The nursing staff seemed to tolerate people who were "classically" mentally ill (psychotic, bipolar, and so forth), even when they had committed horrible crimes. However, nurses quite differently perceived those with a diagnosis of "psychopath" or "severe personality disorder." People with these diagnoses fell out with the legitimating structures of psychiatry. Because there was no clear psychiatric basis or explanation for these patients' actions, nursing staff linguistically isolated them from the rest of the patients and ascribed a new "diagnosis" to them: *evil*. Using the language of evil meant that, in significant ways, nurses wrote off these patients as not fully human beings; the nursing staff linguistically shifted them from *persons* to *evil monsters*.

Bestowing Evil and Creating Monsters

Interestingly, allocation of the label "evil" was neither random nor a purely pejorative act. Rather, this labeling reflected what the researchers described as a "formulation of a rule-structured taxonomic ordering."[15] This is outlined in table 1 below.

Table 1. A Taxonomic Ordering of Evil in Nursing Discourse

Absence of medical descriptors
 Evil was only employed if there was no evidence of physical or psychiatric symptoms.

Nature of the attack
 To qualify as evil, the nature of the attack or assault had to be seen as deliberate, planned, and purposeful.

---

15. Mercer *et al.,* "Good and Evil in the Crusade of Care," p. 16.

Extinction of moral bonding

Evil was linked to the transgression of practical and abstract boundaries, implying free will, choice, intelligence, and unrestrained "instinct."

Adjacent pairing of opposites

Evil was associated with offences where there was a generational gap between victim and perpetrator, for instance, rape of children or the elderly.

Reality testing

Acts were more likely to be described as evil if a pattern of "deviant" behavior had been established over time and "tested out" in the world.[16]

Nurses applied the label "evil" when the patient was deemed to be aware, reasonable, and morally responsible for the particular actions he or she participated in. Significantly, psychiatric diagnosis appeared to "expurgate the demons" and free the person from the accusation of being evil. Thus, such language as "an evil no-hoper," "this one is beyond help," "just rotten through and through," "evil, pure evil," and "the only way out for this man is in a box [coffin]" sat in uneasy tension with the nurses' expressed clinical aims for the patients, such as caring, developing self-esteem, and enabling meaningful relationships.[17] The researchers end their report with this unsettling statement: "These perceptions conceptually move the patient beyond the possibility of rehabilitation or, at least, beyond the ability of psychiatry to effect a cure."[18] The nurses perceive that psychiatry can no longer help these "evil creatures." They judge the "evil person" "untreatable" and in a sense "untouchable," and they employ particular strategies (physical and psychological) to move him or her out of the world of persons and therapeutic intervention and into the realm of lepers, monsters, and "untreatability." Such language not only degraded the patients, but it also forced the mental health caregiver into a position where the danger of inhumane practices becomes a

---

16. Mercer *et al.,* "Good and Evil in the Crusade of Care," p. 15.

17. Mercer *et al.,* "Good and Evil in the Crusade of Care," p. 16.

18. Mercer *et al.,* "Good and Evil in the Crusade of Care," p. 17. For a fascinating exploration of the wider implications of the language of evil for psychiatry see H. Prins, "Psychiatry and the Concept of Evil," *British Journal of Psychiatry* 165 (1994): 297-302.

real possibility, a danger that has been embodied historically in institutions such as this one.

This is an important point. James Waller, in his exploration of the roots of extraordinary evil, observes the role that language plays in the process of dehumanization, which can open the way for the perpetration of evil actions. In all of the genocidal situations Waller examines, at some point a movement towards what he describes as *linguistic dehumanization* occurred. In the Holocaust "the Nazis redefined Jews as 'bacilli,' 'parasites,' 'vermin,' 'demons,' 'syphilis,' 'cancer,' 'excrement,' 'filth,' 'tuberculosis,' and 'plague.'"[19] In Rwanda, the Hutu extremists named the Tutsi *inyenzi,* meaning "cockroaches" or "insects." Waller notes that this linguistic move is a central aspect of the process of dehumanization. Labeling people as evil or as monsters can easily function in a way that dehumanizes them and opens the way for the perpetration of further acts of evil. You don't treat "evil monsters" in the same way as you treat humans. "Creating monsters" in response to evil acts not only destroys the liveliness of the patient but also that of the caregiver and in this way becomes an evil in itself, an insidious form of evil, which in the long term makes all participants less than human.

Evil Breeds Evil

This problem of evil breeding evil and the ways in which it is possible for people, often unknowingly, to get caught up in it is highlighted in the public responses to one of the United Kingdom's most notorious child murderers, Myra Hindley. Her experience helps show how "monster-making" occurs and also illustrates crucial aspects of a faithful response to evil actions.

Britain's "Most Evil" Woman

Myra Hindley was a notorious British murderer who, along with her lover Ian Brady, was jailed for life in 1966 for killing two children. Later she confessed to killing three other children. The couple also tortured some of the children they abducted. They tape-recorded their abuse of one of

---

19. James Waller, *Becoming Evil: How Ordinary People Commit Genocide and Mass Killing* (New York: Oxford University Press, 2002), p. 246.

**Myra Hindley,
Britain's "Most Evil" Woman**

the children, Lesley Ann Downey. This tape, played at Hindley's trial, devastated listeners. Hindley bore the label of "the most evil woman in Britain" and, prior to her death in 2002, there were frequent and vehement public outcries each time it was suggested that she might be released. Despite the fact that she committed these crimes more than three decades ago, the public's perception was still shaped by the picture taken in 1966, a picture that freezes and defines her eternally — hollow-eyed, defiant, and sinister. In the press she is often referred to as "a beast,"[20] an "evil monster," and "the most evil woman of all time."[21] In a strange way, it seems as if we need her to be a monster in order to make sense of her horrific actions.

But of course, Hindley was not a monster. She died as an aging woman with arthritis, angina, and a distance learning degree in humanities from the Open University. Indeed, in her later years she became a born-again Christian, apparently with a deep faith and what appeared to be a genuine

20. *Daily Mirror*, 1997.
21. *The Sun*, 1997.

love for Jesus. Chilling as Hindley's crimes undoubtedly were, another dimension of her story is, in a sense, equally chilling. Before those two years in which she lured five children to their deaths, she lived an exemplary life and was even in demand as a babysitter. Throughout her imprisonment, she showed no criminal tendencies, and experts were unanimous in the opinion that she posed no threat to society. The detective who took her confession in 1986 has no doubt: "Had she not met Ian Brady and fallen in love with him, she would have got married and had family and been like any other member of the general public."[22] Her actions were evil, but it appears that calling her an "evil person" may be inaccurate. And yet, right up to her death, she remained a monster in the eyes of the public; she was the epitome of evil. None of this is intended in any way to justify or minimize Hindley's terrible crimes. The point is that the evidence seems to suggest that she was, in significant ways, "just like us."

Once a Monster, Always a Monster?

In 1994, Hindley made a public statement, saying she had been "wicked and evil" and had behaved "monstrously."[23] It would seem that Hindley herself recognized the seriousness of her actions and used the language of evil and monsters to describe herself: "Without me, these crimes could probably not have been committed."[24] This is true, of course. She was guilty and she did behave, in a sense, monstrously, but does that make her a monster? After describing herself in the language of monsters Hindley goes on to say: "However, . . . *I ask people to judge me as I am now and not as I was then.*"[25] Clearly, Hindley felt that there had been a significant change in her life, a change that, at least in her perception, moved her from being a monster back to being a person. This movement from monster to person was acknowledged in 1999 by Hindley's prison therapist Joe Chapman, who said that Hindley had admitted her own guilt and become genuinely remorseful, even if in public she still tended to blame Brady.

---

22. H. Brand, "Myra Hindley," *Third Way* 24 (April 2000).

23. BBC News Online, Thursday 21 November 2002, http://news.bbc.co.uk/1/hi/england/2497335.stm.

24. BBC News Online, Friday 15 November 2002, http://news.bbc.co.uk/1/hi/uk/581580.stm.

25. Guardian Unlimited, Friday 15 November 2002, http://www.guardian.co.uk/crime/article/0,2763,841041,00.html.

Notably, he said: *"I think Myra was evil then but is not evil now."*[26] Chapman and Hindley indicate that "evil" may not be an ontological character trait but rather a transient action or set of actions that do not necessarily define the entirety of the person who commits them.[27]

The Social Construction of Evil

It is also useful to recognize the role that Hindley's gender played in the construction of her as an "evil monster." Meg Barker, reflecting on the gender implications of the ascription of the label "evil," uses Myra Hindley's situation as an example of the way in which gender stereotypes and negative cultural assumptions combine to create "monsters." She quotes from a British TV Channel 4 documentary interview with Alexander Carr from the Cheshire Constabulary. Carr was the police officer who arrested Myra Hindley. His comments are telling:

> "I came to think of her [Hindley] as being worse than Brady because, for the opposite reason, because she was a female and she had participated in these awful crimes which, to my mind, was terrible." (Interviewer asks, "Why did her being female make a difference?") "Well . . . she . . . there was . . . usually they portray some motherly instinct or protective instinct to the young, but that was absent wasn't it? . . . That mug shot of Myra Hindley portrayed her as she really was. She was a brassy blond, with staring eyes and an impassive expression on her face."[28]

In Carr's eyes, not only were Hindley's crimes shocking, but the fact that she was a woman and behaved in this way was equally shocking. Women are meant to be nurturing, caring, and protective.[29] To act in any other

---

26. BBC News Online, Friday 15 November 2002, http://news.bbc.co.uk/1/hi/uk/581580.stm.

27. Not everyone agrees with this line of thinking. Haybron, for example, argues for the existence of evil as a recognizable character trait that is qualitatively different from other forms of behavior (D. M. Haybron, "Moral Monsters and Saints," *The Monist* 85, no. 2 [2002]: 260-84). However, as we shall see, the argument for evil as qualitatively different from other forms of human behavior is open to significant challenge.

28. Meg Barker, "Women, Children, and the Construction of Evil," http://www.wickedness.net/Barker.pdf.

29. For further discussion of the gender implications of evil, see M. Barker, "The Evil That Men, Women, and Children Do," *The Psychologist* 15, no. 11 (2002): 568-71.

way challenges the cultural stereotype and moves the woman into a position where people can no longer identify with her or her actions. This leaves the woman open to the public's ascription of the label of "evil." In her book *Moving Targets,* Birch notes the incongruity between Hindley's public portrayal and the portrayal of her accomplice Ian Brady and of another child murderer, Raymond Morris, who sexually assaulted and killed three girls around the same time as Hindley and Brady's crimes.[30] The men were quickly forgotten. Birch attributes the apparent inequalities in treatment between Hindley and others who have committed similar crimes to her "unhinging our assumptions about women." Not coincidentally, the tabloid press has consistently focused on Hindley's lack of femininity, her physical looks, and her apparent lack of emotion at her trial. She failed to present herself as a victim and challenged many of the stereotyped images of what a woman should be and how a woman should behave. Birch argues that Hindley fits well the cultural stereotype of the treacherous and sexually active peroxide blond that was prevalent in post–World War Two cinema (such as the *femme fatal* in *film noire*) and that continues to be in popular movies such as *Basic Instinct,* with Sharon Stone playing precisely such a blond, manipulative, and sexually deviant character. Birch clearly highlights the interplay between cultural assumptions about gender and gendered behavior and the creation of "evil monsters," as well as the tendency to see evil as absolutely *other* from that which is perceived as good. While evil is clearly real, Birch's point is that it also involves complex social and psychological dimensions, causing it to be constructed in quite particular ways.

None of this is intended in any way to justify Hindley's actions or to excuse what she did. Her actions were unimaginably evil, brought devastation to many families, and challenged people's faith in the providential goodness of God in profound ways. To suggest that she was a person, not a "monster," is not in any sense to absolve her of responsibility or guilt, nor does it minimize the magnitude of what she did. It also does not challenge the need for justice and punishment within the law. The point is that despite, her evil actions, Hindley was not a monster; she remained a person capable of remorse, repentance, and, it would appear, redemption. It would seem that, at least in Hindley's case, merging evil actions with the

---

30. H. Birch, *Moving Targets: Women, Murder, and Representation* (London: Virago Press, 1993).

all-consuming category of "evil people" may not stand up to scrutiny. If this is true for Hindley, it may also be true for others.

When Grace Arrives Unannounced

Let us explore this suggestion more fully by considering the implications of an incident with similar dynamics. In March 2005 at 2 a.m., Ashly Smith went out to buy a pack of cigarettes. Within the hour, Brian Nichols, a man wanted for raping one woman and murdering another woman and three men, had forced her into her apartment, tied her up in the bathtub, and told her, "I'm not going to hurt you if you just do what I say." Smith was faced with the type of dilemma that inhabits many of our nightmares. How should she respond in the presence of such a "monster"? Smith's mode of resistance was to talk with him. As Andrew Sullivan recounts the story in his essay "When Grace Arrives Unannounced,"[31] Smith

> saw him not as a monster but as a human being. She talked with him. She told her story — how her husband had been stabbed in a dispute and had died in her arms, how she then had developed a drug habit, had been caught for speeding and drunken driving, had been arrested for assault (the charges were dropped), had ceded custody of her young daughter to her aunt. She showed him her wounds as a human being. And she saw in that man a wounded soul.

More than that, she, in a most interesting way, drew the encounter into the presence of God. Sullivan suggests that "Smith's weapon, it appears, was a hugely popular book, *The Purpose-Driven Life,* by Rick Warren, an unabashedly Christian guide to making it through life's highs and lows by constantly asking what God intended for you. The book . . . insists on the notion that God knows all of us intimately, especially sinners."

Through her sharing of her experience and the powerful challenge of Warren's book, the possibility of redemption and deliverance became a reality for Nichols, a possibility that he appears to have grasped. The power of this story lies in its ordinariness. Smith was not an angel and

---

31. Andrew Sullivan, "When Grace Arrives Unannounced," *Time,* 28 March 2005, www.time.com/time/magazine/article/0,9171,1039693,00.html.

Nichols, it seems, was not a demon. Each contained elements of both. Sullivan concludes:

> We latch onto this story not just because it's a riveting end to a high-stakes manhunt. We find ourselves transfixed and uplifted by the sordid ordinariness of it all. He was an alleged rapist and murderer. She was tied up in a bathtub, clinging to the wreckage of a life that was barely afloat. One was a monster, the other a woman unable to care for her five-year-old, looking for cigarettes in the dark. And out of that came something, well, beautiful. He saw his purpose: to serve God in prison, to turn his life around, even as it may have been saturated in the blood and pain of others. She saw hers: to make that happen. These people weren't saints. Grace arrives unannounced, in lives that least expect or deserve it . . . the message of the Gospels is that God works with the crooked timber of human failure. That was an exceptional moment of redemption.

Smith and Nichols remind us that it may be that even "evil monsters" can find redemption.

The Myth of Pure Evil

If this is so, then it raises an important question: *why do we embark on this process of "monster-making" in the face of evil?* What can we learn from it? At the heart of the processes we have been exploring is what Roy Baumeister has described as *the myth of pure evil.*[32] This myth relates to the general view that people who commit evil acts are significantly abnormal, that they are fundamentally different from other people and have an inbuilt and unexplainable propensity for harming others for little or no reason. Often, it is assumed, they gain some sort of sadistic pleasure from their cruelty. The myth of pure evil assumes evil to be wholly *other,* the irrational and incomprehensible actions of distant monsters. The myth makes an absolute bipolar division between that which is good and that which is evil. Victims are necessarily all good and without responsibility, and perpetrators are necessarily all bad without the possibility of redemption.

---

32. Roy F. Baumeister, *Evil: Inside Human Violence and Cruelty* (New York: Henry Holt, 1997).

This myth gains currency from the images of evil produced by the media and cultural myths. These images portray simple black/white battles between the clearly defined forces of good and evil. Evil people have no obvious reasons for acting in the ways that they do; they seem to be sadistic and evil for the sake of it. Baumeister offers eight characteristics that, he argues, comprise the myth of pure evil:[33]

1. It involves the intentional infliction of harm on people.
2. It is driven by the wish to inflict harm merely for the pleasure of doing it.
3. The victims of evil are innocent and good.
4. Evil people are outsiders, the enemy, not part of the in-group.
5. Evil is as old as creation.
6. Evil represents the antithesis of order, peace, and stability.
7. Evil people are driven by egotism.
8. Evil people have difficulty maintaining control over their feelings, especially rage and anger.

Reflecting on the examples of evil we have explored so far, we can see this myth at work. The myth of pure evil distances us from evil, making it an aberration that is carried out by distorted individuals who bear little if any resemblance to "us."

The problem is that the myth of pure evil is simply not true, as the stories of Hindley and Nichols have suggested. It really functions as a cultural defense mechanism to hide aspects of ourselves and our cultures that are distasteful and problematic. Baumeister shows clearly that there is no such category as "evil people" from whom we can legitimately distance ourselves and to whom we can refer as "the epitome of evil." Very rarely is evil carried out for sadistic purposes. Most acts of evil are carried out in an attempt to fulfill personal or idealist goals. They are not carried out by "monsters" but by ordinary human beings who have become desensitized to the moral and personal significance of their actions. The worrying implication of such a suggestion is, of course, the possibility that *everyone* has the potential to behave in evil ways.

---

33. Baumeister, *Evil*, pp. 72-75.

Becoming Evil

Baumeister argues that, given the correct circumstances and the appropriate level of desensitization, most, if not all, people will engage in or fail to notice the significance of acts that are profoundly evil. He argues that ordinary people engage in evil acts because they find them useful in the pursuit of their own goals or ideological hopes. They simply do not take seriously the harm that their actions cause other people. Only around five percent of people engaging in evil actions actually enjoy what they are doing.[34] Even when people come to enjoy the evil they do, it is through a process of desensitization that begins with revulsion and then moves on to normalization and, for a small minority, pleasure. Baumeister gives as an example the way that German police involved in mass killings in Poland during World War Two gradually became desensitized to killing.

> The accounts of the first massacre indicated that most of the men were profoundly shocked and upset by what they had done. The evening after those first killings, the men sat quietly, shaken, unable to talk about what had happened or about anything else. They ate little and drank a great deal of alcohol. Some had nightmares. But as they participated in further massacres, they showed fewer signs of distress. Although killing people may have remained an unpleasant duty, it became far less upsetting. After a day's work the men would sit together at meals, talk, laugh, play cards, and do other normal activities. The later killings were apparently not a moral and psychological shock to their systems the way the first ones were. Part of the explanation was that they devised ways of performing those duties that made them easier, but it also appears that they were less shocked and upset by shooting people. The involvement in killings, like the rest of the job, had faded into an ordinary routine.[35]

These police officers were not mentally deranged. They were normal people who under normal circumstances would not have indulged in such

34. This small percentage does, of course, receive high-profile media coverage. (See for example B. Carey, "For the Worst of Us, the Diagnosis May Be 'Evil,'" *The New York Times,* 8 Feb. 2005.) This, in turn, contributes significantly to the myth of pure evil. Nevertheless, bearing in mind the level of evil there is in the world and the types of statistics presented in the previous chapter, it is clear that it is not only high-profile criminals who commit horrendous acts of evil.

35. Baumeister, *Evil,* p. 286.

evil. However, given particular circumstances, they willingly and eventually quite nonchalantly perpetrated horrendous forms of evil.

William Styron, in his novel *Sophie's Choice,* makes a similar observation in relation to the Holocaust:

> Real evil, the suffocating evil of Auschwitz — gloomy, monotonous, barren, boring — was perpetrated almost exclusively by civilians. Thus we find that the rolls of the SS contained almost no professional soldiers but were instead composed of a cross-section of German society. They included waiters, bakers, carpenters, restaurant owners, physicians, a bookkeeper, a nurse, a fireman; the list goes on and on with these commonplace and familiar citizens' pursuits.[36]

Both soldiers and civilians went home at night, played with their children, shopped, fell in love, and did all of the things that normal human beings do . . . and yet, they remained capable of carrying out the most despicable of actions.

They Must Be Mad!

We have previously seen how mental illness can be an acceptable and anxiety-relieving explanation of people who perform evil actions. If people perpetrating such actions can be diagnosed as mentally ill, then our fear levels subside and we can rationalize evil in the same way as we tend to rationalize many other problems in our society.

A good example of mental illness attribution is found in the public and official reactions to Thomas Hamilton. On 13 March 1996, Thomas Hamilton shot dead sixteen schoolchildren between the ages of five and six, along with their teacher, in the gymnasium of Dunblane Primary School before turning the gun on himself. The crime plumbed the very depths of incomprehensibility and produced tremendous confusion, fear, and frustration across the world. Reading the accounts of Hamilton's life, one is struck by the lack of any obvious psychopathology. Certainly he

36. William Styron, *Sophie's Choice,* 3d ed. (London: Picador, 1992), p. 204. For a deeper exegesis of Styron's work and its implications for the current discussion see C. J. Keeler, "Eichmann in All of Us: Thoughtlessness and the Banality of Evil in *Sophie's Choice*," *Perspectives on Evil and Human Wickedness* 1, no. 3 (2003): 96-105.

was an "odd" loner who quite possibly had a tendency towards homosexual pedophilia. However, he does not appear to show any obvious mental illness, at least not according to official categorizations. Interesting for present purposes, however, was the language that the press, the public, and certain public figures used to try to bring some comprehension into the situation. Several articles described Hamilton as mentally ill and as a "madman," and some prominent public figures and leading politicians at the time appeared in the media explaining the injustice of having to change the gun laws because of the "one off" actions of a "psychotic" such as Hamilton. The myth developed that he somehow *had* to have been mentally ill before he could perpetrate such a crime. But the evidence suggests that he may not have been. Certainly, no one would wish to argue that Hamilton's actions were "normal" in the ordinarily recognized sense of the word; but he was not insane, in the sense that he could be ascribed a recognized psychiatric illness. His actions were evil, but that evil was not, apparently, caused by overt psychopathology. Nevertheless, it is considerably more consoling to the societal psyche to ascribe actions such as these to the realms of mental illness than to the possibility that "a person like us" could have performed such an act.

The evidence would suggest that we cannot find refuge in simply labeling such actions as the product of mental illness. As Thomas Merton observes:

> One of the most disturbing facts that came out of the Eichmann trial was that a psychiatrist examined him and pronounced him *perfectly sane*. I do not doubt it at all, and that is precisely why I find it disturbing. If all the Nazis had been psychotics . . . their appalling cruelty would have been in some sense easier to understand.[37]

In his close study of the mental health of Nazi war criminals, James Waller, a social psychologist, found no evidence of mental illness in those who perpetrated Nazi atrocities. Waller concludes that:

> A myopic focus on the proposed psychopathology of perpetrators, or on their alleged extraordinary personalities, tells us more about our own personal dreams of how we wish the world to work than it does

---

37. Thomas Merton, *Raids on the Unspeakable* (New York: New Directions, 1966), in Waller, *Becoming Evil*, p. 55.

about the reality of perpetrator behavior. In that role, such explanations satisfy an important emotional demand of distancing *us* from *them*. The truth seems to be, though, that the most outstanding common characteristic of perpetrators of extraordinary evil is their normality, not their abnormality.[38]

Evidence suggests, then, that "ordinary" human beings, for whatever reason, are capable of acting in ways that can only be described as evil. It may be that the potential for horrendous evil is present within us all. Evil exists and suffering inevitably accompanies it, but those who behave in such ways, despite our initial instincts, are not qualitatively different from those who don't.

It could, of course, be argued that not everyone placed in similar circumstances would behave in the same way. Not everyone in Germany participated in or supported the Holocaust; not everyone in the Balkans or Rwanda or the Sudan committed rape and genocide; not everyone who faced Hindley's circumstances committed similar crimes. This is true, of course. If that was not the case, then this book would be meaningless. The conclusion to be drawn from the discussion thus far is not that all people *would* behave in such ways under such circumstances, but only that all people *could* behave in such ways given the correct circumstances. People are capable of resisting evil even in the midst of the most trying circumstances. Nevertheless, the evidence suggests that many if not most of us have a propensity to be dragged into the darkness rather than to move away from it. This is why we need consciously to practice goodness in a way that will protect us from evil.

Evil Is Not Only in the Other

The point in engaging in this exploration of the perpetrators of evil is not in any sense to try to explain evil or justify evil actions. The point has been to try to show that evil does not exist only in the "other"; the potential lurks within us all. This being so, evil actions can never exhaustively define what a person is. Despite their evil actions, those who perpetrate evil remain human beings, ultimately made in God's image and poten-

---

38. Waller, *Becoming Evil*, p. 87.

tially capable of change, repentance, and redemption. In significant ways, people who commit evil actions are not unlike "us."

The Scandal of Forgiveness

This is important for our understanding of Christian forgiveness. Both the comfort and the scandal of Christian forgiveness are that it offers the potential of redemption to *all* people, even those who have committed the most horrendous forms of evil. *Salvation remains a possibility for all of us, no matter where we have been and what we have done.* Those who commit evil are not qualitatively different from those who do not. Evil actions do not finally define persons, and repentance, forgiveness, and salvation are always possibilities in the eyes of God.

Reframing evil actions in this way opens the way for an alternative to revenge and destructive dehumanization. In recognizing the humanness of the "other," we begin to pave the way for the possibility of forgiveness. This offers a crucial starting position for the practice of forgiveness. Miroslav Volf puts it this way:

> As Christians [we] must develop a will to embrace and be reconciled with our enemy. This will to embrace is absolutely unconditional. There is no imaginable deed that should take a person outside our will to embrace him, because there is no imaginable deed that can take a person out of God's will to embrace humanity — which is what I think is inscribed in big letters in the narrative of the cross of Christ.[39]

That is not to say that we are called to forget past evil and let bygones be bygones. Christians are called to take their experiences of evil, suffering, and rage to the foot of the cross and allow that event to reframe their response. We remember well the injustice of an evil that has been perpetrated against us, and we cry it out to God in lament. But as we do that, the vicious circle of revenge, retribution, and evil is broken. When this happens, we can at least acknowledge our call to forgive as we recognize the significance of the cross, a place where God renders judgment on all and offers forgiveness to all.

39. Miroslav Volf, "To Embrace the Enemy," *Christianity Today,* 17 September 2001, http://www.christianitytoday.com/ct/2001/138/53.0.html.

Remembering Differently: A Theology of Forgiveness

Thus far we have used the term "forgiveness" without trying to tie down the specifics of what that term might mean. A glance at the plethora of literature on forgiveness indicates that the term has many different meanings. For some it is a therapeutic term, relating to the way in which forgiveness helps people to cope and deal with trauma.[40] For others, forgiveness is a term that relates to a life of discipleship and commitment to Christ, a way of being rather than a series of discrete actions.[41] Others relate it to justice and reconciliation at a social and political level.[42] For others it is primarily a pastoral construct,[43] and for others it is simply impossible.[44] Forgiveness, as it will be developed here, is not perceived primarily as a therapeutic technique or intervention (although it may function in this way), nor is it a mode of conflict resolution. Rather, forgiveness is a way of life that produces a fresh understanding of the way that the world is and how we should respond as we experience it. It is not something we simply do. It is something that defines what and whose we are.

The Epistemology of Life

Underpinning everything we do, see, and understand is a particular theory of knowledge: an *epistemology*. Our epistemology offers us a framework within which we can assess what is knowledge and what is not accepted as knowledge. Our epistemology can be based on the understanding of the world provided by, for example, religion, science, Marxism, or neo-liberal politics. The particular epistemology that individuals or societies choose to underpin the principles, values, and interpretations of the world profoundly affects the way they see the world and the ways in which they learn

40. D. Davenport, "The Functions of Anger and Forgiveness: Guidelines for Psychotherapy with Victims," *Psychotherapy* 28, no. 1 (1991): 140-44.

41. G. L. Jones, *Embodying Forgiveness: A Theological Analysis* (Grand Rapids: Eerdmans, 1995).

42. Desmond Tutu, *No Future without Forgiveness* (New York: Doubleday, 1999).

43. David Augsburger, *Helping People Forgive* (Louisville: Westminster/John Knox Press, 1996).

44. D. Blumenthal, *Facing the Abusing God: A Theology of Protest* (Louisville: Westminster/John Knox Press, 1993).

to act within it. Post-Enlightenment western culture is liberal in its epistemology, assumptions, and expectations. Liberalism emphasizes the importance of reason, rationality, independence, and self-advocacy. Because
liberalism has no particular telos or goal apart from the personal happiness of the individual, goods, both material and social, tend to take on an
instrumental, almost eschatological, quality. We will explore the importance of the commodification of human life further in the next chapter. At
this point, the thing to recognize is that within a liberal epistemology, forgiveness easily takes on the quality of a good or a commodity. The commodification of forgiveness is revealed in the way it has been grafted into
the therapeutic paradigm and assumed to be similar to any other therapeutic tool that might be available to practitioners,[45] even to the extent that we
have developed forms of therapy that enable people to "forgive God."[46]
The bizarre reversal of roles implicit in such an approach borders on the
idolatrous and offers a therapeutic model of forgiveness that bears little
connection to the cross, which is the true source of forgiveness. The problem with such a therapeutic perspective on forgiveness is that, as Greg
Jones correctly points out,

> When forgiveness is seen primarily in individualistic and privatistic
> terms, we lose sight of its central role in establishing a way of life *not
> only* with our "inner" selves *but also* in our relations to others.[47]

45. A particularly good example of the therapeutic approach to forgiveness is found in
Beverly Flannigan's work, *Forgiving the Unforgivable* (New York: Wiley Publishing, 1992).
Flannigan works out a therapeutic framework for understanding and dealing with experiences that are considered to be unforgivable. The problem with Flannigan's work is that the
forgiveness she explores is one with no need for God. The individual and particular therapeutic techniques are all that seem to be required to enable the act of forgiveness. Clearly,
her starting point and goal are quite different from those discussed in this chapter. See
Jones, *Embodying Forgiveness,* for an extended discussion of the theological and practical
distortions that a therapeutic approach to forgiveness can bring about. Useful pastoral alternatives to Flannigan's approach that take seriously the role of theology and the church include J. Patton, *Is Human Forgiveness Possible? A Pastoral Care Perspective* (Nashville:
Abingdon Press, 1985), and Jones, *Embodying Forgiveness.*

46. Julie Juola Exline, Ann Marie Yali, and Marci Lobel, "When God Disappoints: Difficulty Forgiving God and Its Role in Negative Emotion," *Journal of Health Psychology* 4
(1999): 365-79.

47. Greg Jones, "The Judgment of Grace: Forgiveness in Christian Life," *Theology
Matters* 3, no. 4 (July/August 1997): 7-16, 9.

When forgiveness becomes therapeutic, it turns into a personal task and achievement (or failure) rather than a way of living life in community.[48] Such an understanding of forgiveness is a distortion of a Christian understanding of forgiveness. As Lewis Smedes rightly points out:

> It is hard to imagine Saint Paul exhorting his readers to forgive one another "for each of you has a right to be healed of hate." It is typical of them to forgive one another because Christ has forgiven them and in so doing they will be like Christ, or for the sake of harmony in the church, or because in forgiving one another we will become fit for the Kingdom of God or ready for the judgment day. In other words, when asked for a rationale for forgiveness, Paul does not speak in *therapeutic* terms, but instead in terms of what is *fitting*, given certain beliefs about the history of God's actions, the character and actions of Jesus, the nature of the church and the coming Kingdom.[49]

Understanding forgiveness as a way of life or a character trait formed by constant practice, rather than as merely a series of individual events, is the key to how and why the type of forgiveness we have been building up to in this chapter may be possible. The important point to bear in mind is that, according to this understanding, we cannot work out our theology of forgiveness on the extremes or around particular horrific examples of violence, abuse, and apparent "unforgivability." To understand forgiveness, we must practice it as a way of life, as a way of being within a community that perceives itself as forgiven and forgiving. Such a community and such a practice of forgiveness demands a specific epistemology: *the epistemology of the broken body.*

The Epistemology of the Broken Body

The stunning piece of art on page 162 was painted by the German artist Matthias Grunewald in 1515. Grunewald created the altarpiece for the Hospital of St. Anthony in Isenheim, a small town in southern Alsace.

---

48. This is not to suggest that forgiveness cannot be therapeutic. The point is that this is not its primary intention or function.

49. Lewis Smedes, *Forgive and Forget: Healing the Hurts We Don't Deserve* (New York: Harper and Row, 1984), p. 27.

Matthias Grunewald, *Crucifixion,* a panel from the Isenheim Altar (ca. 1515)

Photo credit: Erich Lessing / Art Resource, NY

The painting is a complex polyptych containing various panels and wings, each of which depicts a different aspect of the crucifixion and the resurrection of Jesus. When the work is closed, the scene of the crucifixion comes to the fore. In contrast to earlier images of the crucifixion, which tended to show Christ hanging sublimely on the cross, apparently disconnected from the pain and suffering of the experience, Grunewald's work clearly shows Christ in agony. His body, scarred and beaten, hangs broken and helpless. His arms are bent with the force of gravity pulling down on his body, and his hands are twisted and contorted due to the muscle spasms caused by the impact of the nails. His hands curl up in sheer agony. The heaviness of Jesus' broken body symbolizes the way he bears the great weight of sin that rightly belongs to all of humanity. Bonhoeffer's "rejected Christ" is revealed clearly in Grunewald's artistry. Jesus' bent head reflects the reality of his suffering. Here we see no indication of a triumphalist glorification of suffering, only brokenness and isolation from those around him and from God. Significant in this picture is the height of the cross, not lifted high above the earth but noticeably low. Grunewald seems to emphasize that Christ's suffering for the world is driven low into creation.

In our exploration of lament, we examined the silence of Christ and the way in which the experience of evil separated him from God. Recognition of this separation from God is important. When Jesus, who is God, cried "My God, my God, why have you abandoned me?" he was expressing an inner alienation similar to experience that all victims of evil and intense suffering endure — abandonment, brokenness, apparently unending hopelessness. And yet, one of the mysteries of the cross is how Jesus, who is God, could have felt that God had abandoned him. How can God abandon God? Jesus felt it and it was a reality for him, but abandonment was not the final word. In the passion of Christ we discover such genuine identification with human suffering that Jesus undergoes precisely the abandonment and inability to feel the presence of God that is a primary mark of the human experience of evil. Jesus felt abandoned . . . and yet, ultimately he was not. Sufferers feel abandoned, but in reality God never abandons them.[50] In this way, Jesus legitimates the sufferers' feeling of abandonment in the face of evil, framing it as a spiritual experience rather than a mark of doubt or faithlessness. The resurrection showed clearly that Jesus' experience of abandonment was, at most, transient and temporary, that there was hope of relief even though, during his time of deep suffering, Jesus struggled to find it. In identifying with Jesus in this way, sufferers can begin to move towards a similar framing of their own experiences.

The drama is magnified in Grunewald's painting by the deep, dark sky, which mirrors the darkness of Jesus' pain, suffering, alienation, and ultimate death. The darkness that surrounds Jesus' broken body reflects the darkness that surrounds each one of us as we participate, willingly or otherwise, in the continuing sin of the world. Jesus takes all of this upon himself in order that the possibility of forgiveness and reconciliation with

---

50. Deuteronomy 4:31: "For the LORD your God is a merciful God; he will not abandon or destroy you or forget the covenant with your forefathers, which he confirmed to them by oath."

God can become a reality for all human beings. Forgiveness is not cheap, and because it is not cheap it is not limited. The open arms of Christ reach out in an embrace that both condemns and welcomes even the worst of sinners.

In the broken body of Christ we discover a new way of interpreting and understanding the world. The world is saved from the power of evil not by might and power, humanly defined, but by brokenness, suffering, and vulnerability. The broken body of Christ offers us an image of God, a response to evil, and a radically new epistemology that recognizes evil in all of its fullness, but that refuses to respond to it in ways that would encourage further evil.

Solidarity with Victims

There is, however, another dimension to Grunewald's painting that it is vital to note. The painting was originally hung within a monastery which, at the time, was a hospital for victims of the plague. If we look closely at the painting, we can see that Jesus' body is speckled with small, red marks. These represent the sores that marked the bodies of people who had the plague. In adding this dimension to his painting, Grunewald emphasizes Christ's solidarity and identification with the victims of evil suffering in the world. While the open arms of Christ embrace all of humanity, God identifies in a particular and embodied way with those who are the victims of evil. God offers a universal embrace within which the perpetrators of evil are always free to engage. However, God does not identify with them in their evilness or offer them solidarity in the way that he does the victims of evil and suffering. He calls the evil-doer to repentance; his offer is genuine and creatively redemptive. He calls to the evil-doer to come to him. But he sits in solidarity with the sufferer. He asks for a response from the victims of evil, but the call comes from a position of solidarity and friendship rather than judgment. Both the evil-doer and the victim are called to repentance and reconciliation with God. *Without repentance, there is no possibility of experiencing God's intimate love and solidarity.* The cross opens up the possibility of universal forgiveness for all, a suggestion that is scandalous and, at times, difficult to accept. And yet, the call to repent sounds different to victims, who hear it not as judgment but as a gentle call from a friend who sits alongside them in their suffering and pain. Grunewald's painting reminds us that Jesus is with the victims of evil and suffering in a way that is both similar to and profoundly different from the way he is with evil-doers.

More than that, the parable of the sheep and the goats in Matthew 25 suggests that Jesus is, in a real sense, *in* the poor, the victim, the wounded one. He does not simply identify with the poor and the wounded; in a real sense he becomes like them. Grunewald's observation reminds us that Jesus does not simply sympathize or even empathize with the victim. He, in a very real sense, takes their pain upon himself. He becomes the wounded one who sits with all wounded ones and, in the power of the resurrection life, offers the possibility that there is more to their lives than their wounds.

The Suffering of God

The epistemology of Christ's broken body resonates with the theology and experience of Dietrich Bonhoeffer. In his *Letters and Papers from Prison,* Bonhoeffer sketches a theology of a God who suffers with and for human beings. For Bonhoeffer, crucial dimensions of the power of God are revealed in the suffering of Christ.

> God is weak and powerless in the world, and that is exactly the way, the only way in which he can be with us and help us. Matthew 8:17 makes it crystal clear that it is not by his omnipotence that Christ helps us, but by his weakness and his suffering . . . only a suffering God can help.[51]

Bonhoeffer's point is not that suffering is a good thing or that the suffering God is merely a helpless companion on our journeys of pain. Rather, his point is that recognizing the dimension of vulnerability and suffering within the person of God enables us to see new strands of a providential understanding of life and God's action within that life. It challenges us to think about the possibility that a genuinely Christ-like response to evil, suffering, and forgiveness may be very different from what we might assume. God's power is revealed *in the midst of* suffering and evil, not as a triumphalistic conquering power that strives to annihilate evil, but rather

51. Dietrich Bonhoeffer, *Letters and Papers from Prison* (London: Collins Fontana Books, 1953), p. 164.

as a suffering presence that transforms evil not with force and might, but with the practice of persistent, vulnerable love.

The Centrality of Repentance

Before we move on to explore some ways in which we might embody this new epistemology, one crucial point needs to be made clearly: *Without repentance, there is no possibility of redemption.*[52] That is the ultimate tragedy of the deaths of Flores and Iqbal: Neither, as far as we know, repented and thus neither found himself able or willing to accept God's gracious gift of forgiveness. Forgiveness is available for all, but in order to find reconciliation with God and to experience God's solidarity, it is necessary to repent of one's actions and begin to live a forgiven life. To repent means to turn around and walk away from one's previous ways and to take on the new way of the kingdom. It means a full acknowledgement of one's sinfulness and the sinfulness of one's previous actions and a meaningful movement into a new way of being wherein the values of God become one's own values. Repentance means taking one's past to the foot of the cross, acknowledging the significance of Christ's sacrifice and the new epistemology that emerges from such recognition, and beginning to live differently. When we repent, we see our past lives for what they are; there is no rationalization, no false justification, and no excusing. Repentance means being exposed for what we truly are and, in recognizing what we are, receiving new life. Above all else, repentance requires an acceptance of God's forgiveness and a consequent living out of that gift.

Forgiveness inevitably requires judgment.

> We need to recognize that God's judgment does not come apart from an acknowledgement of, and confrontation with, human sin and evil. God does not simply "overlook" or "ignore" our destructiveness. If that were the case, then there would be no need for Christ's death. Rather, God confronts sin and evil in all of its awfulness. In so doing, God exposes our wounds, both those which have been inflicted upon us and those we have inflicted on others. There clearly is a judgment in God's

---

52. 2 Corinthians 7:10: "Godly sorrow brings repentance that leads to salvation and leaves no regret, but worldly sorrow brings death."

work in Jesus Christ. . . . However, God's confrontation with sin and evil is *not* for the purpose of condemning us. Indeed, it is for the explicit purpose of forgiving us and healing our — and the world's — wounds. It is a judgment of *Grace*.[53]

Thus we are judged by grace, our sins and evils are exposed for what they are, and the possibility of forgiveness becomes a reality. Without such repentance, forgiveness is impossible.

The Practice of Forgiveness: Stepping onto the Road

Theologically, forgiveness is crucial. Unless we understand the theological meaning of forgiveness and its implications for living faithfully within the coming kingdom, forgiveness appears to be a ridiculous suggestion. Why would we even try to forgive the terrible things that happen to us and others if it were not for our particular understanding of the cross and resurrection of Jesus? In order to understand why we should try to forgive that which often appears to be unforgivable, we need to understand the true meaning of the cross. We are a forgiven people who are called to practice forgiveness in the light of the cross and the resurrection of Jesus.

Nevertheless, the actual practice of forgiveness is not easy. While it is clearly the call of all Christians to accept and to offer forgiveness, forcing victims of evil to heed the call to forgive in a legalistic or judgmental way risks turning people into *victims of grace,* that is, people who feel oppressed, downtrodden, and dispirited because they cannot match the standard that grace sets for them. Forgiveness is a difficult, and for some impossible, task. Miroslav Volf is a theologian who has wrestled with the theology of reconciliation. Volf, a Croat, speaks from his experience of destruction and violence within the former Yugoslavia. In his book *Exclusion and Embrace* he develops an influential theology of reconciliation. Yet even he, with all of his intricate theological knowledge, finds the practice of forgiveness difficult. During a lecture on the theology of reconciliation, German theologian Jürgen Moltmann asked him a crucial question: "Can you embrace a *Cetnik?*" Volf writes:

53. Jones, "The Judgment of Grace," p. 10.

It was the winter of 1993. For months now the notorious Serbian fighters called Cetnik had been sowing desolation in my native country, herding people into concentration camps, raping women, burning down churches, and destroying cities. I had just argued that we ought to embrace our enemies as God has embraced us in Christ. Can I embrace a Cetnik — the ultimate other, so to speak, the evil other? What would justify the embrace? Where would I draw the strength for it? What would it do to my identity as a human being and as a Croat? It took me a while to answer, though I immediately knew what I wanted to say. "No, I cannot — but as a follower of Christ I think I should be able to."[54]

For the victims of evil, this is crucial. As Christians we know that we should forgive, even if at times it is an incredibly difficult thing to do. Indeed, for some, it may prove to be impossible. Does this mean they are condemned to failure and guilt, or worse, are permanently excluded from grace? The answer depends on whether we assume forgiveness to be a *process* or an *event*. If we assume that forgiveness is an event, then for many of us the act of forgiving will be impossible. However, if we assume it to be a *process* that we participate in not simply as individuals but also as communities, then the frame changes and forgiveness, or at least the slow and sometimes painful movement towards forgiveness, becomes a possibility. Volf's encounter with Moltmann would suggest that, for him, forgiveness is a process rather than an event. It is initiated by the act of repentance and the acknowledgement of the new epistemology that we discover in the broken body of Christ. In our earlier discussion, we saw the way in which God loves the world and acts gracefully towards it. We also acknowledged that Jesus identified fully with the pain of the world and in particular with the pain of the victims of evil. Jesus understands human pain and why it is so difficult to forgive the experience of evil. Jesus does not expect us to be Jesus. He fully understands the dynamics of human pain, the difficulty of human forgiveness, and why, for some, it is difficult if not impossible to forgive. Humans must at least acknowledge the significance of forgiveness and a flickering desire to step onto the road towards forgiveness. Volf's words "No, I cannot — but as a follower of Christ I think I should be able to" are a beginning point on the road to granting forgiveness. The goal may never be fully achieved, but the jour-

54. Volf, *Exclusion and Embrace*, p. 9.

ney will bring degrees of healing and possibly reconciliation. To try to force victims beyond this point can indeed make them victims of grace. But to work with them in friendship and community, to enable them to come to this point, and to hope and pray that they can move on along the road towards forgiveness is an act of healing love. Reconciliation may never be possible, but the road to forgiveness begins with the words "No, I cannot — but I know I should."

Loving One's Enemies and One's Self

It should be made clear that the call to forgive does not mean that victims of evil should put themselves in danger. As Wadell puts it, "Jesus tells us to love our enemies, not necessarily to live with them, and certainly never to allow them to destroy us."[55] If we are to take seriously the command to love God, others, and ourselves,[56] then placing ourselves in danger in the name of love of the other is clearly inappropriate. We may be called to forgive, but reconciliation may be impossible. You may desire to transform enemies into friends, but if your enemy refuses to be your friend and if she acts as one who has not yet learned what it means to be forgiven, then the hope for forgiveness and reconciliation will always remain just that: a hope.

Paul Wadell sums all of this up neatly:

There is an enormous difference between loving an enemy and loving a friend. Jesus summons us to love all our neighbors, but not in the same way. He tells us to love those who wish us harm, but never expects us to have the same loyalty, affection, and devotion for our seasoned enemies that we do for our lifelong friends. We love our friends with an intensity, depth, and joyfulness we obviously do not have with an enemy, because friendships originate in love and are meant to be a life together in love. We are challenged to love our enemies, but we would dishonor our friends if we showed to those who hate us the same affection and con-

55. Paul J. Wadell, *Becoming Friends: Worship, Justice, and the Practice of Christian Friendship* (Grand Rapids: Brazos Press, 2002), p. 166.
56. Mark 12:30-31. "'Love the Lord your God with all your heart and with all your soul and with all your mind and with all your strength.' The second is this: 'Love your neighbor as yourself.' There is no commandment greater than these."

cern we owe to our friends. Similarly, we may have to forgive an enemy, but much more is lost if we are unwilling to forgive a friend. The bond of love between friends, the history they have shared together, and the happiness they have brought one another indicate not only why forgiveness among friends is so crucial but also why Jesus never expects the love we risk on enemies to be equal to the love we shower on our friends.[57]

As we seek to enable a ministry of forgiveness and reconciliation for the victims and the perpetrators of evil, Wadell's words take on a pertinence that we need to hear.

Raging with Compassion: Speaking Out Our Anger

In closing, let us reflect on some pastoral responses that might initiate this process of forgiveness. One of the great barriers to forgiveness at an interpersonal level is people's inability to deal with the outrage that the experience of evil induces. The sense of outrage, humiliation, and isolation that emerges as part of the experience of evil can be devastating. Of course, one can take various therapeutic approaches to deal with this. Here we will focus on one approach that holds particular pertinence for faithfully practicing forgiveness. In concluding this chapter, we will return to the psalms and explore a particular way of approaching the issue of rage that resonates with our previous discussion of psalms of lament and opens up new possibilities for living lives that are forgiven and forgiving.

The Moral Dynamics of Forgiveness: Judgment and Punishment

When one is injured by another, that injury inevitably produces some kind of moral judgment. We feel *outraged* and demand that others see and acknowledge what has been done to us as wrong. Ideally, we would like the perpetrator to recognize the devastation his actions have caused, but we realize that may not be possible. We pronounce a *judgment* on the

57. Wadell, *Becoming Friends*, p. 166.

treatment we have received, one primarily presented as an accusation against the evil-doer. We pass judgment and we demand justice in the form of appropriate punishment for the abuser. Such punishment at least goes some way to redressing the balance and easing our outrage at what has happened to us.

Important as punishment may be for the abused, there is an important difference between judgment and punishment. A judgment is an *accusation* aimed against a perpetrator of some moral violation. Within the law, the one against whom the offense is perpetrated hands over the issue of punishment to a third party. Punishment is similar to a "verdict rendered in a court of law: one is pronounced guilty or innocent. Punishment is like a *sentence* imposed by the court."[58] Within a legal system, judgment can be carried out by the victim, but punishment is the prerogative of the system. Punishment is carried out by a person or persons who, for good reasons and after due process, accept the judgment of the abused and mete out a punishment that will match the seriousness of the crime.

In this way, the victim fully expresses her pain and violation and in so doing is freed from self-blame. The judgment has been heard and taken seriously, and the victim has no need to blame herself. The judge has proclaimed her innocent and the perpetrator guilty and has promised to punish the evil-doer for his crimes. The victim can now trust the judge to do that which is right. In this way, the victim's inevitable and understandable feelings of outrage are aired and dealt with in a healing and satisfactory way. Feelings of anger, hurt, and resentment may still remain and will have to find resolution and healing, but the *outrage* has been dealt with.

The difference between "outrage" and "anger" (rage) is important. Ray Anderson observes that: "Outrage is grounded in a moral sense, while anger is primarily an emotion capable of cognitive reframing. Bringing forth a judgment against an offender draws outrage to its conclusion."[59] Outrage is the feeling of being incensed at the unfairness and injustice of what has happened. In affirming the judgment, the legal court helps to dissipate the moral outrage at what has happened; the judge's and community's acknowledgement of the evilness of the actions dissipates its sharpness. "What happened was wrong and everyone knows it . . . but I

58. Ray S. Anderson, *The Shape of Practical Theology: Empowering Ministry with Theological Praxis* (Downers Grove, Ill.: InterVarsity Press, 2001), p. 297.

59. Anderson, *The Shape of Practical Theology*, pp. 297-98.

am still very angry." But that anger, assuming the victim is certain that the punishment fits the crime, is of a different moral order from outrage and can be dealt with in different ways. It is therefore right and proper that evil-doers should be held to account both in terms of the law and ultimately before God.

Previously we explored the idea that vengeance belonged to God and that it is necessary to hand issues of revenge over to God. Vengeance is God's. But, *anger belongs to the victim.* The question is, how can the victim express his righteous anger in a way that will not trap him in a vicious spiral of bitterness and hatred?

The Pastoral Power of the Imprecatory Psalms

An answer to this question is found, once again, in the psalms. In the previous chapter, we explored the pastoral significance of the psalms of lament and how they provided a language and grammar in the face of evil and suffering. Here, as we consider how to help victims embark on the road to forgiveness, we can usefully turn again to the psalms, this time to the imprecatory psalms. These psalms are a portion of scripture that we are never quite sure what to do with. They seem to express attitudes and responses that clash in fundamental ways with the teachings of Christ and his movement towards a peaceful kingdom. Take, for example, Psalm 137.

> By the rivers of Babylon we sat and wept
> when we remembered Zion.
> There on the poplars
> we hung our harps,
> for there our captors asked us for songs,
> our tormentors demanded songs of joy;
> they said, "Sing us one of the songs of Zion!"
> How can we sing the songs of the LORD
> while in a foreign land?
> If I forget you, O Jerusalem,
> may my right hand forget its skill.
> May my tongue cling to the roof of my mouth
> if I do not remember you,

if I do not consider Jerusalem my highest joy.
Remember, O LORD, what the Edomites did
on the day Jerusalem fell.
"Tear it down," they cried,
"tear it down to its foundations!"
O Daughter of Babylon, doomed to destruction,
happy is he who repays you
for what you have done to us —
he who seizes your infants
and dashes them against the rocks.

At first glance, we find in this psalm a desperate plea for revenge against the perpetrators of evil. Psalms such as these express rage, anger, and the desire for violent revenge. Strangely, they pronounce blessings on those who would kill the children of the psalmist's enemies! There seems to be a total disconnect between these psalms and the model of forgiveness that has been developed in this chapter. But, if we change the frame a little, we will see things slightly differently. Many people who have been the victims of evil experience this type of anger and desire for vengeance. When you are hurt and broken, very often you want to hurt and hit back. To deny such feelings to self or others is to turn the anger within, which can have devastating psychological effects. The psalmist refuses to keep his anger within. He is angry and he wants to hurt those who have hurt him . . . or does he? His rage is very real, but, if we look a little closer, *he* is not in fact threatening to avenge his suffering. He is asking *God* to do so. The imprecatory psalms are ritual prayer. By praying in this way, the psalmist is not expressing a desire to take revenge himself. Rather, he is giving his very real anger and genuine desire for revenge over to God. This pattern of expressing rage and handing it over to God is common within the imprecatory psalms. As Billman and Migliore note:

> [A]lmost without exception the psalmist prays that *God will justly repay the enemies* rather than asking for the personal power to act out vengeance. It is one thing to leave judgment to God and quite another to take judgment into one's own hands.[60]

---

60. K. D. Billman and Daniel L. Migliore, *Rachel's Cry* (Cleveland: United Church Press, 1999), p. 121.

As Bonhoeffer puts it in his sermon on a psalm of vengeance (Psalm 58), given in July 1937 in the midst of the Nazi persecutions and imprisonments:

> Whoever entrusts revenge to God dismisses any thought of ever taking revenge himself. Whoever does not take revenge himself still does not know whom he is up against and still wants to take charge of the cause by himself.[61]

So within the imprecatory psalms we find the psalmist expressing torrents of real rage; but this rage is contained within the context of conversation with God. In a strange way, the imprecatory psalms may point to a way out of the slavery of revenge and into the freedom of forgiveness. In enabling us both to express and hand over our rage to the crucified God, as Bonhoeffer puts it:

> The psalms of vengeance lead to the cross of Jesus and to the love of God that forgives enemies. I cannot forgive the enemies of God by myself, only the crucified Christ can; and I can forgive through him. So the carrying out of vengeance becomes grace for all in Jesus Christ.[62]

The victim cannot forgive. But by handing over his rage and unforgivingness to the God, who offers forgiveness to all, the victim makes a first move towards the possibility of forgiveness. For the followers of the crucified Messiah, the main message of the imprecatory psalms is this:

> *rage belongs before God* — not in the reflectively managed and manicured form of a confession, but as a pre-reflective outburst from the depths of the soul. This is no mere cathartic discharge of pent up aggression before the Almighty who ought to care. Much more significantly, by placing unattended rage before God we place both our unjust enemy and our vengeful self face to face with a God who loves and does justice.[63]

The psalmist's rage is real and his desire for vengeance is equally as pressing. However, he does not scream to God to allow *him* to destroy his ene-

---

61. Dietrich Bonhoeffer, "A Bonhoeffer Sermon," trans. Daniel Bloesch, ed. F. Burton Nelson, *Theology Today* 38 (1982): 469.

62. Dietrich Bonhoeffer, *Life Together: Prayerbook of the Bible* (Minneapolis: Fortress Press, 1996), p. 175.

63. Volf, *Exclusion and Embrace,* p. 124.

mies. Rather he gives over his rage to God and asks God to take revenge. Whether or not God acts in a vengeful manner is, of course, God's business. For the psalmist the key thing was to have the faith and the certainty in God and God's justice that would allow the victim to let go of his rage and leave it in the hands of the compassion, or the vengefulness, of God. In the same way, all of us need to learn to bring our rage and our outrage before God and to allow it to be transformed through the cross of Christ. Volf puts it this way:

> By placing unattended rage before God we place both our unjust enemy and our own vengeful self face to face with a God who loves and does justice. . . . In the light of the justice and love of God, however, hate recedes and the seed is planted for the miracle of forgiveness. Forgiveness flounders because I exclude the enemy from the community of humans even as I exclude myself from the community of sinners. But no one can be in the presence of the God of the crucified Messiah for long without overcoming this double exclusion — without transposing the enemy from the sphere of monstrous inhumanity into the sphere of shared humanity and herself from the sphere of proud innocence into the sphere of common sinfulness. When one knows that the torturer will not eternally triumph over the victim one is free to rediscover that person's humanity and imitate God's love for him. And when one knows that God's love is greater than all sin, one is free to see oneself in the light of God's justice and so rediscover one's own sinfulness. In the presence of God our rage over injustice may give way to forgiveness which in turn will make the search for justice for all possible. If forgiveness does take place it will be but an echo of the forgiveness granted by the just and loving God — the only forgiveness that ultimately matters, because, though we must forgive, in a very real sense no one can either forgive or retain sins "but God alone" (Mark 2:7).[64]

Of course, as we noted previously, it is possible to pray the imprecatory psalms in ways that are destructive and violent. However, this need not be so. As Shults and Sandage correctly point out,

> Emotional disclosure that leads to reframing the meaning of a conflict and that provides a sense of coherence is associated with psychological

64. Volf, *Exclusion and Embrace*, p. 124.

health and healing. The translation of the emotions chaos of relational estrangement into language is the poetry of lament.[65]

Ellen Davies offers a good example of the ways in which we might use the imprecatory psalms to facilitate the movement towards forgiveness:

> As a young seminarian, I had a bitter experience of betrayal by a close friend within the community. . . . But my pastoral theology professor saw my need, and he gave me a list of psalm numbers with the advice: "Go into the chapel when no one else is around and shout these at the top of your lungs." It was the most helpful advice anyone gave me at that time — especially the part about shouting. That the psalms provided a vent for my anger is obvious. Less obvious, and much more important, they helped me move beyond blind rage. After a few days and nights, my own loud rantings began to sound a little different in my ears. Angry as I still was, I could hear in them a faint note of self-righteousness, even pettiness. . . . Like a wise friend, these psalms were giving me company in my anger and at the same time instructing me through my self consciousness. For the cursing psalms confront us with one of our most persistent idolatries, to which neither Israel nor the church has ever been immune: the belief that God has as little use for our enemies as we do, the desire to reduce God to an extension of our own embattled and wounded egos.[66]

The epistemology of the broken body challenges and enables us to reframe our natural responses to the experience of evil and to reflect seriously on how we might resolve the inevitable tension between our desire for revenge and the reality of the open embrace of Christ on the cross.

The imprecatory psalms gives us a means and a language that enable us to hand our rage over to God and in so doing open up the possibility of forgiveness and compassionate action. If we incorporate this pastoral use of the imprecatory psalms into our practices, we can begin to live forgiven and forgiving lives even in the face of evil.

---

65. Shults and Sandage, *The Faces of Forgiveness,* p. 95.
66. Ellen Davies, *Getting Involved with God: Rediscovering the Old Testament* (Cambridge, Mass.: Cowley Publications, 2001), p. 26.

Conclusion: Practicing Unreasonable Love

Understood in the ways outlined in this chapter, Christian forgiveness is both scandalous and unreasonable.[67] It demands that we totally reframe our natural responses and respond to evil in a way that is countercultural but potentially transformative. More than that, as Bonhoeffer puts it, *forgiveness is a mode of sharing in the suffering of Christ.* "Forgiving sins is the Christ-suffering required of his disciples. It is required of all Christians."[68] While our own ability to forgive does not atone for sin, it does bear witness to the magnitude of God's grace in Christ and the practical implications of the cross. To embark on the road to forgiveness can be costly, painful, and unreasonable.

Forgiveness becomes even more unreasonable if we think that it is something that we do occasionally and alone. But if forgiveness is the way in which we live peaceably in the world, then we cannot do it alone. Granting forgiveness is possible only when one is accompanied by one's friends. We will explore the importance of friendship more fully in chapter eight. Friendship is the fabric of community and a vital aspect of discipleship. As disciples we are called to become friends of God,[69] and as such we are expected not simply to accompany our friends and show solidarity with them but also to die for them.[70] Our friends sit with us in our suffering, understand our bitterness and hate, and pray for a time when we will be freed from our burdens. When we realize that we have friends like this, we receive the courage and confidence that we need to step onto the road towards forgiveness and, perhaps, reconciliation. "In this respect, the love of friendship helps us not to hate our enemies but to pity them and, perhaps, to see them as more than the persons who have hurt us."[71] Our friends cannot forgive on our behalf. But they can provide a context in which we feel secure enough and at home with ourselves and

---

67. Wadell, *Becoming Friends,* p. 165.

68. Bonhoeffer, *Life Together,* p. 88.

69. John 15:15. "I no longer call you servants, because a servant does not know his master's business. Instead, I have called you friends, for everything that I learned from my Father I have made known to you."

70. For a further development of this model of friendship see John Swinton, *Resurrecting the Person* and *From Bedlam to Shalom: Towards a Practical Theology of Interpersonal Relationships and Mental Health Care* (New York: Peter Lang, 2000).

71. Wadell, *Becoming Friends,* p. 166.

others that the possibility of opening up ourselves to forgive may be at least possible. Friends cannot forgive by proxy, but they can pray with and for the wounded one. The victim of evil can be surrounded by the prayers of her friends, prayers that are filled with empathy and understanding for the pain and apparent impossibility of the talk of forgiveness but that remain tinged with the hope that with God all things are possible. Such prayers enable the victim at least to begin to say, "I can't, but as a Christian I know that I should."

Forgiveness, then, is perhaps the most radical gift that God calls us to accept and share as we struggle to resist the evil that surrounds us. Enabling forgiveness and resurrecting the humanness of those who have been dehumanized by our desire for vengeance is a primary task of the church, not only in its pastoral ministry but in every dimension of its ministry and mission. Jesus' cry "Father, forgive them" draws us uncomfortably to the realization that we are sinners and that we need to be forgiven *and* that even the worst sinner is loved by God and worthy of respect, forgiveness, and possibly reconciliation. To forgive is the ultimate form of resistance to evil and an unmistakable mark of the coming kingdom.

CHAPTER SEVEN

Practicing Thoughtfulness:
What Are People For?

[There is] "a strange interdependence between thoughtlessness and evil."

Hannah Arendt

Could the activity of thinking as such, the habit of examining and reflecting upon whatever happens to come to pass, regardless of the specific content and quite independent of results, could this activity be of such a nature that it "conditions" men against evil-doing?

Hannah Arendt

Lament and forgiveness form the bedrock of an effective practical theodicy. Taken together they offer important and faithful ways in which the church can build communities that will absorb suffering and enable perseverance until Christ returns. Lament and forgiveness are practices that can reframe the world. When we learn to respond to evil and suffering with lament and forgiveness instead of hopeless despair and a lust for vengeance, we can see the world differently, and when we see the world differently we will act differently in the world.

One of the primary results of practicing such gestures of redemption is the renewal of our minds, which enables us to think and respond differently in the face of evil and suffering. In Romans 12:2 Paul instructs us:

Do not conform any longer to the pattern of this world, but be transformed by the renewing of your mind. Then you will be able to test and approve what God's will is — his good, pleasing, and perfect will.

The suggestion that through the power of the Holy Spirit we should embark on the practice of renewing our minds is interesting. We renew our minds as we pray and interact with scripture and with one another in community. When we allow our ideas and thoughts to be formed and reformed by this interaction, we begin to think differently. Our thoughts, our values, and our interpretations of the world are reframed into a challenging and inevitably, at times, countercultural form.

However, in reality we rarely allow our minds to be transformed. We are all implicitly and explicitly embedded within forms of culture that often run contrary to the ways in which the gospel teaches us to think. Unless we learn the practice of critical thinking — a mode of thinking that approaches the everyday, mundane dimensions of the world with a theological hermeneutic of suspicion — we risk drifting into thought patterns and subsequent forms of action that are not only dissonant with the gospel but that can, in fact, become profoundly evil. In this chapter we will develop a third dimension to practical theodicy: *the practice of thoughtfulness.* Thoughtfulness is vital if we are not to find ourselves seduced into complicity with some of the hidden evils in our societies.

The definition of evil developed in chapter three made it clear that evil is not something that only "evil people" do. Preventing people from seeing and experiencing God's providential hope and love does not require active involvement. Simply by not doing something or not noticing something, people can find themselves excluded or excluding others from their primary source of providential hope. We can easily become complicit with evil if we are not vigilant and thoughtful. If this is so, then developing the practice of critical thoughtfulness is an essential dimension of practical theodicy.

The Evils of Thoughtlessness and Lack of Attention

In our consideration of forgiveness in the previous chapter, we explored the complexities of the relationship between good and evil. Our culture often thinks of good and evil as polar opposites. In reality, the distinction is far from clear-cut. In his book *Good and Evil,* Martin Buber explores in some detail this tension.[1] For Buber, good is the product of striving for truth and beauty. Such goodness does not occur accidentally. Rather it emerges from intentional practices of caring about and paying attention to particular noble goals. Evil, according to Buber, is of a different order. Evil requires no such purposefulness. One must work to be good, but one happens to be evil. Evil occurs when one strays from the path of truth and beauty. Such straying can be conscious and intentional, but it need not be so. Important for this chapter is Buber's assertion that evil is the consequence of distractions and in particular of *inattention.* In order to achieve the good, one needs to consciously strive towards it. To move towards evil requires no formal work, only inattention to the good. One stumbles into evil by being distracted and inattentive.

The Banality of Evil

Otto Adolf Eichmann, a prominent member of the Nazi government, was responsible for the annihilation of millions of Jewish people during World War Two. The psychiatrist who examined him described Eichmann as "a man obsessed with a dangerous and insatiable urge to kill," "a perverted, sadistic personality." In the eyes of the public, Eichmann was truly a monster. His crimes belonged to a different order from most others. His actions placed him in the realm inhabited by people who are "not like us," the realm of monsters and demons. Eichmann was a prime illustration of the myth of pure evil and the social construction of monsters.

There is, of course, no question about the heinousness of Eichmann's crimes. They were monstrous, even if, for the reasons outlined in the previous chapter, we would not describe him as a monster. Yet, when one takes a closer look at Eichmann, something rather strange emerges. In her reflections on Eichmann's trial in Jerusalem, Hannah Arendt, herself a Jew, makes some startling observations.[2] What she noticed, above all else, was the apparent ordinariness of Eichmann as he sat before the court. Indeed,

1. Martin Buber, *Good and Evil: Two Interpretations* (New York: Charles Scribner's Sons, 1953).

2. Hannah Arendt, *Eichmann in Jerusalem: A Report on the Banality of Evil* (New York: Penguin Books, 1994).

as the trial unfolded, Arendt concluded that he was "not sinister at all." She points to the fact that "[t]he deeds were monstrous, but the doer . . . was quite ordinary, commonplace and neither demonic nor monstrous."[3] Yet this apparently ordinary man was responsible for the transportation of millions of Jews to concentration camps and ultimately to their deaths. For Arendt the tension between what she saw in Eichmann and the public profile that had been created around him was dissonant. Arendt was looking for a monster and instead she discovered a bureaucrat. Rather than being radical, that is, rooted in evil motives or demonic forces, the evil carried out by Eichmann was rather banal, the product of close attention to the workings of bureaucratic systems and an inattention to the consequences of his actions. Arendt concluded that the horrendous evil for which Eichmann was responsible was the product of *an inability to engage in critical thinking.* The key was Eichmann's *thoughtlessness.* As she puts it:

> the only specific characteristic one could detect in his past as well as in his behavior during the trial and the preceding police examination was something entirely negative: it was not stupidity but a curious, quite authentic inability to think . . . he was neither perverted nor sadistic . . . [but] terribly and terrifyingly normal, and without any "diabolical or demonic profundity"; what characterized him was "sheer thoughtlessness," "extraordinary shallowness," and a "quite authentic inability to think."[4]

Thoughtlessness as the reason for perpetrating evil is not unique to Eichmann. It could, at one level, be aimed at the whole of Hitler's Germany. The entire nation was implicated in gross acts of evil without necessarily recognizing that fact. There were many acts of thoughtlessness and inattention within Nazi Germany. Presumably someone had to grout the tiles in the gas chambers, build the chimneys for the ovens, and lay the foundations for the building of Auschwitz. Did these workers know or think about what they were doing? If even the most overt forms of evil can be carried out through inattention and the lack of critical thinking, this should raise our consciousness to the possibility that there may be more subtle, covert modes of evil within our own societies in which we are all

3. Hannah Arendt, *The Life of Mind — Thinking — Willing* (New York/London: Harvest/HBJ, 1978), p. 4.

4. Hannah Arendt, "Thinking and Moral Considerations: A Lecture," *Social Research* 38, no. 3 (Fall 1971): 417.

complicit because we have never bothered to think about them or remain attentive to their implications.

The Practice of Thoughtfulness as Resistance

Arendt asks the crucial question:

> Could the activity of thinking as such, the habit of examining and re-flecting upon whatever happens to come to pass, regardless of the spe-cific content and quite independent of results, could this activity be of such a nature that it "conditions" men [sic] against evil-doing?[5]

Thinking is such a mundane aspect of our lives that we rarely reflect on its significance. However, if Arendt is correct, then we need to be aware of the dangers of thoughtlessness and the importance of critical thinking. The practice of thoughtfulness is a vital dimension of practical theodicy that can raise our consciousness to aspects of ourselves and our implication in implicitly evil practices that we may never otherwise have recognized.

If Arendt and Buber are correct in their reflections on thoughtless-ness and inattention, then learning the practice of critical thinking and avoiding the evil of thoughtlessness are crucial practices for the church to learn. However, one might ask, how does such talk of inattentiveness, thoughtlessness, and the banality of evil affect the church today? Most readers of this book do not live in totalitarian regimes and few would con-sider themselves thoughtless enough to participate, even implicitly, in evil. But is that really the case? Let us begin to think together.[6]

Thinking about Joanne

Joanne was two years old and had profound and complex needs, which meant that she was totally dependent on others for everything. The mus-cles in her legs and arms were frequently in spasm due to a condition simi-

---

5. Arendt, "Thinking and Moral Considerations," p. 418.
6. Kerr, Shakespeare, and Varty offer a fascinating and important history of genes, eu-genics, and people with disabilities that has particular relevance to the following discussion. A. Kerr, T. Shakespeare, and S. Varty, *Genetic Politics: From Eugenics to Genome* (Chelten-ham, England: New Clarion Press, 2002).

lar to cystic fibrosis. Thus, she was never able to walk or to hold anything or anyone in her arms. Joanne had to get daily, often painful, physiotherapy in an attempt to ease the stiffness of her muscles and allow her some degree of movement. She was incontinent and would be in diapers for her entire life. Due to a congenital narrowing of her esophagus, Joanne was unable to eat or swallow properly and all of her food had to be softened and sometimes liquefied and fed to her. She also suffered from epilepsy, probably caused by a lack of oxygen at birth. When she was born she had to be resuscitated several times. The medics were surprised that she survived. Some felt it might have been better if she had not.

Joanne was beautiful, not in a conventional sense, but beautiful nonetheless. Her mouth was small and rigid, and her teeth were black from a combination of medication to control her epilepsy and the fact that the tenseness of her muscles made effectively cleaning her teeth very difficult. But Joanne's eyes ... her eyes were truly beautiful — pale blue and expressive, oceans of calm and mystery in a world that was often marked by apparent hopelessness and uncertainty. Joanne may not have been able to communicate with words, but her eyes communicated a multitude of feelings and experiences. They laughed, they danced, they cried, they reminded us of the fullness of her personhood even in the midst of her apparent brokenness.

I have to be honest, though; Joanne scared me. Not because of anything that she actually was or did, but because of what she represented and how she challenged me and the way that I saw and continue to see the world. Her absolute dependency, lack of cognitive ability, and total vulnerability always made me very uneasy. These qualities made me uneasy because they brought to the fore awkward questions about my own expectations for life, my values, my basic assumptions about what I mean by "quality of life," and ultimately my own mortality. Her vulnerability and "weakness" reminded me that my apparent "able-bodiedness" was necessarily temporary. Joanne uncomfortably highlighted the repressed reality that at any given moment what I have can be taken from me by accident, disease, or the unstoppable ravages of time.

But that is not all. Joanne's life raised other, deeper questions about what it means to be human and to live humanly, and in the end that big question: *What are people for?* Her vulnerability, dependence, and powerlessness; her inability to compete in the "marketplaces of life"; and her "non-productiveness" run wholly against those aspects of humanness that my culture has taught me to revere. In a culture that assumes people are primarily made for competition and striving after power, Joanne clearly falls well short of the mark. Joanne may have spoken no words, but the challenge that her life communicated to me and indeed to all of us who knew her was immense. If Joanne was fully human, and if her life was as valuable as my life, then what does it *really* mean to be human and to live humanly? It obviously doesn't mean what many of us assume. When I remember the liveliness exuding from Joanne's beautiful blue eyes as she gazed mysteriously upwards, silently seeking out my eyes and catching them in a momentary hold that touched my soul, ideas of the primacy of the intellect melt away. As I watched a deep smile pass across Joanne's face as her caregiver ran the back of her hand slowly across Joanne's stomach, I sensed the presence of love. At these fleeting but beautiful moments the words of Peter Singer and Helga Khuse, *"We think that some infants with severe disabilities should be killed,"*[7] seem to crash in from another world.

When Joanne died a few months ago, after a particularly destructive series of epileptic fits, I cried . . . we all did. At the funeral, I watched Joanne's parents' pain and sadness; I watched her other caregivers *truly* mourn for the loss that they had experienced. I saw that when Joanne left this world, something changed, and it was not a change for the better. We miss her.

But *why* should we care? Why should we care for someone who misses the cultural mark in such significant ways? In a hyper-cognitive culture in which "clarity of mind and economic productivity determine the value of a human life,"[8] why would we bother to offer care to Joanne and others like her? *Why should this child live?*

Thinking about Persons: When Is a Person Not a Person?

"We think that some infants with severe disabilities should be killed." Elsewhere, Singer argues that in the case of all disabled children, "a period of

---

7. Peter Singer and Helga Khuse, *Should the Baby Live? The Problem of Handicapped Infants* (Oxford/New York/Toronto: Oxford University Press, 1985), p. 1.

8. S. G. Post, *The Moral Challenge of Alzheimer's Disease: Ethical Issues from Diagnosis to Dying* (Baltimore: Johns Hopkins University Press, 2000).

twenty-eight days after birth might be allowed before an infant is accepted as having the same right to live as others."[9] Khuse and Singer want to make the case that if a child will not bring an appropriate degree of happiness to its parents, then the parents should have the right to end the child's life. These authors assume that disability is a problem to be solved, an obstacle to the happiness of the parents. In this case, the "solution" is to kill the person who is disabled. But of course, in Khuse and Singer's eyes, there is no *person* to kill. Joanne has no moral significance.

Is It Acceptable to Kill Disabled Children?

Peter Singer is an Australian philosopher and teacher who is currently Ira W. DeCamp Professor of Bioethics at Princeton University's Center for Human Values. Singer is arguably one of the most influential philosophers in the world today. He has published widely in the area of philosophy and ethics, and his influence is great, particularly in the area of animal rights, where his book *Animal Liberation* has played a crucial role in shaping the contemporary animal rights movement. This book, along with his other influential work, *Practical Ethics,* has been translated into fifteen languages and is taught in courses worldwide. Singer has profoundly influenced the shaping of philosophical thinking about issues of life and death. While our initial reaction may be to ridicule and reject out of hand the suggestion that infanticide can be justified, we must bear in mind the intellectual weight and influence that Singer brings with him. His opinions deserve to be taken seriously.

More recently, Singer has modified his position on giving medics and parents twenty-eight days to decide whether or not to kill the child, acknowledging the number is arbitrary. However, he insists that the central point is that "the life of a newborn baby is of less value than the life of a pig, a dog, or a chimpanzee is to the nonhuman animal."[10] In Singer's opinion, Joanne's life was worth less than the life of a pig.

In his book *Practical Ethics,* Singer further unpacks some of his thinking about the worth of disabled children:

9. Peter Singer, *Rethinking Life and Death* (New York: St. Martin's/Griffin, 1996), p. 217.

10. Peter Singer, *Practical Ethics,* 1st ed. (Cambridge: Cambridge University Press, 1979), pp. 122-23.

When the death of a disabled infant will lead to the birth of another infant with better prospects of a happy life, the total amount of happiness will be greater if the disabled infant is killed. The loss of a *happy* life for the first infant is outweighed by the gain of a *happier* life for the second. . . . killing a disabled infant is not morally equivalent to killing a person. Very often it is not wrong at all.[11]

The question at stake here is the *personhood* of the child. The question of personhood — what it is, and how and why we bestow it on some individuals and not on others — is an important one. To answer these questions, we must begin by exploring precisely what we mean by the term "person."

Personhood as a Protective Notion

Paul Ramsey, in his book *The Patient as Person,*[12] uses the notion of "person" to protect individual patients against the excesses of depersonalizing medical technologies within a modern health care system. He develops the term "person" to prevent medicine, and in particular experimental medicine, from falling into a dangerous form of utilitarianism wherein the welfare of the individual is sacrificed to the needs of the greater number of patients. Ramsey argues that reconciling the welfare of the individual with the welfare of the wider human community is a major issue for medicine. Medicine is called to serve both, but not at the cost of one or the other. Within this context, Ramsey emphasizes the importance of understanding the moral significance of personhood and its necessary role in reminding medicine of the importance of the unique individual who stands in its immediate presence. Thus, as Stanley Hauerwas points out,

> Ramsey's emphasis on "person" is an attempt to provide the basis for what he takes to be the central ethical commitment of medicine, namely, that no person will be used as a means for the good of another. Medicine can serve mankind [sic] only as it does so through serving the individual patient.[13]

11. Peter Singer, *Practical Ethics,* 2d ed. (New York: Cambridge University Press, 1993), p. 191.

12. Paul Ramsey, *The Patient as Person* (New Haven: Yale University Press, 1970).

13. Stanley Hauerwas, "Must a Patient Be a Person to Be a Patient? Or, My Uncle Charlie Is Not Much of a Person but He Is Still My Uncle Charlie," in John Swinton, ed., *Critical*

Importantly, this use of the term "person" focuses the physician's attention on the *person* experiencing the disease, rather than on the disease process viewed in abstraction. Thus, "the notion of 'person' functions for Ramsey as a Kantian or deontological check on what he suspects is the utilitarian bias of modern medicine."[14]

Personhood as an Exclusive Notion

However, the notion of "person" plays quite a different role in the thinking of Singer and others who hold similar positions. In his case, "person" is not used as a *protective* notion but rather as a *permissive* notion that enables modern medicine to make difficult decisions without having to reflect on the potential moral implications of particular forms of action. Such thinking assumes that if we can say with a degree of certainty that such-and-such is not a person, then our responsibility is not the same as it is towards those whom we do decide are persons. If one can argue a human being out of the realm of persons, then it becomes quite acceptable to do to him things that one would never consider doing to those labeled persons. Thus we may be comfortable aborting a "fetus" (a non-person), but we would never consider destroying a child (a person). In this way, the notion of "person" acts as a boundary concept that defines those who are to be protected by the moral community and those who are to stand outside of it and who do not have that protection.[15] Singer's view, therefore, both reflects and illustrates the type of moral position from which Ramsey's idea of personhood seeks to protect patients.

Preference Utilitarianism

In order to understand Singer's thinking, we must understand his philosophical presuppositions. Singer's position on the worth of disabled infants emerges from his philosophical foundation of *preference utilitarianism*. According to this theory, one should behave so that the result of one's

---

Reflections on Stanley Hauerwas' Theology of Disability: Disabling Society, Enabling Theology (New York: Haworth Press, 2005), p. 115.

14. Hauerwas, "Must a Patient Be a Person?" p. 115.

15. There is an interesting connection here between the notion of "person" as protective and the notion of the terms "evil" and "monster" as permissive. The latter terms act as permissive concepts that allow people to dehumanize others and to act accordingly.

behavior is, to the greatest extent possible, in accordance with the *preferences* of those who will be affected by it, whether directly or indirectly. For Singer, the key with regard to the worth of disabled infants is whether or not the baby will bring an adequate degree of happiness to the parents. If the child will bring unhappiness, then the parents should have the right to kill the baby so that they can have the opportunity to have another child that will enable them to maximize their happiness.

The pivotal point for Singer is his definition of personhood. He draws on the definition of a person proposed by John Locke, "a thinking intelligent being that has reason and reflection and can consider itself, the same thinking thing in different times and places."[16]

Singer does not address the question of why these aspects of humanness and not others should be so highly significant. He simply states these things as crucial for personhood and moves on to develop the implications of such a position. Certain assumptions emerge from this definition, key among them being that human life has no intrinsic value. Within that general assumption, it is presumed that human beings have no inherent rights unless they are deemed to be persons. Unless a human being knows she is a person she cannot be classified as a person. The inevitable conclusion to this is that some human beings have a right to life and others do not.

Given this philosophical position, it is not difficult to understand why Singer would struggle to see the moral significance of a life like Joanne's. By his definition, she never was and never could be a person. Singer's response to Joanne's life experiences is to rationalize her out of the world of persons, and thus make her unworthy of moral consideration and protection. Because she could not, in Singer's opinion, bring the maximum amount of happiness to her parents, it would have been morally appropriate to eliminate her. In Singer's thinking, Joanne is a non-person and as such is *replaceable*. This "principle of replaceability" assumes that newborn babies[17] don't have names, personalities, or unique identities. It assumes that they are simply commodities whose existence is justified not by what they are in and of themselves, but by their ability to bring happiness to others by their presence, or if that doesn't work, by their absence!

16. John Locke, *Essay Concerning Human Understanding*, bk. 2, ch. 27, sec. 9 (Oxford: Clarendon Press, 1894).

17. Note that, in principle, Singer's argument applies to all babies. He may have gained some notoriety by focusing on disability, but in fact his position is much broader than disability alone.

Eugenics, Genetic Testing, and the
Principle of Replaceability

Outrageous we might think! Perhaps, but as will become clear, Singer's position, while apparently extreme in some significant senses, may not be as far from the culturally accepted norm as it first appears to be. I want to draw out this suggestion by focusing on two dimensions of Singer's thinking, the principle of *replaceability* and the concept of *personhood.*

The following quotation from a recent document on pregnancy and childbirth will help us focus on the issues:

> *Professional and governmental bodies recommend that various problems be routinely screened for in pregnancy and postnatally including HIV, hepatitis B, and Down Syndrome antenatally and domestic violence postnatally.*[18]

The deviance juxtaposition in this phrase is extraordinary. To apparently compare Down Syndrome with *HIV, hepatitis,* and even more bizarrely *domestic violence* is unusual, to say the least! This statement clearly shows the dangers of making disability a problem, as well as the major issues that surround genetic testing and, in particular, amniocentesis, which can lead to the abortion of disabled children. We will return to this latter point as we move on. For now, it helps to consider the implications of this statement as it relates to the negative attitudes toward disabled children. By doing this, we will discover that such deviance juxtaposition may reflect a cultural assumption implicit in some of our accepted forms of practice.

Let us begin by thinking about the moral implications of genetic testing for disability. At one level, one could argue that it is a good thing insofar as it enables parents to prepare for a child who may need additional care. However, this is clearly not the way that such testing is used.[19] Ris-

---

18. Jane Henderson, Leslie L. Davidson, Jean Chapple, Jo Garcia, and Stavros Petrou, "Pregnancy and Childbirth," http://hcna.radcliffe-oxford.com/pregnancy.htm.

19. The Foundation for People with Learning Disabilities in the UK offers some challenging statistics:

> The number of babies aborted because of deformities has increased by eight percent in a year, figures have revealed (2003-2004). There were more fetuses with Down Syndrome aborted than babies born with the condition in 2002 — 372 abortions compared with 329 births. Overall 1,863 abortions were carried out under Ground E of the Abortion Act, which allows termination where "there is a substan-

ing rates of abortion on the basis of disability would indicate that the accepted "solution" to the "problem" of the imminent arrival of a child with disabilities is to end the pregnancy. This is considered morally appropriate because it is assumed that such a child is somehow not fully human, or at least not fully a person. The underlying implication is that the child will not bring its parents (or society) adequate happiness. Therefore, the parents should be freed from the bonds of unhappiness caused by the disabled child so that they can have another child that *will* bring them happiness. This, of course, is part of Singer's argument — that we already do what he recommends, the only difference being that he is prepared to take the child's life *after* birth. (Note that under the 1967 Abortion Act in the U.K., fetuses with severe disabilities can be aborted at any point during a pregnancy.) Thus, thinking through the implications of Singer's perspective has raised our consciousness to a degree of thoughtlessness that may lead to our implication in evil actions.

The Problem with Prenatal Testing

At one level, prenatal testing appears to be a reasonable response to the imminent arrival of perceived suffering. However, if we dig a little deeper, it becomes clear that certain forms of prenatal testing, such as amniocentesis, are usually euphemisms for the destruction of "defective fetuses," primarily, but not exclusively, those with Down Syndrome. Unlike preventive inoculation against smallpox or measles, prevention in this case means killing the unborn child. As my friend John, who has Down Syndrome, put it, "That doesn't make us feel very welcome, does it?"

While those who favor prenatal testing argue that such treatments of disability prior to birth are in no way intended to reflect on the lives of disabled people *once they are here,* in reality such procedures cannot do anything other than cast a dark shadow of devaluation over the lives of people with disabilities. As Hans Reinders puts it, what message does this state of affairs present to people with disabilities? To quote Reinders:

---

tial risk that if the child were born it would suffer from such physical or mental abnormalities as to be seriously handicapped." The number of abortions carried out because of chromosomal abnormalities such as Down Syndrome increased by seventeen percent — from 591 in 2001 to 690 in 2002.

The first message says "Since you're here, we're going to care for you as best we can," but the second says, "But everyone would be better off if you were not here at all."[20]

What does this tell us about the popular, or at least the medical, understanding of the humanness of people with genetic disabilities? Reinders again points out that

> the only reasonable answer to the question of why a disabled child should be born is by reference to what one thinks about the lives of people actually living with the same disorder.[21]

Certainly, genetic technology that tests unborn children with a view to ending their lives if a disability is found has unrecognized *social side-effects* for people with disabilities who are "already here." Such social side-effects leave all people with disabilities with some serious questions about society's perception of their value, worth, and dignity and leave us wrestling with questions relating to the validity and authenticity of the humanness of people labeled "disabled." Advances in genetic technology *appear* to bring liberation from many forms of impairment. In some cases this may be true. Some dimensions of this technology should perhaps be welcomed. Nevertheless, we need to realize that these technologies bring with them side-effects that are often hidden from the public's eyes. These side-effects can be places where evil resides unnoticed. Indeed, current developments in genetic technology may present the greatest challenge to our understandings of humanness and human living.

Commodifying Our Children

This is a serious situation, not just for people with disabilities, but for all reasonably minded people who sense that there is more to being human than can be explained by genetics and philosophical ethics alone. To develop an alternative perspective, we must explore the cultural dynamics that lie behind our easy acceptance of the death of disabled infants before they are born or, in Singer's opinion, "when they are here."

---

20. Hans S. Reinders, *The Future of the Disabled in Liberal Society: An Ethical Analysis* (Notre Dame, Ind.: University of Notre Dame Press, 2000), p. 4.
21. Reinders, *The Future of the Disabled in Liberal Society*, p. 8.

Gail Landsman suggests that a key dynamic within the issues we are discussing is the ways in which we commodify our children.[22] She argues that the concept of personhood is crucial to the way in which we develop this process of "child-commodification" and use it to protect ourselves from the reality of some of the hard decisions we are forced to make. To think through this suggestion, we need to examine what we mean by the term "commodity." Landsman describes commodities thus:

> Commodities have use value and can be exchanged in discrete transactions; the transaction itself indicates that a counterpart has an equivalent value. Saleability and exchangeability for other things thus suggests that an item has something in common with other exchangeable items that "taken together, partake of a single universe of comparable values."[23]

Landsman points out that in order to be "saleable" or exchangeable, a thing must be common and able to be generalized rather than being singular, unique, and therefore not exchangeable for anything else. She points out that within western thought a division exists between commodities and non-commodities. This division implicitly and explicitly marks the division between *things* and *people.*

> The universe of commodities is understood to be comprised of things (physical objects and rights in them), while at the opposite pole we place people, who represent the natural universe of individuation and singularization. [Within western culture], the establishment of personhood is critical for defining a human being as outside the realm of commoditization. Human beings to whom personhood has been attributed are neither saleable nor exchangeable; each is unique and irreplaceable. Human beings who fall outside the category of full persons are, in contrast, potentially replaceable.[24]

Understood in this way, the ideas of replaceability and exchanging one life for another in the name of "happiness" becomes much more intelligible.

22. Gail Landsman, "'Too Bad You Got a Lemon': Peter Singer, Mothers of Children with Disabilities, and the Critique of Consumer Culture," in *Consuming Motherhood*, ed. Janelle Taylor, Danielle Wozniak, and Linda Layne (New Brunswick, N.J.: Rutgers University Press, 2004), pp. 100-121.
23. Landsman, "'Too Bad You Got a Lemon.'"
24. Landsman, "'Too Bad You Got a Lemon.'"

When the child (either before or after birth) is diagnosed as "disabled," she is moved from the world of persons into the world of commodities, from the status of "I" to the much more ambiguous status of "it." We treat "its" very differently from the way that we treat "I's." Clearly, the term "person" acts as a *permissive* notion that moves a child into the world of morality where he is protected by rights and laws. The child who fails to gain the label of "person" is transported out of this moral universe and into the world of commerce and commodification, where his value, worth, and ultimate survival depend on his fulfilling his primary function as the "bringer of happiness."

This idea of commodification lies at the heart of Singer's thinking and forms a central but hidden dynamic within the process of prenatal testing for disability. By commodifying and depersonalizing children with disabilities, we can make "hard decisions" without having to face up to the fact that *these "hard decisions" have names.* To kill a "disabled infant" who is considered not to be a person is qualitatively different from killing a baby called David, Marcia, or Joanne. The tears of Joanne's parents and those others who cared for her would attest to this as fact. If this is so, then our society has indeed been both inattentive and thoughtless.

What Are People For?

In his book of the same title, American poet and novelist Wendell Berry asks the question *What are people for?*[25] It's a good question. Within a consumerist culture such as ours, wherein the value and function of most things is determined by their abilities to perform appropriately within the market place, it is unclear exactly what is the purpose of people. One problem is that we, as individuals and as a culture, have lost a unified and unifying sense of purposeful movement. What is the common goal to which we all strive? As Alasdair MacIntyre points out, a primary problem with contemporary western culture is that it has lost its unifying sense of telos, its communal direction and shared sense of purpose and meaning.[26] The answer to the question "What are people for?" is not at all clear. In-

25. Wendell Berry, *What Are People For?* (New York: North Point Press, 1990).
26. Alasdair MacIntyre, *After Virtue: A Study in Moral Theory* (Notre Dame, Ind.: University of Notre Dame Press, 1981).

deed, the question itself may sound strange to our ears. "Surely the answer is obvious. The main task people need to perform is to ensure personal happiness and to make sure that they don't intrude on the happiness and freedom of others." However, the discussion thus far would cast a shadow on such a naive and unreflective view of human fulfillment. Are we really here simply to bring each other happiness with no particular goal beyond the fulfillment of our individual selves? If that is so, then Singer is probably right. Killing babies is, in fact, acceptable. However, we Christians claim not just to live in the "world" but also that the world in which we live is a "creation." If that were not so, we would find it necessary also to assume that we have a purpose that is merely focused on the fulfillment of our own desires and happiness. Indeed, the epistemology of the broken body would indicate that happiness, as culturally defined, may not be central to the purpose of what human beings should be.

Of course, introducing the term "creation" into the discussion significantly alters the moral and the theological dynamic. If it is true that we reside within God's *creation* rather than simply on "planet earth" (and as Christians we necessarily make this basic assumption), then we inevitably discover that the moral dynamic within which we address and seek to understand the types of debate we have engaged in thus far, is quite different from those who imagine that they do not live in such a creation.

Choosing Our Children?

In his essay entitled "Having and Learning to Care for Retarded Children," Christian ethicist Stanley Hauerwas states that our attitudes towards children with disabilities cannot be based on whether or not they enliven or dishearten certain families. The purpose of having children does not relate to personal happiness, at least not in the way that people like Singer would suggest. Instead, Hauerwas argues, we must ask *what kind of families and communities we should be in order to welcome such children into our midst regardless of the happy or unhappy consequences they may bring.* Central to Hauerwas's argument are the ideas that, contrary to prevailing wisdom, parenting should be considerably more than a matter of personal choice, and children are considerably more than commodities that we choose either to have or not to have. If we think that we have children simply to fulfill our personal desires and aspirations, then we have fundamentally misunderstood the basis for Christian parenting. Motivation for parenting based only on the desire for personal happiness leaves us totally unprepared for what we should actually do with children when we have them.

> We thus seem trapped to live and raise our children as if the only object is to secure for them a better basis for the acquisition of goods than we had, e.g. that they go to a better college than we did, have a better job, home, boat etc. . . . the sacrifice, what we do for our children, becomes a way of claiming our children as our own. They are made our property by our choice to have them and by what we do for them — they are our product.[27]

Because children are our product, we desire them to be perfect. Hauerwas continues, "After all the effort we have put in, the least we can expect is for them to get a decent job that we can be proud of!" In this way of thinking, our children inevitably always let us down and fall short of our expectations. The danger of such an approach to parenting (which effectively commodifies our children, at least implicitly), is that the child can become totally subsumed to the desires, expectations, and hopes of her parents. Of course, this tends to happen with *all our children*. The disappointment that some parents feel in having a disabled child is common to all experiences of parenting. The only difference is the disappointment happens earlier!

Hauerwas moves on to suggest that a better way to understand the place of children within the family is to see them as *gifts* rather than possessions.

> [O]nly when we understand that our children are gifts can we have an intelligible story that makes clear our duties to them and the form of our care and in particular the care of our children born retarded.[28]

Thus, giving birth to children is an act of faith that witnesses to the type of world the Christian hopes for now and in the future.

---

27. Stanley Hauerwas, "Having and Learning to Care for Retarded Children," in John Swinton, ed., *Critical Reflections on Stanley Hauerwas' Theology of Disability*, pp. 152-53.

28. Quoted in John Swinton, *Critical Reflections in Stanley Hauerwas's Theology of Disability* (New York: Haworth, 2005), p. 153.

[O]ur having children draws on our deepest convictions that God is the Lord of this world, that in spite of all the evidence of misery in this world, it is a world and existence that we can affirm as good as long as we have the assurance that he is its creator and redeemer. That even though we know that this is an existence racked with sin and disobedience, our Lord has provided us with the skills to deal with sin, in ourselves and others, in a manner that will not destroy us or them. Children are, thus, our promissory note, our sign to present and future generations, that we Christians trust the Lord who has called us together to be his people.[29]

Thus, having children makes sense only when we understand ourselves as a people who are charged to carry the story of God, who gives us the basis for our existence as a people. Having children is a vocation and as such is a high calling within the Christian community. This means that we do not parent on our own. As parents we raise our children *on behalf* of the community and ultimately with and on behalf of God. In other words, we do not raise our children to conform to what we as individuals might desire; rather, as parents we are agents of the Christian community, which in turn is an agent of God and a participant in Christ's continuing mission of redemption.

This view of parenting and why we have children will help us rethink our understandings of personhood and the moral significance of lives like Joanne's. Understanding children as gifts changes the texture of the debate. To have children is to welcome them as gifts. A gift is something to be received with thankfulness and love for what it is, not for what it might become, and it is certainly not to be rejected for what it is not. A gift is loved because it is a gift. A gift is both given and accepted in love. A gift may not always be what we want it to be, but when it is given by one whom we love, we accept and graciously care for it and appreciate it as a token and a revelation of that love. If children are, in fact, gifts given to the Christian community as a revelation of the hope of God's reconciling movement towards the world in the midst of evil and suffering, then to destroy children for whatever reason is clearly evil.

29. Stanley Hauerwas quoted in Swinton, *Critical Reflections*, p. 153.

The Moral Significance of Love

This focus on gift is crucial for making a genuinely Christ-like response to the issues we have been discussing in this chapter. One word notably missing from Singer's vocabulary, and indeed from the field of medical ethics in general, is "love." The word sits uneasily in the midst of the complex philosophical and medical language that defines the field. Yet, love informs the telos of most, if not all, human beings. We are made to love, and all of our lives we seek after loving relationships. Human beings are designed to be persons-in-relation. It seems strange then that the word "love" is not central to the types of ethical debates that we explored in the early part of this chapter. We need to introduce the language of love and relationship into the discussion of the nature of persons and the moral significance of people with disabilities. Josef Pieper explains love in this way:

> In every conceivable case love signifies much the same as approval. . . . It is a way of turning to him or it and saying, *"It's good that you exist; it's good that you are in this world!"* . . . Human love, therefore, is by its nature and must inevitably be always an imitation and a kind of repetition of this perfected and . . . *creative* love of God.[30] (italics added)

The primary reason we should argue against the practices put forward by Singer and those who endorse prenatal testing for disability without thinking through the consequences of such a practice relates to this idea of love and the Christian virtue of hospitality. *These are inhospitable and loveless practices.* They stand in dissonance and conflict with the virtue that would say to another person, "It's good that you exist; it's good that you are in this world." Such a statement, "It's good that you exist," forms the very fabric of meaningful human relationships and a genuinely inclusive, moral community.

Barbara Katz Rothman offers an insightful analysis of the complexities — psychological and moral — of prenatal diagnosis. Rothman argues that prenatal technology allows and indeed encourages mothers to distance themselves from their unborn children. Such technology allows them to learn much about the child, and ultrasound testing (a sonogram)

---

30. Quoted in Gilbert Meilaender, "Learning from Pieper: On Being Lutheran in This Time and Place," *Concordia Theological Quarterly* 63, no. 1 (1999): 37-49.

even allows them to visualize the child.[31] However, in doing this, the natural connections between mother and child are reversed.

> Without such technologies, mother and child began with an inseparable attachment and moved towards birth, the beginning point in their distancing and the separation of their individual identities. But prenatal testing means that *the relation of mother and child begins with separation and distancing and moves towards birth,* which is now understood as the moment of attachment or "bonding."[32]

Such forms of screening encourage people to understand pregnancy as a movement from separation toward attachment, with the option of the bond being completely severed if the woman so chooses. Rothman thus notices that pregnancy tends to become "tentative," unless and until the process of genetic screening produces results that encourage the woman to acknowledge the fetus in positive ways. Before this, the woman must maintain a certain distance because she remains uncertain as to whether she will choose to sustain the bond with this particular fetus. Thus, as Meilaender observes,

> prenatal screening with abortion as a possible "treatment" in view if test results are unsatisfactory has a subtle effect on the meaning of motherhood (and eventually fatherhood). For it makes the commitment of parent to child tentative, conditional.[33]

While Hauerwas presses the importance of understanding our children as gifts to be accepted and loved for what they are, rather than for what they are not, and Pieper emphasizes the importance of love-as-welcoming-and-appreciating-the-other, it is clear that the type of relationship that emerges due to the availability of the option of prenatal testing for disability is of a different kind. Rather than assuming that parenthood may necessitate a moral and relational bond that first manifests itself as it is embodied in the mother child unit, prenatal testing encourages distancing between mother and baby, assuming that it is during

31. Barbara Katz Rothman, *The Tentative Pregnancy: Prenatal Diagnosis and the Future of Motherhood* (New York: Penguin Books, 1987).

32. Gilbert Meilaender, *Bioethics: A Primer for Christians,* 1st ed. (Grand Rapids: Eerdmans, 1996), p. 53.

33. Meilaender, *Bioethics,* p. 54.

the process of bonding *after birth* (or the test) that these two individuals come together. Thus we begin with individuation, separation, and distancing and move towards unity and relationship, a unity and relationship that is *optional, tentative,* and *dependent* on the child fulfilling certain criteria.

Such a view of relationships is much in line with our cultural norm. Neo-liberal capitalism offers a picture of human beings as fundamentally individual beings who choose to join together to form societies, the primary purpose of which is to attain the greatest benefits for the largest number of individuals. In other words, the individual *precedes* the community. The process of commodification and the idea of distancing and seeing bonding as a secondary process following individuation are not untypical of the way we see many, if not most, relationships within our society. Within such a philosophical and cultural context, the logic of Singer's position is easier to recognize, even if we still feel uneasy about its implications.

How can the mode of evil highlighted thus far be resisted and transformed? Despite the cultural power of individual conceptions of personhood, we can examine the question of personhood in another way, one that protects children with disabilities and that challenges us to rethink and be more attentive to our practices in fundamental ways.

Practicing Love, Hospitality, and Thoughtfulness

Tony Bland was a young man who was seriously injured in the Hillsborough disaster in the United Kingdom. It occurred on 15 April 1989 on a soccer field in England. Six minutes into the game, the referee was forced to call a halt to the proceedings because a sudden influx of supporters in the Leppings Lane end of the ground was causing a major crush, which ultimately took the lives of ninety-six people. Tony Bland survived the disaster but was left in a persistent vegetative state.[34] Many high profile and complex ethical and moral debates followed about

34. Persistent Vegetative State (PVS) is a condition in which the cerebral cortex (the part of the brain that relates to thought and feeling) ceases to work. People in this condition cannot understand anything that is going on around them and cannot communicate or make voluntary movements. However, the brain stem is largely unaffected and so such people can continue to breath and function at a certain level without assistance.

whether he should live or die and, ultimately, whether or not his personhood remained intact in the midst of his suffering.

However, in the midst of the welter of intellectual energy being spent on deciding whether he should live or die, important gestures of redemption took place unnoticed by many. One such gesture deserves our reflection. On his birthday, Tony's mother spoke movingly about the huge number of birthday cards that he received. For her this was clearly an affirmation that Tony remained valued and that in the eyes of those who loved him he remained fully a person. Tony's mother's affirmation of her son's personhood was confirmed and sustained in the sentiments of friends, family, and strangers embodied in those cards. In a very real sense, his personhood was sustained by the love of those around him. Although Tony was no longer able to tell his own story, his story was held and uplifted by those around him. When he was unable to remember his personhood, the community remembered him. The community's love for him sustained his personhood. Ultimately, hard decisions had to be made, and after much legal debate it was decided that food and water should be withheld from him and that he be allowed to die. Whether these decisions were made on the basis of other understandings of personhood is difficult to assess.

Tony Bland's story echoes the earlier story of Joanne. Joanne was never anything less than a person in the eyes of those who loved her. Her caregivers' loving touches, meaningful caresses, and gentle relationships ensured that Joanne was always a person and that, we hoped, she felt that. Certainly she didn't meet Singer's criteria for personhood. But if we expand or change those criteria to include such things as relatedness, love, warmth, and beauty, then her personhood shines through.

A Theology of Community-as-Personhood

Such words as relatedness, love, hospitality, warmth, and beauty resonate with a theology and spirituality that is of particular importance for this discussion: *ubuntu* theology as put forward by Desmond Tutu. Tutu's perspective offers us a constructive way forward and a useful counter to Singer and the excesses of our thoughtless actions in relation to genetic technology.

The idea of ubuntu emerges from an African worldview and relates to the very essence of being human. Michael Battle notes that

According to much current African scholarship, African epistemology begins with the community and moves to individuality, whereas Western epistemology moves from individuality to community.[35]

Ubuntu assumes that individuals are not *purely* individuals.

The African view of personhood denies that a person can be described solely in terms of the physical and psychological properties. It is with reference to the community that a person is defined. The importance of the community in self-definition is summed up by Mbiti, "I am because we are, and since we are, therefore I am."[36]

Rather than perceiving human beings as discrete, unconnected individuals, ubuntu views them to be constituted as individuals through their relationships and affiliations to other individuals, communities, and ultimately to God. Within this worldview, personhood is not an individual possession. It is a gift that is bestowed on others within community. Tutu describes ubuntu in this way:

> When we want to give high praise to someone we say *Yu, u nobuntu'*; hey, he or she has *ubuntu*. This means they are generous, hospitable, friendly, caring, and compassionate. They share what they have. It also means my humanity is caught up, is inextricably bound up, in theirs. We belong in a bundle of life. We say, "a person is a person through other people." It is not "I think, therefore I am." It says rather: "I am human because I belong." I participate, I share. A person with *ubuntu* is open and available to others, affirming of others, does not feel threatened that others are able and good; for he or she has a proper self-assurance that comes from knowing that he or she belongs in a greater whole and is diminished when others are humiliated or diminished, when others are tortured or oppressed, or treated as if they were less than who they are . . . what dehumanizes you, inexorably dehumanizes me.[37]

35. Michael Battle, "A Theology of Community: The Ubuntu Theology of Desmond Tutu," *Interpretation,* April 2000, p. 179.

36. N. Kkhizie, "Culture, Morality, and Self, in Search of an Afrocentric Voice," unpublished manuscript, University of Natal — Pietermaritzberg, Department of Psychology, South Africa Initiative, 1998.

37. Desmond Tutu, *No Future without Forgiveness* (London: Random House, 1999), pp. 34-35.

Michael Battle contrasts an ubuntu perspective on personhood and humanness with western suppositions about the nature of personhood:

> Many Western views of personhood focus primarily on the lone, self-determined individual. The African view of a person depicts a person in the context of that person's surrounding environment. In the African concept of ubuntu, human community is essential for the individual's acquisition of personhood; however, in Western thought, especially in existentialism, the individual alone defines self-existence. Jean-Paul Sartre's individual illustrates this Western attribute. The Western individual is "nothing [and] will not be anything until later, and then he will be what he makes himself." This Sartrean view defines person as a "free unconditioned" being, a being not constrained by social or historical circumstances. Such Western individualism flies in the face of African beliefs.[38]

From the ubuntu perspective, Joanne's personhood is inextricably tied in with my personhood and indeed with the personhood of each one of us. We are *gifts* given to one another for the purpose of living out meaningful relationships. What we are allowed to become is a gift that is given to us as we interact with others. To destroy or prevent the birth of a disabled child is to make a telling statement about who we are and how we view our relationship with the rest of humanity and the rest of creation. Ubuntu theology understands personhood as a *relational concept* that has to do with the individual's inextricable connectedness with the relational matrix that *is* life. Within this understanding, each of us is a gift to the other and should be respected and treated as such irrespective of our physical or cognitive abilities. Our personhood is constituted by our relationships with the other, and ultimately with God. Tutu's perspective means that Joanne's personhood is assured by the fact that those around her love her and that ultimately she is loved by God without boundaries. To denigrate Joanne and to claim that she is not a person in order that we can justify killing her is not only derogatory to her, but it also denigrates our own humanity. The ubuntu answer to the question "What are people for?" is "To be with and for one another and ultimately to be with and for God."[39]

38. Battle, "A Theology of Community," p. 180.

39. This way of viewing personhood resonates with the counter-Cartesian perspective of Scottish philosopher John Macmurray, who in his 1966 Gifford Lectures presented a

The Image of God as Relationship

The suggestion that human beings are inherently relational finds its theological correlate in a particular understanding of the image of God. In developing this more fully, we will find it helpful to turn to the book of Genesis. In the Genesis account of creation, God creates the world and all that is within it and is pleased. God creates Adam in God's own image (Gen. 1:27). However, on his own Adam is unfulfilled. It is not until God creates Eve from Adam's own flesh and bone that Adam feels fully human. Thus as Karl Barth points out, the basic form of humanity is cohumanity (Gen. 2:18). From the beginning, interpersonal relationships were vital for identity and humanness. Human beings were created for relationships.

However, they are not sustained only by relationships on a vertical level. One of the criticisms of the relational construction of personhood as it has been presented here is that it appears to be dangerously anthropocentric.[40] What if a person has no relationships? What if he is so damaged that he cannot relate; what if no one around him has any desire to relate to him? Does this mean that he ceases to be a person? The answer, of course, is a resounding no! While human relationships are important, ultimately it is God's relationship with human beings that is definitive and sustaining of human personhood.

In the Genesis account of creation, God creates Adam from the same

---

strong case for the relational basis of human personhood. For Macmurray, it is a person's *relationships* that constitute who they are as persons. "I exist as an individual only in personal relation to other individuals. Formally stated, 'I' is one term in the relation 'You and I' which constitutes my existence" (John Macmurray, *Persons in Relation* [London: Faber, 1961; rpt. 1991], p. 44). We become who and what we are according to the types of relationships that we experience within our lives, including those relationships that we have with God. In a very real sense, we are responsible for the construction of the personhood of those whom we choose to relate with.

40. Of course Tutu's use of ubuntu is thoroughly theological. His intention is to merge this traditional worldview with the Christian understanding of forgiveness, repentance, and reconciliation. The intention, or at least the consequence of this constructive theological melding, was that subtle pressure was put on those people who testified and offered forgiveness to their abusers at the South African Truth and Reconciliation Commission. The point being made was that it is only through forgiveness and the recognition that the wrongdoer is in fact a human being "just like us" that testifiers could effectively reclaim their own humanity. In this vital way, ubuntu is significantly connected with our previous discussion on forgiveness.

stuff from which God creates the rest of the world. God breathes the same *nephesh* (spirit) into all creatures, including the human creature. At that level, human beings are creaturely, which accounts for the similarities that humans have to other forms of life.[41] What marks Adam out as somehow different from the other creatures is God's willingness to enter into a personal relationship with him (Gen. 2:16). God does not offer such relationship to any other creature. God does not speak to the animals, the birds, or the trees; only Adam receives this honor. This being so, we can argue that it is this unique, primal relationship with God who is in and of himself self-relationship and love[42] that is the definitive way in which we should understand the image of God in human beings. It is as Adam enters into meaningful personal relationships with God and with Eve that the image of God is made manifest in his life and his personhood is confirmed and assured. God sustains human beings in relationship irrespective of their own capacity to respond or reciprocate. Understood in this way, the fact that relationships should be so central to human life and human development at physical, psychological, and spiritual levels is an inevitable consequence of being made in the image of a relationship-seeking God who is love.

The Practice of Adoption:
Why We Don't Have to Choose Not to Have Disabled Babies

Clearly, there is great need for a serious critique of current practices around disability and prenatal testing. Critique, of course, is relatively easy. However, it is much more complex and demanding to think through a possible alternative. For many parents, both single and married, it is difficult and perhaps impossible for them to cope with a child with a severe disability. It is not enough simply to pour guilt on people and to assume that because you have your theological and ethical principles right, the pastoral aspect will automatically work out. It won't. But if the arguments presented above are correct, then the responsibility for the child does not lie solely with the parents, but rather it is a responsibility of the community as a whole.

41. For a further development of this approach see Ray Anderson, *Becoming Human* (Pasadena, Calif.: Fuller Seminary Press, 1991).

42. John Swinton, *From Bedlam to Shalom: Towards a Practical Theology of Human Nature, Interpersonal Relationships, and Mental Health Care* (New York: Peter Lang, 2000).

But what might that mean in practice? Effective resistance requires radical thinking. To conclude this chapter, we will look at one response that the church-as-community might offer that can resist the type of evil we have been discussing and help to alleviate the pain and guilt of parents who find that, for whatever reason, they cannot cope with a disabled child yet deeply desire that the baby lives. We will explore hospitality as it works itself out in the practice of *adoption*. By examining the practice of adoption as a radical form of hospitality, we will see that adopting disabled babies is a profound mark of faithfulness and resistance.

A Culture of Adoption

Let me begin with my own story. I belong to an interesting family. I am adopted, my brother and sister are adopted, my cousins are adopted, and four out of five of my own children are also adopted. So adoption is the norm within our family narrative and culture. All of us have grown up assuming that adoption is a normal and pretty mundane way of doing family. However, three years ago, "out of the blue" and against all medical expectations, my wife Alison became pregnant with our youngest daughter Naomi. We were and are of course delighted! Not because Naomi is in any sense special (or at least not any more than the rest of the children), but because she has been a wonderful addition to our family. Nevertheless, the mode of her acquisition does raise some interesting and awkward questions, primary amongst them being: *How are we going to explain to Naomi that she is not adopted!?* Will she be scarred by the news that she has only one mum and dad? Will she feel different, out of place, excluded because the way in which she has entered our family is odd? These questions may seem strange to some, but within our family culture, adoption is normal and not to be adopted is odd. It may be hard for "outsiders" to see the significance of this. People still tell us what wonderful people we are for "taking on" "other people's children," how they "don't know how we can do it," and that they "take their hats off to us." We simply tell them to put their hats back on and realize that family is not necessarily the way that they assume it to be and that adoption is not an act of charity, but an act of hospitality, a welcoming of a greatly loved child into one's life, one's family, and one's world.

My point in telling this story is to set a context for proposing that an authentic and faithful Christian alternative to the evil of aborting disabled children is offering them the hospitality of adoption. If the birth parents don't want or feel they cannot cope with a disabled child, then would it not be a better option for others to accept the gift and take on the task of parenting? This seems a strange and challenging suggestion, particularly bearing in mind how heavily stigmatized adoption can be in the eyes of some. However, as my own story indicates, if we had a culture in which adoption was an accepted and desirable norm, then things would look very different. The creation of precisely such a culture is an act of faithful resistance to the type of evil that we are all implicated in. A culture of adoption is one of hospitality where those who are not wanted can find a place where they are welcomed and where individuals and families open up their lives in ways that embody the fact that "it's good that you exist; it's good that you are in the world!" *Adoption is a radical alternative that the church can offer to the world's advocacy of abortion.*

Worshipping an Adopted God

But, one might respond, creating a culture of adoption is a nice idea, but it's never going to happen! Where and how would you initiate such a thing, even if you wanted to? The answer is that a Christian culture that does not recognize it is fundamentally a culture of adoption has failed to recognize and think through an essential dimension of the gospel. To talk about developing a culture of adoption is neither idealistic nor unrealistic; it is, in fact, a radical reflection of a crucial but often overlooked aspect of the incarnation. Adoption is a key theological motif.

> For you did not receive a spirit that makes you a slave again to fear, but you received the Spirit of sonship. And by him we cry, "*Abba*, Father." The Spirit himself testifies with our spirit that we are God's children. Now if we are children, then we are heirs — heirs of God and co-heirs with Christ (Rom. 8:15-17).[43]

To be a Christian is to be adopted into the family of God; to become sons and daughters, not by birth but through the graceful movement of God

43. A particularly good resource for developing a deeper understanding of the theology of adoption is J. Stevenson-Moessner, *The Spirit of Adoption: At Home in God's Family* (Louisville: Westminster/John Knox Press, 2003).

through the Holy Spirit towards human beings. This graceful movement is not based on what we can or cannot do, nor is it based on what we may or may not be able to achieve. It is simply a movement of loving acceptance embodied in the work and person of Jesus. In the incarnation, God is with us, affirming that it's good that we exist; it's good that we are in the world! Adoption is a key aspect of our salvation.

However, adoption is also present, in a slightly different way, in the incarnated life of Christ. Thinking through the implications of two passages will help us to see something most interesting. The first chapter of Matthew gives us some interesting insights into Joseph's experience of the news that Mary is pregnant:

> . . . an angel of the Lord appeared to him in a dream and said, "Joseph son of David, do not be afraid to take Mary home as your wife, because what is conceived in her is from the Holy Spirit. She will give birth to a son, and you are to give him the name Jesus, because he will save his people from their sins." . . . When Joseph woke up, he did what the angel of the Lord had commanded him and took Mary home as his wife. (1:20-21, 24)

I often wonder what it would have been like for Joseph. His betrothed informed him that she was pregnant and that the father of the baby was God! Not surprisingly, his immediate reaction was to distance himself from Mary and look for a way to separate. It was only when God intervened in a dream and persuaded him that the marriage should go ahead that Joseph finally decided to make a commitment to stay with Mary.

What, then, was Joseph's relationship with Jesus? He was not his biological father, yet he seems to have brought Jesus up as his own along with his other children. Matthew 13:55-56 gives us an interesting insight into Jesus' wider family:

> Isn't this the carpenter's son? Isn't his mother's name Mary, and aren't his brothers James, Joseph, Simon and Judas? Aren't all his sisters with us? Where then did this man get all these things?

If Jesus was Joseph's son, and if Joseph was not his biological father, then presumably *Joseph must have, in some sense, adopted Jesus.* He must have taken him into his family as his adopted son who shared brotherhood and sisterhood with Joseph and Mary's "natural" children. This being so, *the*

God whom we worship is an adopted God! Adoption was the mode of parenting that God used upon entering into the human condition. Adoption was the first mode of parenting that God used to initiate the new kingdom and the new humanity. Adoption is not an act of charity or a "good thing to do." The act of adoption mirrors and embodies a primary redemptive action of God.

To suggest that adoption is a radical and faithful alternative that the church can offer as a mode of resistance to the evil of aborting disabled children is to call the churches' attention to the particular way that God has acted in the incarnation of Jesus. If adoption was deemed an appropriate mode of parenting for the upbringing of the son of God, then one would imagine that creating a culture within which adoption is normal should be a natural response by the community called into existence to follow the son.

Certainly, adopting disabled infants raises its own issues and challenges. Nevertheless, if the arguments presented in this chapter are correct, then *all* babies are gifts and should be treated and respected accordingly. The challenges of adopting a child with a disability must be carefully balanced against the call to be loving and hospitable. In the words of Stanley Hauerwas, "Christians witness to wider society . . . by welcoming the children that the wider society does not want."[44] "The crucial question for us as Christians is what kind of people we need to be to be capable of welcoming children into this world, some of who[m] may be born disabled and even die."[45] The practice of adoption helps us to become such people.

Nothing Can Separate Us from the Love of God

This chapter has aimed to engage us in a process of critical thinking to help us recognize that the choices that we assume to be logical, obvious expressions of individual freedom and personal rights may be highly problematic for those who seek to follow the gift-giving God. The choices that liberal culture offers us may appear to be "natural" and "obvious," but when we

---

44. J. Berkman and M. Cartwright, *The Hauerwas Reader* (Durham, N.C.: Duke University Press, 2001), p. 620.

45. Berkman and Cartwright, *The Hauerwas Reader,* p. 619.

view them in a theological frame that recognizes the given-ness of our children, we find these choices to be at best limiting and at worst evil in the sense that this term has been worked out within this book.

Thinking in this way can be painful. Making decisions around beginning-of-life issues is incredibly complex and messy. In focusing on the utilitarian dimensions of the process of prenatal testing for disability, I have not meant to suggest that people selfishly search after happiness irrespective of the consequences to self and others. Prenatal testing may well be performed for utilitarian reasons, but not everyone who receives prenatal testing for disability necessarily has utilitarian intentions. People make difficult decisions about whether or not they should bring a child with disabilities into the world for many and varied reasons that do not necessarily revolve around purely personal happiness. Deciding whether to bring a disabled child into the world can be incredibly painful and difficult. I have no wish to minimize the personal and social problems involved in making such decisions and the pain that people go through before and after they decide one way or the other. I also acknowledge that there are times when people, even with the best intentions, feel that they cannot bring a disabled child into the world. This chapter is not intended to make people feel unloved or alienated from God or others. Nothing can separate us from the love of God!

> For I am convinced that neither death nor life, neither angels nor demons, neither height nor depth, nor anything else in all creation, will be able to separate us from the love of God that is in Christ Jesus our Lord. (Rom. 8:38-39)

Nevertheless, the fact that people may feel compelled by circumstances to decide not to have a child because it has a disability does not make such an action right. If circumstances appear to dictate that we must choose not to bring such a child into the world, our actions remain wrong, even if we feel that such a choice is the lesser of two evils. If we have made such a choice, we need to think about the reality of what we have done and repent. As we have seen, forgiveness is always available to those who approach God with a repentant heart. Irrespective of the mistakes we have made in the past, or our failure to fully think things through in the present, God's love remains steadfast and sure. Nothing can separate us from that love. It is therefore vital to note that the practice of thoughtfulness cannot be separated from the practice of forgiveness and lament. For those of us who, upon reflecting on the discussion in this chapter, find ourselves hurt, broken, or in pain, Paul's words offer a healing balm. This healing may begin with silent reflection on where we have been; it may even move to lament. But the healing dynamic as it is revealed in genuine repentance always moves us towards forgiveness and reconciliation with the God who will never leave us or forsake us because he loves us. Our past actions may not be excusable (indeed, attempting to rationalize our previous mistakes leads only to denial and alienation from ourselves and from others), but they are forgivable. The key thing is to ensure that we do not repeat the mistakes of the past in the present. When we achieve such a task, we become able to resist evil, and we feel assured of healing and reconciliation with God, self, and others.

Conclusion: The Interconnectedness of the Practices

Within this relational theodical movement, the practices of *thinking, hospitality,* and *adoption* have emerged as key aspects. Once again the interconnectivity of Christian practices as they work together to form a faithful way of living is clear. These three practices are necessary for us to discover a faithful response to the evil of thoughtlessness. However, as we have moved on, it is clear that other practices such as lament, listening to silence, forgiveness, and friendship are also necessary for the effective practice of thoughtfulness.

In conclusion, when we think about it, it is a very bad idea to kill disabled babies. Caring for and protecting the lives of children with disabilities is vital for the health of our society, morally, psychologically, and spiritually, and for the faithfulness of our communities. A society that is inattentive to the essential interconnectedness of its participants is a society that is open to the possibility of justifying abuse and forms of practice that can be deadly for the weakest and most vulnerable members of our society. Children with disabilities are extremely vulnerable both in utero and when they are here. In this chapter we have examined the dangers of the ways in which we understand the concept of "the person" in medical ethics and the ways that this has become a vehicle for avoiding making hard decisions about vulnerable people. Ultimately, I have suggested, personhood is a gift that is bestowed on persons in community. The idea of personhood is a reminder that we are deeply connected and that the way I act towards you reveals something important about the way I see the world and human beings.

Stephen Post, reflecting on the position of people with Alzheimer's disease, another condition that falls out with Singer's definition of personhood, makes the following poignant observation:

> We must set aside the distorted position that a person's worth, dignity, and status as a human being depend entirely on cognitive capability. We must develop a view of personhood that takes into account the emotional, relational, symbolic, and even spiritual capacities of the person. We live in a culture that is dominated by heightened expectations of rationalism, clarity of mind, and productivity. We internalize these expectations; thus when someone we love is diagnosed with early dementia, our reaction is likely to be despair. Our goal, however, must be to remember that persons with dementia are neither "shells" nor "husks"; they have not become subhuman; they remain part of our shared humanity. About this we must be clear, lest we succumb to the banality of evil.[46]

The way we treat disabled infants like Joanne and those unborn children who bear the deadly label of "disabled" embodies the answer to the question: *What are people for?* How we answer that question calls us to a place of judgment, decision, and thoughtfulness. In attempting to justify the killing of disabled infants, either before they are born or when they are with us, perhaps we end up being lesser persons ourselves.

46. Stephen Post, "Alzheimer's and Grace," *First Things* 142 (April 2004): 12-14.

CHAPTER EIGHT

Friendship, Strangeness, and Hospitable Communities

Don't forget to show hospitality to strangers, for some who have done this have entertained angels without realizing it! . . . Remember also those being mistreated, as if you felt their pain in your own bodies.

Hebrews 13:2-3 (New Living Translation)

In national and international fora, the dominant considerations regarding displacement of people have deteriorated from assistance and hospitality to rejection and hostility.

Migrants' Rights International

When I Was a Stranger . . . You Invited Me into Your Home

Yaffa Eliach is a professor of history and holocaust studies at Brooklyn College, New York. In her book *Hasidic Tales of the Holocaust*, she narrates Zvi's story:

> In the Lithuanian shtetl or town of Eisysky, the Jewish population of four thousand was liquidated on September 25, 1941. In groups of two hundred fifty, first the men and then the women, the people were taken to the old Jewish cemetery in front of the open ditches. They were ordered to undress and stand at the edge of the open graves. They were shot in the back of the head by Lithuanian guards with the encourage-

ment and help of the local people. The chief executioner was the Lithuanian Ostrovakas. Dressed in a uniform, a white apron, and gloves, he personally supervised the killing. He reserved for himself the privilege of shooting the town's notables . . . and he practiced sharpshooting at the children, aiming as they were thrown into the graves.

Among the Jews that September 25, 1941, in the old Jewish cemetery of Eisysky was one of the shtetl's . . . teachers, Reb Michalowsky, and his youngest son, Zvi, age sixteen. Father and son were holding hands as they stood naked at the edge of the open pit, trying to comfort each other during their last moments. Young Zvi was counting the bullets and the intervals between one volley of fire and the next. As Ostrovakas and his people were aiming their guns, Zvi fell into the grave a split second before the volley of fire hit him.

He felt the bodies piling up on top of him and covering him. He felt the streams of blood around him and the trembling pile of dying bodies moving beneath him.

It became cold and dark. The shooting died down above him. Zvi made his way from under the bodies, out of the mass grave into the cold, dead night. In the distance, Zvi could hear Ostrovakas and his people singing and drinking, celebrating their great accomplishment. After eight hundred years, on September 26, 1941, Eisysky was . . . cleansed of Jews.

At the far end of the cemetery, in the direction of the huge church, were a few Christian homes. Zvi knew them all. Naked, covered with blood, he knocked on the first door. The door opened. A peasant was holding a lamp which he had looted earlier in the day from a Jewish home. "Please let me in," Zvi pleaded. The peasant lifted the lamp and examined the body closely. "Jew, go back to the grave where you belong!" he shouted at Zvi and slammed the door in his face. Zvi knocked on other doors, but the response was the same.

Near the forest lived a widow whom Zvi knew too. He decided to knock on her door. The old widow opened the door. She was holding in her hand a small, burning piece of wood. "Let me in!" begged Zvi. "Jew, go back to the grave at the old cemetery!" She chased Zvi away with the burning piece of wood as if exorcising an evil spirit. . . . "I am your Lord, Jesus Christ. I came down from the cross. Look at me — the blood, the pain, the suffering of the innocent. Let me in," said Zvi Michalowsky. The widow crossed herself and fell at his bloodstained feet. . . . "My

God, my God," she kept crossing herself and praying. The door was opened.

Zvi walked in. He promised her that he would bless her children, her farm, and her, but only if she would keep his visit a secret for three days and three nights and not reveal it to a living soul, not even the priest. She gave Zvi food and clothing and warm water to wash himself. Before leaving the house, he once more reminded her that the Lord's visit must remain a secret, because of His special mission on earth.

Dressed in a farmer's clothing, with a supply of food for a few days, Zvi made his way to the nearby forest. . . .[1]

At the beginning of chapter six, we highlighted the massive scale of human destruction and death that has been a mark of the twentieth century. The various wars and acts of mass violence have had wide-ranging consequences. Primary among these has been a massive displacement of human beings, people forced to move from their homes and their countries for fear of death and torture. Worldwide approximately 125 million displaced people are living temporarily or permanently outside of their countries of origin. Two-thirds of the world's refugees live in developing countries, often in camps. In the Sudan alone, four million people have been forced to leave their homes.[2] Zvi's experience of the horrors of genocide and unspeakable acts of evil have been multiplied in our own time in many countries and contexts from Bosnia, to Rwanda, to Sudan. Refugees and those who are escaping the many horrors of the world are "the stranger" whom we encounter in the world today.

The epistemology of the broken body of Christ informs us that God is with those who suffer such outrages; God is with them in solidarity and real presence. God does not merely empathize with or watch over human beings "from a distance." Rather, God is so deeply involved in the suffering of the world, that it inevitably creates deep suffering for God.[3] As

---

1. Yaffa Eliach, *Hasidic Tales of the Holocaust* (New York: Vintage Books, 1988), pp. 53-55.

2. More than half a million people have fled the country, mainly to neighboring countries such as Chad. Yet, fewer than one thousand Sudanese applied for asylum in the United Kingdom in 2003. Contrary to popular myth, it is *poor countries* and not rich western countries that look after the majority of the world's refugees. The tension between the truth of the situation and the cultural myths that surround asylum-seekers is deeply concerning.

3. For a further classic development of this suggestion see Jürgen Moltmann, *The Cru-*

God offers hospitality towards strangers such as these, so also the church, which has received and understands something of divine hospitality, is called to offer hospitality towards these same strangers. In this chapter we will explore the implications for pastoral theodicy of the Christian practice of hospitality towards strangers. We will do this by focusing on the significance of God's actions in the world in and through the practice of Christian friendship, which can be understood as a type of hospitality. By examining the critical role of hospitality-in-friendship as a mode of resistance to evil, we will discover ways of creating communities-of-friends that care for strangers, resist evil, and absorb suffering.

Friendship as Resistance

To understand the theodical potential of friendship, we must first understand what is meant by the term "Christian friendship." Elsewhere I have written extensively about the theological and practical importance of friendship, particularly with regard to the experiences of marginalized people.[4] Here I will draw on and develop some of that thinking to explore the theodical significance of friendship and its particular application in the cases of people in situations similar to that of Zvi. First, we will look at what friendship is and what it is not.

Becoming Friends

Friendship is a basic and vital human relationship that forms the social fabric of our lives. It is in and through friendships that we discover our identity, gain our sense of value and place in the world, and learn what it means to participate in community. As our reflections on ubuntu theology in chapter seven clearly revealed, friendships aid the development of our self-identity. Through friendships, we discover where we want to go

cified God, trans. R. A. Wilson and John Bowden (New York: Harper & Row, 1974; Minneapolis: Fortress Press, 1974).

4. John Swinton, Resurrecting the Person: Friendship and the Care of People with Severe Mental Health Problems (Nashville: Abingdon Press, 2000); John Swinton, From Bedlam to Shalom: Towards a Practical Theology of Human Nature, Interpersonal Relationships, and Mental Health Care (New York: Peter Lang, 2000).

in life and how we should relate with others and with God. Friends help us to *recognize* one another and the world.

The Politics of Recognition

In his book *Multiculturalism,* Charles Taylor reflects on the link between *recognition* and *identity,* which is a person's self-understanding of who she is and what her defining characteristics are as a human being.[5] Taylor suggests that human existence is dialogical, meaning that we acquire our identity not as dislocated individuals, but through interaction with significant others, most notably by means of the language they use to describe us.[6] For Taylor, the "monological ideal [so prevalent within western cultures] seriously underestimates the place of the dialogical in human life."[7] Hence, recognition, whether it is given or withheld, has a significant impact on the identity of individuals and individual cultures.[8] The way in which we recognize others and are recognized by others can shape the way in which we identify ourselves.

> The thesis is that our identity is partly shaped by recognition or its absence, often by the misrecognition of others, and so a person or group of people can suffer real damage, real distortion, if the people or society around them mirror back to them a confining or demeaning or contemptible picture of themselves. Non-recognition or misrecognition can inflict harm, can be a form of oppression, imprisoning someone in a false, distorted, and reduced mode of being.[9]

We see and respond to things within a particular frame of recognition. We do not, however, develop such a frame-of-recognition in a vacuum. That frame is determined by our implicit and explicit assumptions about the world, ourselves, our environment, our values, expectations, hopes, and so forth. In other words, we learn to recognize things and people in

---

5. Charles Taylor, *Multiculturalism,* ed. Amy Gutman (Princeton: Princeton University Press, 1994).

6. Taylor, *Multiculturalism,* pp. 32-33.

7. Taylor, *Multiculturalism,* p. 33.

8. Taylor, *Multiculturalism,* p. 36.

9. Taylor, *Multiculturalism,* p. 25.

particular ways. In chapter six we examined the myth of pure evil, which separates good from evil in an absolute way and is created by media images, popular culture, and fantasies that evil resides exclusively in a realm inhabited by "evil monsters" who are "nothing like us." Recognition of identity, as Taylor develops it, shares some important similarities with the myth of pure evil. We learn to recognize one another, both positively and negatively, through the same shaping forces that comprise the myth of pure evil. And, like the myth of pure evil, much of what we learn to recognize in others is mythical, false, and sometimes dangerous. This mythical creation of false identity in the other significantly affects how we respond to those we choose to call strangers.

Being recognized by another can be uplifting or terrorizing. To be recognized in a crowd by a friend who rushes to greet you is enhancing and positively impacts your identity. To be recognized as different from the crowd and singled out by someone for humiliation or derogatory comments destroys your positive identity. Taylor cites the feminist example of how women adopt negative and oppressive self-identities when they are forced to internalize images of inferiority. Once they internalize such images, their negative self-identity persists even when the cultural and political barriers that caused their oppression begin to come down. In chapter seven we explored the idea of thoughtlessness and its implications for people with disabilities. Recognition and thoughtlessness are connected. Because people with disabilities are recognized in a particularly negative way, thoughtlessness regarding the ways in which they are treated is almost inevitable. If this is so, then

> misrecognition shows not just a lack of due respect. It can inflict a grievous wound, saddling its victims with a crippling self-hatred. Due recognition is not just a courtesy we owe people. It is a vital human need.[10]

How we recognize those around us will determine whether or not they are perceived as "insiders" or "outsiders," "strangers" or "friends." Recognition, therefore, has the power to re-humanize or to dehumanize, to be an agent of good or an agent of evil.

10. Taylor, *Multiculturalism*, p. 26.

Recognition and Radical Friendship

The power of friendship as a form of resistance to evil lies in the fact that friends *recognize* one another in particularly constructive and health-bringing ways. The importance of friendship is demonstrated in the way Jesus practiced it as a mode of recognizing and offering hospitality to strangers.

In John 15:15-17, Jesus says:

> I no longer call you servants, because a servant does not know his master's business. Instead, I have called you friends, for everything that I learned from my Father I have made known to you. You did not choose me, but I chose you and appointed you to go and bear fruit — fruit that will last. Then the Father will give you whatever you ask in my name. This is my command: Love each other.

When Jesus shifts the disciples' identities from servants to friends, he offers them a mode of recognition and a form of identity that was not available previously. In making this shift, Jesus acknowledges and embodies the fact that human beings can become friends of God. Friendship with God radically changed the identity of Jesus' disciples and enabled them, in turn, to recognize God differently and, by extension, to recognize one another differently. In this graceful act of recognition, Jesus makes friendship with him the basis of their understanding of who they were and what they were in the world to do. Knowing Jesus' radical recognition of them as his friends gave them a new identity and helped them begin to understand what it might mean to be and to live as friends of God. True, the full meaning of that friendship did not become clear until after the resurrection, for Jesus' friendship unto death far surpassed the disciples' ability to reciprocate. Nevertheless, this episode in their lives was a vital turning point of identity and recognition.

Friendship unto Death

It would be a mistake to underestimate the challenge offered by Jesus in his gift of recognition-in-friendship. The type of friendship that Jesus called the disciples to experience was quite different from friendship in the market-driven economy of western culture. Jesus called his disciples to a friendship that required faithfulness and solidarity unto death: "Greater love has no one than this, that one lay down his life for his friends" (John 15:13). Friendship framed as a radical commitment unto death has a distinctive shape and goal. The solidarity, commitment, sacrifice, and ongoing faithfulness that God shows to human beings in friendship with them is also to be embodied and practiced by those who are called to recognize themselves as God's friends. This holy friendship differs from the cultural norm, not only because of its depth of commitment, but also because of its focus and intention. In western culture, we develop relationships based on two principles: the principle of *social exchange* and the principle of *likeness*.[11] The principle of social exchange assumes that we gauge our relationships according to what we can get from them. Thus, *I* enter into a relationship with another person with the hope that *I* will get particular things back that will satisfy *me* and encourage *me* to stay in the relationship. No inherent moral or theological obligation binds our friendships together, only the quest for personal satisfaction and happiness. Consequently, if *I* am not getting what *I* want from a relationship, *I* will move on to one in which *I* can feel more fulfilled and satisfied. In such a market-driven approach to friendship, it is not surprising that many of our friendships are transient and self-centered. We might lay down our lives for our families, but for our friends?

Deeply tied in with the principle of social exchange is what I have described elsewhere as *the principle of likeness*.[12] This principle assumes that friendships are constructed between individuals who have particular things in common. Thus, our friendships tend to be based on the idea that like-attracts-like. However, the friendships of Jesus are based on a very different principle: *the principle of grace*.[13] In Jesus' incarnation we discover that which is radically unlike humanity, God, entering into friendships with humanity and setting a radically different pattern for forming human relationships in general and friendship in particular. The principle of grace suggests that it is not what we have in common at a temporal level — our common interests, similar personalities, shared experiences, and so on — that forms

11. Swinton, *Resurrecting the Person*, p. 45.

12. John Swinton, *From Bedlam to Shalom: Towards a Practical Theology of Human Nature, Interpersonal Relationships, and Mental Health Care* (New York: Peter Lang Publishers, 2000), p. 84.

13. Swinton, *From Bedlam to Shalom*, p. 86.

the basis of our friendships. It is what we have in common at the transcendent level that provides a different basis for the practice of friendship. Our friendships are based on the shared knowledge that we are recognized by God as God's friends and called in and with God's grace to recognize the world and others within it in ways that differ greatly from the assumed norm.

Sitting with "Strangers"

This has important implications for the ways in which we choose to practice friendship. Jesus sat with those who were socially and religiously unlike him — tax collectors, sinners, women — those considered socially and religiously unclean. More than that, he considered them his friends. When Jesus was derided for being a friend of tax collectors and sinners, his accusers unknowingly made a profound statement about Jesus and, indeed, about God, for Jesus said:

> The Son of Man came eating and drinking, and they say, "Here is a glutton and a drunkard, a friend of tax collectors and 'sinners.'" But wisdom is proved right by her actions. (Matt. 11:19)

Notice that it was not "reformed sinners" or even "repentant sinners" that Jesus sat with. These were people marginalized by society and with no access to the cleansing rituals of the temple; they were condemned as sinners (at least in the eyes of the religious authorities) with no obvious way out of that state. But Jesus recognized them differently, sat with them, and offered them friendship rather than condemnation. His friendships were open, unbounded by culture or public opinion; in particular, he offered friendship to those whom society marginalized, stigmatized, and demonized. In fact, by sitting with the marginalized and offering them God's friendship, Jesus shifted the margins. Now it was the religious people, who assumed that they knew God and that "God was on their side," who became marginalized, even though they did not realize it. Such a repositioning of the margins challenges our church communities by raising the question: *Are we sitting where God is sitting?*

Friendship and Lament

Such a practice of friendship offers a context for the practices that we have focused on in this book. I have argued that we need to become a people who know what it means to experience sadness faithfully. But how do we learn to become a people who are capable of lamenting in faithfulness? Chapter five laid out some initial strategies designed to enable church communities to learn the practice of lament. These suggestions are important, but in order to succeed at them, communities need to understand and practice them in a context of friendship.

Thinking back to the narrative that opened the book, we can see why this might be so. When Gemma died so suddenly and tragically, who heard George's lament, "Why me?" It was me, George's friend. I wrestled with the fact that I had nothing to say, that I could not explain why God would allow this to happen to George and Martha. I felt helpless . . . useless . . . and yet, I heard George's lament; I recognized his pain. But I did not recognize it in hopelessness; I recognized it hopefully. George may have experienced the "abandonment" of God: "My God, why have you abandoned me?" But as his friend, I held onto God for him in silence, in prayer, and in solidarity. When he could not hope, when lament was the only language available, I, in holy friendship, could hope on his behalf. My friendship with George gave him a way to express his lament and pain within a safe relationship based on a shared faith that, even now, there might be hope. He could not have experienced that hope at that moment; his sense of abandonment truly echoed Jesus' lament from the cross. Nevertheless, in silent advocacy I still hoped and sustained faith in the God who had "abandoned" him.

Alongside all of his friends, I hoped and had faith for him. George was paralyzed with pain and grief, but his friends were able to drop his suffering down through the roof of the pain house and ask for Jesus' healing touch. Friends can hope for one another even when all hope seems to be gone. Without friendship and a hopeful place to express real pain and suffering, the practice of lament can never flourish. My silence was awkward and frustrating, yet it provided a sounding board for George's pained prayer of complaint to God. There may have been nothing to say in explanation, but George's lament and my silently spoken prayers said volumes. I had nothing to say to George . . . but . . . I could give him myself in the silent bond of friendship.

Friendship and Forgiveness

Friendship is the place where forgiveness begins. We practice forgiveness with and towards our friends. At the deepest level, forgiveness begins when we recognize the immensity of human sin and the breadth of God's desire to forgive. We begin our understanding of human forgiveness at the foot of the cross, that place where, in the broken body of Christ, we can clearly see the depth of God's love and the cost of true forgiveness. Seeing God's desire to be reconciled, we also realize our need and desire to be reconciled with God and with one another.

But forgiveness is not easy. Throughout this book, I have used extreme examples of apparently unforgivable behavior to make the point that all human beings can be forgiven. Nothing is beyond God's ability to redeem. However, we may look at such extreme examples and decide that we can never forgive in this way. Then we turn away with heavy hearts, knowing the truth but being unable to practice it. However, looking at our own lives, we find that we don't have to be faced with acts of grotesque evil for us to struggle to forgive. The simplest of slights can become unforgivable if we don't practice forgiveness regularly. The myriad of tiny hurts that we inflict on our friends and that they inflict on us, all of which have the potential to develop into destructive rifts, are overcome and healed as we constantly engage in the practice of forgiveness-in-friendship. Friendship is where we practice forgiveness and learn what it means to be people who do not simply engage in various acts of forgiveness, but who are forgiving in their very being. When we begin to learn to forgive in this way through friendship, our response to other acts of hurt and sinfulness will begin to shift.

As we have seen, forgiveness is not an option for Christians. It is the essence of faithful discipleship. Nevertheless for some, forgiveness is not possible. Sometimes the best that we can do is to recognize that we should be forgiving and struggle honestly and faithfully with the reality that we cannot forgive. That struggle should not involve guilt or shame at our inability to fulfill God's desire. But it should demand that we take our pain to the foot of the cross and realize that we can frame our experience in other ways and that forgiveness, not revenge, is our goal, even if we struggle to achieve it. Our friends sit with us in that struggle and offer us a safe space where we can lament, express our rage and outrage, and be led and encouraged, gently, to put our feet on the complex and sometimes painful road towards forgiveness.

Hospitality towards Strangers

The practice of friendship is thus integral to the other practices that we have looked at. However, as well as supporting and containing other theodical practices, Christ-shaped friendship also offers a mode of resistance to evil in its own right. In Matthew 25, Jesus tells a story that adds a challenging dimension to the practice of friendship and hospitality. In that parable, Jesus reflects on the final judgment and the relationship of God to those whom the world considers to be strangers. On the last day, Jesus will sit on the seat of judgment and separate those who were for him in this life, the sheep, from those who were against him, the goats — the sheep to the right and the goats to the left:

> Then the King will say to those on his right, "Come, you who are blessed by my Father; take your inheritance, the kingdom prepared for you since the creation of the world. For I was hungry and you gave me something to eat, I was thirsty and you gave me something to drink, I was a stranger and you invited me in, I needed clothes and you clothed me, I was sick and you looked after me, I was in prison and you came to visit me."
>
> Then the righteous will answer him, "Lord, when did we see you hungry and feed you, or thirsty and give you something to drink? When did we see you a stranger and invite you in, or needing clothes and clothe you? When did we see you sick or in prison and go to visit you?"
>
> The King will reply, "I tell you the truth, whatever you did for one of the least of these brothers of mine, you did for me."
>
> Then he will say to those on his left, "Depart from me, you who are cursed, into the eternal fire prepared for the devil and his angels. For I was hungry and you gave me nothing to eat, I was thirsty and you gave me nothing to drink, I was a stranger and you did not invite me in, I needed clothes and you did not clothe me, I was sick and in prison and you did not look after me."
>
> They also will answer, "Lord, when did we see you hungry or thirsty or a stranger or needing clothes or sick or in prison, and did not help you?"
>
> He will reply, "I tell you the truth, whatever you did not do for one of the least of these, you did not do for me."
>
> Then they will go away to eternal punishment, but the righteous to eternal life. (vv. 34-46)

In this passage, Jesus clearly identifies himself as the *xenos,* the stranger, the one whom many would not befriend. Jesus calls his people to recognize the stranger as the one whom they are obliged to protect and care for. Those who offer hospitality and friendship towards the stranger will be welcomed into the kingdom of heaven. Those who fail to offer such hospitality to the *xenos* will depart from the presence of the Lord into everlasting fire. In offering friendship towards strangers, one encounters Jesus. Note that Jesus does not simply entreat people to pursue acts of charity towards the stranger. ("If you know me, then you will act in this way.") The relationship between Jesus and "the stranger" seems to be quite different. Jesus is not simply *with* the poor and the oppressed; in a very real sense, he *is* the poor and the oppressed. He states quite clearly that such acts of charity and friendship towards strangers are in fact gestures of love towards Jesus. Indeed, one might even go so far as to suggest that such acts of friendship towards strangers are, in fact, acts of worship. They are worship in the sense that to minister to and value the sick, the poor, the hungry, and the victims of evil is to minister to and value Jesus. Showing hospitality is an act of love, worship, and devotion to God. By calling his disciples to perform radical acts of hospitality and to recognize the theological significance of those acts, Jesus places "the stranger" under divine protection and his followers under divine obligation to offer hospitality towards the stranger. One way in which Jesus practiced hospitality was through friendship.

"I Am Your Lord"

In the light of Matthew 25, the encounter between Zvi and the Christian woman that opened this chapter takes on a new meaning. Zvi's panicked cry, "I am your Lord," was a desperate deception to save himself from death or worse. And yet, his cry contained a hidden truth, probably unrecognized by him but perhaps recognized by the woman, who felt a disturbing resonance with something deep within her religious tradition. God was in Zvi in the same way God is in all "strangers." In clothing Zvi and giving him food and warm water to wash himself, the woman was recognizing Jesus in the stranger, and in so doing, she ministered to God in a way that stood in stark, resistant contrast to the acts of evil that surrounded her. Her initial reluctance to minister to the stranger echoes the reluctance of many Christians to face up to the practical implications of this difficult teaching, particularly when offering hospitality to strangers can bring danger. But her reluctant faithfulness added a vital theodical dimension to the encounter, which echoes the response of Jesus' followers in the Matthew 25 parable.

To Know Yahweh Is to Minister to the Stranger

God's strong identification with strangers is not confined to the New Testament. It is also found in the Old Testament, particularly in relation to God's relationship with the poor and the outcast. In Jeremiah 22:16 we read: "'He defended the cause of the poor and the needy, and so all went well. Is that not what it means to know me?' declares the Lord." This is a fascinating proposition. In its wider context, the text speaks about good and bad kings and offers Josiah as a model of a good king because he cared for the poor and the needy. This text points to Jesus' teaching on his presence in the stranger. Brueggemann notes that

> This is an extraordinary text which shows how Yahweh is understood in terms of a social practice. Note well, the text does not say that if one takes care of the poor and needy, then one will get to know Yahweh. Nor does the text say that, if one knows Yahweh, then one will take care of the poor and needy. The two elements are not sequential nor are they related as cause and effect. Rather, the two phrases are synonymous. Caring for the poor and the needy is equivalent to knowing Yahweh. That is who Yahweh is and how Yahweh is known. Yahweh is indeed a mode of social practice and a form of social relation.[14]

Taken together, these passages in Matthew and Jeremiah, one speaking of Jesus and the other indicating what it means to love Yahweh, reveal the social location of God in relation to the stranger, the poor, and the outcast, along with the modes of social practice that emerge from such recognition. If Jesus is in the stranger, the poor, and the oppressed, and if social practices that offer care and protection to the poor and the oppressed are a mode of knowing Yahweh, then the foundational call of the church must

14. Walter Brueggemann, "The Practice of Homefullness," *Church and Society*, May/June 2001, p. 12.

be to recognize the poor, the outcast, and the stranger and to ensure that, through its social practices, the church protects and cares for the stranger (in whatever form the stranger comes to us). As the church practices in this way, it ministers faithfully to God and to the body of Christ. Friendship is precisely such a social practice. To offer Christ-like friendship to the poor, the outcast, the victims of evil is to minister faithfully to God. To love God is to act in such a way. As such, friendship is a key dimension of practical theodicy.

Who Is the Stranger?

Since friendship is an important mode of resistance to evil, it will be helpful to asking the apparently simple question, *Who is the stranger?*

Basically, a stranger is someone we do not know. She is an outsider who does not (or at least is not perceived to) share our environment, values, and assumptions about the world. The stranger is one who is perceived as significantly other than us. Strangers induce fear and uncertainty precisely because they emerge from environments and hold value systems that are, or are at least perceived to be, quite different from our own. Their presence challenges the boundaries of our safety zones. Strangers intrude on our security and raise issues that we may not want to address. But who are these "strangers"? Bearing in mind the clear call for Christians to offer hospitality towards strangers, we must answer this question.

A World of Strangers

In the previous chapter we looked at some implications of liberal society for the ways in which we understand individualism, community, disability, and humanness. There we noted that where neo-liberal capitalism so strongly influences the way in which we experience the world, a picture emerges of human beings who are discrete, unconnected individuals who choose to get together to form relationships, communities, and societies, the primary purpose of these unions being to attain the greatest benefits for the largest number of individuals. The individual precedes the community. The "meaning of life" lies in self-fulfillment and freedom, and the only real obligation that citizens have towards one another is to ensure that their expressions of personal freedom do not impinge on other people's expressions of freedom. As, at least in the public realm, we have no external authority to ensure that this happens, we need the nation state to create and enforce laws, rights, and structures that will ensure that our freedom will not be impinged upon and our potential for self-fulfillment can receive the greatest opportunity to come to fruition. All of this seems quite natural to us, as this is the frame within which we have been taught to understand the nature of reality.

An interesting idea emerges from a deeper reflection on our basic assumptions: *Within liberal societies we are all strangers!* The beginning and end point for a happy, self-fulfilled life is to maintain one's autonomy, one's separateness from those around us. If the individual precedes the community, then connectedness does not mark us out from one another but estrangement. Sometimes that estrangement is passive and sometimes it is hostile, but it is engrained in the ways in which we perceive the world and ourselves within it. As we saw in chapter seven, we tend to move from being strangers to being in some form of relationship through *choice* rather than *obligation*. We overcome this "natural" estrangement by choosing to enter into particular contracts (formal and informal), around certain areas of our lives: business, work, marriage, friendships, and so on. But even here our relationships with others tend to be limited to particular tasks and areas and are bounded by the ability of that to which we contract to bring us happiness. When this ceases to happen, we end the contract and once again become estranged.

Why Are Some Strangers Stranger Than Others?

Nevertheless, while we may all be in some sense estranged from one another, we do not recognize everyone as being a "stranger" in the same way. Assigning the label "stranger," like the label "evil," has complex social, political, and theological dimensions.[15] We treat some individuals and groups as "stranger strangers" because we are taught to recognize them as clearly "not like us," as dangerous, alien, and potentially lethal.

15. Elie Wiesel, *Inside a Library and the Stranger in the Bible,* Hebrew Union College-Jewish Institute of Religion, 1980.

Zvi had this experience. Creating strangers whom we consider somehow stranger than the others we encounter is a dangerous process in which all of us are implicated, but few of us think critically about it. In a previous book, I looked at how a similar process occurred in the social experiences of people with profound mental health problems.[16] In chapter six, we explored the dangers of creating monsters out of strangers and the implications for people who have carried out actions that are considered to be evil. Here our focus will be on another group of people who are misrecognized within our society, with devastating and potentially evil consequences: *refugees and asylum-seekers*. Exploring the experiences of this group will provide a useful test case for our discussion of Christian hospitality and the dangers of creating "stranger strangers." Focusing on this group will help us understand the potential evils going on within our communities and recognize the theodical possibilities of hospitality-in-friendship towards the "stranger."

Hospitality towards Strangers: Refugees and Asylum-Seekers

Reflection on the ways in which we respond to evil and, in particular, to the victims of evil is important. Take, for example, the terrorist attacks and natural disasters that occur within western countries or that involve significant numbers of westerners. For the most part, victims of such tragedies are treated with the deepest respect, and everything is done to ensure that their suffering is not exacerbated by a negative response to their experiences. People recognize their situation as a personal or national tragedy and tend to respond to their situation with sympathy, compassion, and concern. And this, of course, is exactly as it should be. Not to recognize the depth and reality of the pain experienced by people when they encounter evil is to compound their pain and alienation and to give evil an even deeper victory. However, if we look above our own horizon, we soon discover that not all victims are recognized with sympathy, acceptance, and love. For many victims, their experience of evil is met with hostility and rejection rather than hospitality and acceptance.

---

16. Swinton, *Resurrecting the Person*.

What Do We Mean by Refugees and Asylum-Seekers?

Let us be clear about what we mean by the terms "refugee" and "asylum-seeker." These terms do not refer to illegal immigrants or economic migrants. They refer to a quite different group of people. In article 1(a) of the 1951 United Nations Refugee Convention Relating to the Status of Refugees, a refugee is defined as a person who:

> owing to a well-founded fear of being persecuted for reasons of race, religion, nationality, membership of a particular social group or political opinion, is outside the country of his or her nationality and is unable to or, owing to such fear, is unwilling to avail himself of the protection of that country.[17]

Refugees are therefore not simply immigrants. They are not people who have chosen to emigrate from one country to another for economic reasons or in search of a "better life." Refugees are people whom the host country recognizes as having been forced from their home countries because of conflict, persecution, abuse, and terror. Refugees are the victims of evil. *Asylum-seekers* are people who *claim* to be fleeing from abuse and oppression and have applied to be accepted by the host nation as refugees and legal residents. They are people who claim to be the victims of evil but have still to prove to the host country that this is the case. *There is, therefore, no such thing as a bogus or illegal asylum-seeker,*[18] although there may be such a thing as a failed asylum-seeker, that is, someone who has applied for asylum and not had his request accepted. Until proven otherwise, asylum-seekers are people who claim to be fleeing from the consequences of evil. In the same way that our legal system assumes people are innocent until proven guilty, so asylum-seekers are assumed to be valid until proven otherwise. If their case is proven invalid, then they cease to be asylum-seekers and become illegal immigrants whom authorities will then seek to deport.

17. United Nations, *Convention on the Status of Refugees, 1951* (New York: United Nations, 1951), article 1. Protocol updating the convention was published in 1967.

18. A "bogus asylum-seeker" is, arguably, not an asylum-seeker at all but is someone deemed to be pretending to be escaping from evil who is really looking for a new geographical location for economic or other reasons. I use the term "arguably" because there is debate about the fairness of certain decisions concerning the acceptance of asylum-seekers. Clearly, some asylum-seekers are having their applications turned down and are being forced to return to situations of gross evil and suffering.

If asylum-seekers' applications are turned down, then they would be recognized as illegal immigrants. One of the big problems in the various debates around refugees and asylum-seekers is the conflation of the latter with immigrants (legal or otherwise) who choose to leave their own country in search of a better life. This being so, asylum-seekers and refugees have a particular history and should be recognized in a specific way. Asylum-seekers are, or at least claim to be, the victims of extreme evil; they are seeking refuge in places deemed to be safe and hoped to be welcoming. Sadly, sometimes tragically, and all too often, these places of asylum are neither safe nor welcoming.

Creating Strangers

In light of the state of the world, one might expect any civilized country to immediately see the importance of showing hospitality towards those claiming to be fleeing from evil and suffering. However, this is not the case. Rising incidences of violence, abuse, and even racially motivated killing of asylum-seekers and refugees indicates, not welcome and hospitality, but aggression and hostility towards these "strangers." While many countries do welcome asylum-seekers and refugees, they are generally recognized in disturbing ways. Unhelpful rhetoric from politicians and the media fuels the growing estrangement between "us" and "them," all of which persuades people to view asylum-seekers and refugees in particularly negative ways. Sensational headlines paint the asylum-seeker not only as a stranger but as a *dangerous stranger:*

> "Handouts to refugees are robbing the British poor" (*Evening Standard,* April 2000); "Beggars build mansions with OUR handouts" (*Sun,* 14 March 2000); "Asylum-seekers caught begging will be kicked out in a month" (*Sun,* 20 March 2000); "Refugees get flats with Jacuzzi, sunbeds, and . . . a sauna" (*Daily Star,* 25 March 2000); "We'll lock up all asylum-seekers, promise Tories" (*Express,* 30 March 2000); ". . . [W]e resent the scroungers, beggars, and crooks who are prepared to cross every country in Europe to reach our generous benefits system." (*The Sun,* 7 March 2001); ". . . [I]llegals flooding into UK . . ." (*Daily Star,* 31 October 2001). When asylum-seekers are juxtaposed with terrorists, as was the case after the London bombings — "Bombers are all sponging

asylum-seekers" (*Scottish Daily Express,* 27 July 2005) — the potential for violence and evil becomes immense.[19]

Such implications and accusations are, of course, ill-founded and inaccurate. But they are no less powerful for their lack of substance and truth. We have already seen the dangers of how labeling groups in a derogatory fashion such as this is a precursor for dehumanization, which in turn provides a basis for evil actions. Linguistic dehumanization is clear in the statements offered above. The dangers of labeling asylum-seekers as "robbers," "scroungers," "illegals," "terrorists," and so forth are obvious. A less obvious danger within the general talk about "asylum-seekers" is the creation of a false perception that there is an international movement of people with an overarching strategy to invade "our" countries. The term "asylum-seekers" can become a generalized abstraction that leads to thoughts and actions that subsume the unique situations of the God-loved individuals to the mass of distorted public perception.

The Emergence of Xeno-racism

The negative recognition experienced by refugees and asylum-seekers finds a corporate manifestation in an emerging form of racism that has come to be known as *xeno-racism:* racism towards strangers. This term emerged from a European context, but it applies within other countries who host refugees and asylum-seekers. Xeno-racism has shifted away from traditional forms of racism (although it certainly has not replaced them), which focus on people of color, to a new form of racism that places asylum-seekers and refugees at its heart. This neo-racism is aimed against the displaced, the dispossessed, the uprooted, the *stranger.* Sivandan describes xeno-racism as

> a racism that is not just directed at those with darker skins, from the former colonial territories, but at the newer categories of the displaced, the dispossessed, and the uprooted, who are beating at western Europe's doors, the Europe that helped to displace them in the first place. It is a racism, that is, that cannot be color-coded, directed as it is at poor

19. While the focus here is on Europe, it is clear that similar forms of xeno-racism are prevalent in other western countries such as Australia and the United States.

whites as well, and is therefore passed off as xenophobia, a "natural" fear of strangers. But in the way it denigrates and reifies people before segregating and/or expelling them, it is a xenophobia that bears all the marks of the old racism. It is racism in substance, but "xeno" in form. It is a racism that is meted out to impoverished strangers even if they are white. It is xeno-racism.[20]

Xeno-racists consider asylum-seekers to be "uninvited intruders" who have hidden colonial and financial motives. The stranger will "take our jobs," "steal from the welfare state," and "threaten our security, our values, our heritage." Such dangerous strangers are not people to whom automatic hospitality and friendship should be offered. Indeed, hostility is often deemed necessary in order to protect what we have from these marauding strangers. It is this sense of the presence of unwanted and potentially dangerous strangers that lies at the heart of xeno-racism. Xeno-racism is thus an evil and dangerous reaction against the presence of strangers. In the light of our previous discussion of the relationship between Jesus and the stranger, it is clear that such racism, like all racism, is profoundly evil.

Beyond the Myth

But of course, little, if any, of the picture painted by xeno-racists is actually true. In reality, the number of asylum-seekers looking for refuge in industrialized countries has tumbled since 2002.[21] In fact, the poorer, emerging-world countries carry the burden of most of the world's population who are displaced by the types of evil that have been highlighted earlier in this book.[22] In many countries, asylum-seekers are not allowed to work and are, in fact, forced to exist on state support, which is often

20. A. Sivandan, "Poverty Is the New Black: The Three Faces of British Racism," *Race & Class* 42, no. 2 (2001): 1-5.

21. "Asylum Applications Continue to Tumble in Industrialized Countries," UNHCR News Stories, Saturday 10 September 2005, http://www.unhcr.ch/cgi-bin/texis/vtx/news/opendoc.htm?tbl=NEWS&id=431db6ee4. (Africa and Asia between them host over sixty percent of the world's refugees. Europe looks after just twenty-five percent.)

22. See the statistics presented at Forced Migration Online: A World of Information on Human Displacement, http://www.forcedmigration.org/.

minimal and sub-average. Asylum-seekers do not come in search of free benefits.[23] In fact, they tend to be desperately poor[24] and know very little about the asylum system before they arrive.[25] Also, no evidence suggests that asylum-seekers and refugees are more prone to committing crimes than the rest of the population. Indeed, in such a xeno-racist climate, they are more likely to be the victims of crime. Like all racist ideologies, when the surface of the claims of xeno-racism is scratched, the substance is at best questionable and at worst, dangerously misleading. Nevertheless, people still believe it and still choose to recognize asylum-seekers and refugees in disempowering and dangerously negative ways. This racism is all the more poignant because it is (a) aimed at the dispossessed, the homeless, and those without a country or the protection of community and state and (b) it is rarely recognized and thought about. Because it is not noticed by most people, all of us are apt to become implicated in it through our attitudes, values, or assumptions about how things should be, in particular, about who owns what and why. Furthermore, if the theological reflection we engaged in earlier in this chapter is correct, *xeno-racism is racism against God.*

Recognizing Whose We Are

The problem of xeno-racism relates, at least in part, to the fact that many individuals, communities, and nations have *forgotten whose we are.* The fear of xeno-racists is that *these strangers* will take *our* land, *our* jobs, and *our* homes. Apart from being untrue, such assumptions reveal theological weaknesses in the ways in which we understand ourselves and the world that we have been given. The land is not ours. As we tighten our grip on the security of our nations and as we close our borders in order to become "Fortress Europe" or "Fortress America," we need always to be held in check by the question: *Who actually owns the land in which we live?* The

23. Economic migrants seek after financial benefits, but asylum-seekers have a quite different experience and history.

24. Eighty-five percent of organizations working with them said that their clients experienced hunger, while ninety-five percent said their clients could not afford clothes or shoes (joint study by Oxfam and the Refugee Council, 2002).

25. Home Office Research Study 243, "Understanding the Decision-Making of Asylum-Seekers," 2002.

doctrine of creation suggests that we need to begin any discussion of who owns the land we live in with the acknowledgement that the world we inhabit has been given to us. It is only when we recognize that we are created and sustained in and through the hospitality of the God who demands that we offer hospitality towards the stranger and who is known through the social practices of love, that we can begin to think through the implications of how to respond to refugees and asylum-seekers.

The Old Testament makes it particularly clear how we are to understand ownership of "the land," which is always assumed to be an inalienable inheritance and never a tradable commodity (Micah 2:1-3). The Old Testament writers always perceive the land as a gift from the creator God. Brueggemann makes the point thus:

> The land to Israel is a gift. It is a gift from Yahweh and binds Israel in new ways to the giver. Israel was clear that it did not take the land either by power or stratagem, but because Yahweh had spoken a word and had acted to keep his word. The central memories of Israel were told and retold to recall this very point. Israel had always known it was a creature of his word. It lives because he called it (see Hos. 11:1). Israel knew that in his speaking and Israel's hearing was life. That is why the first word in Israel's life is "listen" (Deut. 6:4)! Israel lived by a people-creating word spoken by this people-creator (Deut. 8:3).[26]

We live in God's creation and everything that we have, including the land in which we dwell, is a *gift*. We may tend to it, develop it, and nurture it with care and concern (or not, as the case may be). But ultimately, the land can never be ours. It can only be understood as a gift that is given to us by God as a foundational act of graceful hospitality; it is a gift that we are asked to care for but that we cannot claim as our own.

The danger is that, from within the frame provided to us by our consumerist assumptions, we presume that the land and the goods that we gain from engagement with it are commodities similar to any other commodity, something that we own, buy, and sell, something that exists primarily to make us happy and fulfilled. We have noticed the way we are inclined to do this with our children. Here it becomes clear that we tend to commodify even the world that has been given to us. Malcolm Brown

---

26. Walter Brueggemann, *The Land: Place as Gift, Promise, and Challenge in Biblical Faith* (Philadelphia: Fortress, 1977), p. 93.

notes how, within consumerist cultures, we shape our understanding of what it means to belong in quite specific ways.

> Culturally, we are more likely to cast ourselves as *owners* — people who have belongings — than as people who are owned. We place a very high premium on being *subjects* not *objects,* on being in control rather than done-unto, on the primacy of our choices and of ourselves as people who choose.[27]

If we take the doctrine of creation seriously, ideas of ownership, belongings, control, and choice are at best relativized and at worst shown to be illusions. Primary to our identity as Christians is the lived reality that we are not our own, that we are owned by God, who is our friend and who, in gracious hospitality, "leases" the land to us free of charge with the stipulation that we use it fruitfully in the cause of God's coming kingdom of love.

If this is so, then we can no longer define our response to "the stranger" by what is ours and what is not ours. None of it is ours. When the stranger comes to us and we offer her friendship, hospitality, and a valued place in our communities, we do not do this "out of the goodness of our own hearts"; we perform such hospitable actions in response to God's gracious act of hospitality towards us revealed ultimately in the redemptive gift of Christ. We should receive the gifts of home and possessions from God with thankfulness, humility, and generosity towards others. If we forget this hospitable dynamic, if we forget whose we are, then it becomes difficult, if not impossible, for us to offer hospitality to strangers. If we believe that this is *our* land and these are *our* possessions, then *we* need to protect them from all intruders. If this is *my* land and these are *my* possessions, *I* have no real need for God; all *I* need *I* have right now. Viewed in this way, xeno-racism (in both its strong and weak forms) proves to be based on idolatry and selfishness. It substitutes recognition of God as creator and landowner for a false claim to ownership of land and possessions, and it places distancing and alienation above offering love to God through loving the stranger. In distinction, Christian hospitality reflects the grace and hospitality that creation has received in Christ. In a sense, we *are* all strangers in a world which is not our own. But

27. Malcolm Brown, "The Big Issue: Asylum Seekers," http://www.eamtc.cam.ac.uk/x/residentials/2004-05/jan2005/MB-asylum-jan2005.pdf.

that strangeness is overcome by the grace of the owner, who longs to share his possessions with his children and who in Christ has called all to remember whose they are.

Friendship as a Mode of Recognition

Now we can see how powerful friendship is as a way to resist the types of racist evil described in this chapter. Christ-like friendships begin from and with the recognition that the followers of Jesus know whose they are and in whose land they live. Within the various controversies and debates about asylum-seekers and refugees, Christians have the critical role to constantly remind the world to whom it belongs and to embody that knowledge in welcoming friendships. This voice will sound foolish to many and will struggle to be heard within the complexities of anthropocentric political systems. But it is nonetheless crucial. When society marks refugees and asylum-seekers as dangerously different and somehow less than human, and when it preys on their vulnerability for political or social gain, the friendship the church offers to such strangers serves as a continuing, embodied reminder to society that this world is not our own and that "these people" are valued friends.

The church is called to share what it has with the stranger, because what it has is not its own. All is gift. Life is a gift, creation is a gift, children are gifts. Augustine argues that friends are God's gifts to us in God's providential will;[28] strangers are gifts given to us so that they can become friends. Thus, opening up our churches, our homes, and our lives to refugees is not an act of charity. Nor is it a moral obligation. Rather, it is a natural response that occurs when we recognize who we are in Christ and where we live. Offering hospitality to the stranger recognizes our own status as "resident aliens" and our desire to acknowledge the wonderful gifts of hospitality that God has bestowed upon us. Offering such friendship counteracts the xeno-racist inclinations of our societies and becomes a powerful mode of resisting this form of evil.

28. See Augustine's discussion on friendship in *The Confessions* (Oxford: The Clarendon Press, 1992).

Practicing Friendship: Guest or Host?

God's hospitality towards creation, made manifest in the life of Christ, is reciprocal. Ana Maria Pineda notes that, as well as meaning "stranger," the word *xenos* means both "guest" and "host." Thus *xenos* signals the essential mutuality at the heart of hospitality. "No one is strange except in relation to someone else; we make one another guests and hosts by how we treat each other."[29] Allen Verhey puts this point slightly differently:

> Jesus is not only the host; he is also the stranger, the guest. He not only signals the hospitality of God; he is also the one who depends on the hospitality of others. The striking contrast fits a pattern, of course. The kingdom that he announced and practiced was a kingdom in which the exalted will be humbled, and the humiliated will be exalted (Luke 14:11). And it fits a second pattern, as well. To welcome the kingdom is to welcome Jesus; to be hospitable to the good future of God is to be hospitable to Jesus. But the contrast, the reversal, is no less striking for all that, and it undercuts any association of status with the roles of guest and host.[30]

This dual meaning of *xenos* is intriguing and important. Reflecting on the life of Jesus, we see the host-guest pattern come up time and again. Sometimes he hosted strangers, sometimes he was the guest, sometimes he *was* the stranger. In the nativity narratives, Jesus is a stranger to Mary, one who comes as an unexpected gift from the Holy Spirit. He was a stranger to Joseph, and he was a stranger to Herod. Indeed, Herod saw him as a particularly dangerous stranger who drew out hostility and violence rather than hospitality.[31] Host and guest, befriender and befriended appear to be inextricably intertwined within the life of Jesus.

This significantly reframes what it means to be hospitable to asylum-seekers and refugees. If the land is not our own, and if the biblical pattern

---

29. Ana Maria Pineda, "Hospitality," in Dorothy C. Bass, ed., *Practicing Our Faith* (San Francisco: Jossey Bass, 1997), p. 33.

30. Allen Verhey, "Hospitality Remembering Jesus," *Reformed Review: A Theological Journal of Western Theological Seminary* 57, no. 2 (Winter, 2003-04), http://216.239.59.104/search?q=cache:jitBSwUcwwoJ:www.westernsem.edu/Pub/04Winter/Verhey.htm+%22allen+verhey%22+hospitality+pohl&hl=en.

31. Verhey, "Hospitality Remembering Jesus."

of hospitality as revealed in Christ alternates between the roles of guest and host, then hospitality relates as much to receiving gifts *from* the stranger as it does to giving gifts *to* the stranger. Offering the gift of friendship needs to be held in tension with receiving the gift of friendship. Colonialism and paternalism have no place within such a mode of hospitality. Hospitality has mutuality and a vital sense of reciprocity.[32] Approaching the asylum-seeker, the refugee, the person who carries the weight of our cultural fears and insecurities, we offer her friendship, and we look for friendship from her. More than that, we recognize that the gifts she brings to us may change or transform how we see the world. The stranger brings strange gifts. To Abraham, the stranger brought the gift of a child; to Mary, the stranger brought the gift of another child — Jesus; to the disciples in their early encounter with the risen Christ, the stranger brought them living proof of the resurrection. The refugee and the foreigner, with their different experiences of living within God's creation, bring the gifts of stories and perspectives that we would never have encountered had we not met with them and shared the gift of hospitality. As Ogletree puts it,

> To offer hospitality to a stranger is to welcome something new, unfamiliar, and unknown into our life-world. On the one hand, hospitality requires a recognition of the stranger's vulnerability in an alien social world. Strangers need shelter and sustenance in their travels, especially when they are moving through a hostile environment. On the other hand, hospitality designates occasions of potential discovery which can open up our narrow provincial worlds. Strangers have stories to tell which we have never heard before, stories which can redirect our seeing and stimulate our imaginations. The stories invite us to view the world from a novel perspective. They display the finitude and relativity of our own orientation to meaning.[33]

---

32. Of course, xeno-racists are also capable of intimate relationships and mutuality. The key is that the friendships described here are Christ-like; that is, they take on the shape, the texture, and the goal of the hospitality of Christ and the importance of offering that hospitality towards those considered strangers. They are not simply pleasant mutual relationships. They are radical modes of embodied theology that seek to reflect and reveal something of the kingdom that is coming.

33. Thomas W. Ogletree, *Hospitality to the Stranger: Dimensions of Moral Understanding* (Louisville: Westminster/John Knox Press, 2003), p. 3.

Offering such friendship and hospitality gives us a way to avoid the evils of fear, racism, and violence. As Verhey puts it,

> A hospitality that remembers Jesus sees the stranger and the rival as (potentially, at least) a friend and a sibling. Members of communities formed in remembrance of Jesus sought not just to protect themselves from the potential violence of strangers and rivals but to perform the hospitality of God, to give some small token of God's good and generous future.[34]

In this way we can begin the process of recognizing strangers as potential friends. This practice of holy friendship in Christ offers a loving mode of resistance to the evils of xeno-racism and provides healing for those who have already suffered from much evil.

Identity in Christ

Such hospitality-in-friendship can come about only as it is worked out in and through a community that finds its primary identity in Christ-the-xenos and seeks to live out the meaning of whose they are. As Letty Russell puts it,

> If a Christian community has no sense of its identity in Christ as the center of its life, it will not have a great deal of generosity and compassion to share with others. Just as persons cannot give themselves away to others if they have no sense of self-worth to share, churches with no sense of identity and worth have little to share. It is our identity in Christ who welcomes the stranger that leads us to join in the task of hospitality.[35]

This is an important point. Friendship with strangers demands integrity and faithfulness. It does not mean that we meet the stranger in an attitude of compromise, pretending that our differences don't really matter or that they don't even exist. Clearly they do, and they are important. Hospitality

---

34. Verhey, "Hospitality Remembering Jesus."

35. Letty M. Russell, "Practicing Hospitality in a Time of Backlash," *Theology Today* 52, no. 4 (January 1996): 483.

towards strangers, particularly strangers with beliefs, values, and world-views that differ from our own, does not involve a search for the lowest common denominator. In the early church communities, we find Christians learning through the power of the Holy Spirit to welcome one another, to respect difference, and to love one another even in their differences. But the integrity of each different group was kept intact.

> The Jew was not required to become a Gentile, or to speak like one, in order to be a member of this community and to have a voice in it. But the Jew was required not to condemn the Gentile for being Gentile. The Gentile was not required to become a Jew or to talk like one, but the Gentile was required not to despise the Jew for being Jewish. Paul exhorted Jews and Gentiles in the Roman churches to hospitality, "Welcome one another, therefore, just as Christ has welcomed you, for the glory of God" (Rom. 15:7).[36]

The Christ-centeredness of hospitality towards strangers indicates that Christ is real and is precisely who he claims to be. The stranger may not know Jesus, and his belief system may stand in stark contrast to those offering hospitality in Christ's name. Our task is to be hospitable to him and to respect and seek to understand the differences that he brings; but that hospitality is offered from a position of faithful integrity and Christ-centeredness. The offer of friendship is made with integrity. It is made from a position of certainty about whose we are in Christ, yet it is always open to the surprise that the stranger will bring and always hoping that the stranger, through our friendships, might come to recognize Jesus as the source of all friendship. In loving the stranger and offering him friendship, we minister to God in the hope that through our friendships the stranger can recognize whose he is and find reconciliation with God despite the terrible experiences that he has had. By sharing God's friendship in this way, we faithfully hope that the stranger will come to know the source of that friendship and to love God as God loves him. Friendship embodies Christian community and the love and acceptance of Jesus and provides a safe space for growth and change. Friendship mediates love; perfect love drives out all evil. As such, friendship is a powerful tool of resistance.

36. Verhey, "Hospitality Remembering Jesus."

Negotiating the Space between Us

Of course, friendship, like all forms of hospitality, requires negotiation and care of self as well as care for the other. There is no guarantee that the stranger is going to accept one's offer of friendship or that her motives for entering into friendship with you are positive. Friendship and hospitality are complicated practices that require much negotiation and care. Jesus commands us to love God and to love one another as ourselves.[37] This command indicates clearly that we are called to love ourselves in the same way that we offer love to God and to others. The creative tensions within this relational dynamic are important. As we offer hospitality towards God and strangers, we must not lose the importance of offering hospitality towards ourselves. Friendship is a negotiated space between two parties who care for one another. It does not require that we collapse ourselves into the other in a way that smothers the self or forces it to take on unnatural shapes and forms. It also does not mean that the other always takes priority over the needs of the self. Indeed, to offer meaningful friendship and hospitality requires that the self is a respected dimension of the relational process. To be hospitably oriented towards the welfare of the other requires that one is hospitably oriented towards oneself.

Genuine hospitality and meaningful friendship takes place in the negotiated space between us, a space where together we learn what it means to be hospitable to God, self, and others. Negotiating this space is always complex and demanding but nonetheless vital if hospitality is to avoid drifting into oppression and restrictive compliance to the questionable demands of the stranger. Failure to properly negotiate this space will lead to the possibility of injustice and abuse.

Offering friendship can be a dangerous business. In telling us that we should love our enemies, Jesus clearly indicates that we will have enemies; not all strangers will be well motivated; some strangers will wish us harm. However, unlike the xeno-racist, our beginning point for negotiating such a hospitable space will not be from a position of fear and alienation, but rather from a place of openness, hospitality, and friendship. Some friendships will not work and some will prove too dangerous to continue. But

---

37. "Jesus replied, 'Do not murder, do not commit adultery, do not steal, do not give false testimony, honor your father and mother,' and 'love your neighbor as yourself'" (Matt. 19:19).

this is so with all people, not only refugees and asylum-seekers. The price we pay for offering hospitality can be rejection, hurt, and sometimes even violence. The epistemology of the broken body of Christ informs us that this was so, for God as God offered his hospitality to the world in Christ. If it was true for Christ, it will be true for those who seek to follow him and practice his gestures of redemption. If, as I have suggested in this book, Christian practices do have an "as-so," or correspondence, structure — *as* God has received us in Christ, *so* we too are to receive our fellow human beings[38] — and if such a correspondence means we have to live with the assumption "as Christ, so we," then we should not be surprised if these same practices bring about in our lives the consequences as well as the benefits of the cross. It is as we negotiate the hospitable space between us and work through what it means to love God, other, and self in all situations that the development of loving friendships of resistance will become a possibility.

Resisting Evil and Loving God

The definition of evil in chapter three argued that the *real* problem of evil was its ability to block us from loving God. In this chapter, I have argued that evil separates us not only from God, but also from one another. Indeed, the arguments presented here show an intricate connection between the ways in which we recognize one another and offer love and friendship to God and the ways in which we offer these things to one another. In blocking us from loving the stranger, evils such as xeno-racism may also be blocking us from loving God. If Jesus truly is in the stranger in the ways that have been suggested, and if the evil of xeno-racism prevents us from recognizing Jesus in the stranger, then that same evil, in fact, blocks us from experiencing aspects of God that are crucial for faithful discipleship. If in loving the stranger we also love God, and if we find ourselves unable to show love towards the stranger for the reasons outlined previously, then evil has won a victory that demands resistance and transformation. Friendship as a mode of hospitality is a practice that enables precisely such resistance and transformation.

38. Miroslav Volf and Dorothy C. Bass, *Practicing Theology* (Grand Rapids: Eerdmans, 2002), p. 250.

Practicing Faithfulness in the Face of Evil

The arguments and examples throughout this book have made it clear that the approach one takes to the problem of evil is defined and, to an extent, determined by the particular frame within which one conceptualizes it. If we approach the problem of evil theoretically, we will see the key issues quite differently than if we approach it from the perspective of practice and human experience. Similarly, one's starting point will determine what one considers to be a satisfactory solution to the problem of evil. The theodicist finds satisfaction in logical coherence within a theistic framework. For the "practical theodicist," consolation of the sufferer and the active practice of resistance to evil constitutes a satisfactory response to the problems that evil brings. The various practices that we have explored in this book do not offer an explanation for the existence of evil and suffering. Rather, they are concrete and faithful ways in which evil can be actively resisted and transformed and sufferers can be delivered from the grip of evil and the danger of losing hope in the providential goodness of God. These practices sustain faith in a loving and powerful God and encourage hope that life has meaning and purpose, despite the way things may appear.

Reframing the Church: Practicing Theodicy

The table on page 245 outlines the key Christian practices that have been presented in this book.

Christian Practices: The Formation of a
Unified Way of Life in the Spirit

Listening to Silence (thoughtfulness, friendship, prayer, patience, perseverance, hope, love)

Lament (prayer, listening to silence, friendship, hope, patience, perseverance, eschatological imagination and hope, love)

Forgiveness (prayer, lament, faith, trust, hope, thoughtfulness, compassion, patience, perseverance, eschatological hope and imagination, love)

Thoughtfulness (hospitality, adoption, lament, listening to silence, forgiveness, eschatological imagination and hope, friendship, love)

Hospitality (friendship, thoughtfulness, compassion, faith, eschatological imagination and hope, perseverance, love)

The table shows clearly the interconnectedness of the various practices and the ways in which they are implicitly and explicitly involved with and dependent on one another. Although our focus has been primarily on the five practices of listening to silence, lament, forgiveness, thoughtfulness, and hospitality, it is clear not only that these practices are reliant on one another, but that they also contain a number of other practices that we have not been able to develop fully within this book. For example, practicing eschatological hope and developing an eschatological imagination are both necessary for effectively carrying out our five practices and also emerge from participation in such practices. Compassion is a crucial underpinning to all five of the practices. Likewise, perseverance is foundational to all of the practices examined in this book. And, of course, underlying everything that has been said is the practice of love in both its divine and human forms. In the end, practical theodicy, which emerges from within this complex web of practices, is the church.

If, as McFarland suggests, "the church as the body of Christ, can be conceived in terms of an interlocking set of practices that serve both to critique and to refashion our vision of the divine so that we may come to know God more fully and more truly,"[1] then it is clear that the church not

---

1. Ian P. McFarland, *The Divine Image: Envisioning the Invsible God* (Minneapolis: Fortress Press, 2005), p. vii.

only *does* theodicy but also *is* a particular mode of theodicy. The church is an embodied theodicy of practice that does not seek to explain how a good, all-loving, all-powerful God could allow evil and suffering, but, through its practices and gestures of redemption, reveals in concrete, tangible forms the various ways in which God responds to evil. Practicing theodicy in this way, the church shows how to continue loving God and worshipping God forever, even in the midst of evil and suffering. Framed in this way, practical theodicy is nothing more (and nothing less) than the church as it strives to remain faithful to its calling to be a community that can absorb suffering and evil and facilitate perseverance and faithfulness among the followers of Christ until he returns and the former things pass away.

Perfect Love Drives Out Fear

Our reflections in chapter nine on the practice of friendship brought us to the end of a complex but crucial journey into the problem of evil. But of course, the journey does not end with the final chapter of this book. Evil still flourishes, people continue to suffer. Yet hope remains. It may be that evil cannot be explained through human reason and logic. But that does not mean that there is no answer to the problem of evil. There is an answer and it is *love*. Only perfect love can drive out fear, and only love can truly conquer evil in all of its forms.[2] The practices explored in this book all have love at their core. Each holds the potential to bring healing, comfort, and reconciliation to those who are battered and broken by the massive sea of evil that saturates our world. Each is intended to enable victims of evil to hold onto their love for God, self, and one another. By practicing this way and learning how to hold onto the love of God, we maintain hope in the providential love and goodness of God even in the midst of evil. In this way, we can resist evil and transform suffering.

Learning to practice in the ways described in this book is much more than just human striving. It is an ongoing task carried out in the power of the Holy Spirit and within a community of *thoughtful, holy friends* who recognize whose they are and remain open to the dangerous possibility of

---

2. "There is no fear in love. But perfect love drives out fear, because fear has to do with punishment. The man who fears is not made perfect in love" (1 John 4:18).

meeting Jesus in the multitude of ways in which the stranger comes to us. Thoughtful, holy friends are open and alert enough to see through the various myths that surround and shape the stranger, whether that stranger is a refugee, an asylum-seeker, or a person with a disability. Such thoughtful friends are aware of the pathologies of society and, through the gift of friendship, stand in solidarity as a plausible, healing alternative to the hopelessness and misery of evil. Friends like these are called to practice critical thinking in order to avoid being sucked into the morass of lies, half-truths, and violence-inducing propaganda against these "strangers." Thoughtful, holy friends recognize their calling to acknowledge and live out the truth of Matthew 25 and to think through the implications of offering hospitality to Jesus as we offer it to the stranger. Thoughtful friends understand the reality of sadness and the need to lament in faithfulness. Thoughtful friends forgive one another for the little things that hold the potential to become sources of evil. Such friends stand in solidarity with the weak, the poor, the suffering, the victims of evil wherever they may be. In this way, we can resist and transform evil and open up the possibility of a hopeful future. In this way, we receive the resources to sustain us until that day when "He will wipe every tear from their eyes. There will be no more death or mourning or crying or pain, for the old order of things has passed away" (Rev. 21:4). Until that day, we are called to live together as faithful and compassionate friends whose task it is to minister faithfully and to love unceasingly even in the midst of the darkest of evils. When we see the Lord face to face, we will know the answer to the question "Why?" For now, it must be enough to learn how to love God in all things and enable one another to find providential hope and meaning even in the midst of the darkest storms until the Lord returns. Our task is to work through the practical implications of Paul's beautiful words of reassurance and hope:

> For I am convinced that neither death nor life, neither angels nor demons, neither the present nor the future, nor any powers, neither height nor depth, nor anything else in all creation, will be able to separate us from the love of God that is in Christ Jesus our Lord. (Rom. 8:38-39)

That is our hope, our vision, our prayer, and our calling.

Bibliography

Ackermann, Denise M. "Lamenting from the Other Side." http://www
.crvp.org/book/Series02/II-6/chapter_viii.htm
————, and M. Bons-Storm, eds. *Liberating Faith Practices: Feminist Practical Theologies in Context.* Leuven: Peeters, 1998.
Adams, M. M. *Horrendous Evils and the Goodness of God.* Ithaca, N.Y.: Cornell University Press, 1999.
Amnesty International. "Women and Torture." *File on Torture,* July 1985.
Anderson, Ray S. *Becoming Human.* Pasadena: Fuller Seminary Press, 1991.
————. *Dancing with Wolves, Feeding the Sheep: Musings of a Maverick Theologian.* Eugene, Ore.: Wipf & Stock Publishers, 2002.
————. *The Shape of Practical Theology: Empowering Ministry with Theological Praxis.* Downers Grove, Ill.: InterVarsity Press, 2001.
Arbuckle, Gerald. *Grieving for Change: A Spirituality for Refounding Gospel Communities.* New York: Continuum, 1991.
Arendt, Hannah. *Eichmann in Jerusalem: A Report on the Banality of Evil.* New York: Penguin Books, 1994.
————. *The Human Condition.* Chicago: University of Chicago Press, 1998.
————. *The Life of Mind — Thinking — Willing.* New York/London: Harvest/HJB Book, 1978.
————. "Thinking and Moral Considerations: A Lecture." *Social Research* 38, no. 3 (Fall 1971).
Augsburger, David. *Helping People Forgive.* Louisville: Westminster/John Knox Press, 1996.
Augustine. *City of God.* London: Penguin Classics, 2003.
————. *Enchiridion.* South Bend, Ind.: Gateway Editions, 1996.
Barker, Megan. "The Evil That Men, Women and Children Do." *The Psychologist* 15, no. 11 (2002): 568-71.
————. "Women, Children and the Construction of Evil." Second Global Con-

ference: Perspectives on Evil and Human Wickedness, 16-21 March 2001, Anglo-American College, Prague, Czech Republic. http://www.wickedness.net/Barker.pdf

Baumeister, R. F. *Evil: Inside Human Violence and Cruelty.* New York: Henry Holt, 1997.

Berkman, J., and M. Cartwright. *The Hauerwas Reader.* Durham, N.C.: Duke University Press, 2001.

Berry, Wendell. *What Are People For?* New York: North Point Press, 1990.

Billman, K. D., and Daniel L. Migliore. *Rachel's Cry.* Cleveland: United Church Press, 1999.

Birch, H. *Moving Targets: Women, Murder, and Representation.* London: Virago Press, 1993.

Blumenthal, D. *Facing the Abusing God: A Theology of Protest.* Louisville: Westminster/John Knox Press, 1993.

Bonhoeffer, Dietrich. "A Bonhoeffer Sermon." Translated by Daniel Bloesch. Edited by F. Burton Nelson. *Theology Today* 38 (1982): 469.

———. *Discipleship.* Minneapolis: Fortress Press, 2003.

———. *Ethics.* Minneapolis: Fortress Press, 2005.

———. *Letters and Papers from Prison.* London: Collins Fontana Books, 1953.

———. *Life Together: Prayerbook of the Bible.* Minneapolis: Fortress Press, 1996.

Brand, H. "Myra Hindley." *Third Way* 24 (April 2000).

Brown, M. "The Big Issue: Asylum Seekers." http://www.eamtc.cam.ac.uk/x/residentials/2004-05/jan2005/MB-asylum-jan2005.pdf

Brueggemann, Walter. *The Land: Place as Gift, Promise, and Challenge in Biblical Faith.* Philadelphia: Fortress Press, 1977.

———. *The Message of the Psalms: A Theological Commentary.* Minneapolis: Augsburg Publishing House, 1984.

———. *Old Testament Theology: Essays on Structure, Theme, and Text.* Minneapolis: Fortress Press, 1992.

———. "The Practice of Homefullness." *Church and Society* (May/June 2001): 12.

———. *The Psalms and the Life of Faith.* Edited by Patrick D. Miller. Minneapolis: Fortress Press, 1995.

———. "Some Aspects of Theodicy in Old Testament Faith." *Perspectives in Religious Studies* 26, no. 3 (1999): 253-68.

———. *Texts Under Negotiation: The Bible and Postmodern Imagination.* Minneapolis: Fortress Press, 1993

———. "Truth-Telling Comfort." http://www.sermonmall.com/WTC/wtc22.html

Buber, M. *Good and Evil: Two Interpretations.* New York: Charles Scribner's Sons, 1953.

Capps, Donald. *Reframing: A New Method in Pastoral Care.* Minneapolis: Fortress Press, 1990.

Carey, B. "For the Worst of Us, the Diagnosis May Be 'Evil.'" *The New York Times,* 8 February 2005.

Davenport, D. "The Functions of Anger and Forgiveness: Guidelines for Psychotherapy with Victims." *Psychotherapy* 28, no. 1 (1991): 140-44.

Drane, John. *The McDonaldization of the Church.* London: Darton, Longman & Todd, 2000.

Eliach, Yaffa. *Hasidic Tales of the Holocaust.* New York: Vintage Books, 1988.

Exline, Julie Juola, Ann Marie Yali, Marci Lobel. "When God Disappoints: Difficulty Forgiving God and Its Role in Negative Emotion." *Journal of Health Psychology* 4 (1999): 365-79.

Farley, Wendy. *Tragic Visions and Divine Compassion: A Contemporary Theodicy.* Louisville: Westminster/John Knox, 1990.

Felderhof, Marius C. "Evil: Theodicy or Resistance?" *Scottish Journal of Theology* 57, no. 4 (2004): 397-412.

Flanigan, B. *Forgiving the Unforgivable.* New York: Wiley Publishing, 1992.

Frankl, Viktor E. *Man's Search for Meaning: An Introduction to Logotherapy.* New York: Washington Square Books, 1984.

Garbarini, Vic. "Death, Rebirth, and the Business of Music: Sting on the Ties That Bind." *Spin,* November/December 1987: http://www.sting.com/news/interview.php?uid=1541.

Gebara, I. *Out of the Depths: Women's Experience of Evil and Salvation.* Minneapolis: Fortress Press, 2002.

Geddes, Jennifer L. *Evil after Postmodernism: Histories, Narratives and Ethics.* New York: Routledge, 2001.

Gerstenberger, Erhard S. *Psalms, Part One: With an Introduction to Cultic Poetry.* The Forms of the Old Testament Literature. Grand Rapids: Eerdmans, 1988.

Goodliff, Paul. *Care in a Confused Climate: Pastoral Care and Postmodern Culture.* London: Darton Longman and Todd, 1998.

Govier, T. *Forgiveness and Revenge.* London: Routledge, 2002.

Govig, Stewart D. *Souls Are Made of Endurance: Surviving Mental Illness in the Family.* Louisville: Westminster/John Knox, 1994.

Gutiérrez, G. *On Job: God Talk and the Suffering of the Innocent.* Maryknoll, N.Y.: Orbis Books, 1987.

Habron, D. M. "Moral Monsters and Saints." *The Monist* 85, no. 2 (2002): 260-84.

Hauerwas, Stanley. *Cross Shattered Christ: Meditations on the Seven Last Words.* Grand Rapids: Brazos Press, 2005.

———. *Naming the Silences.* Grand Rapids: Eerdmans, 1990.

Hedges, C. *War Is a Force That Gives Us Meaning*. New York: Anchor Books, 2002.

Hick, John. *Evil and the God of Love*. Revised edition. New York: Macmillan, 1985.

Hume, David. *Dialogues concerning Natural Religion*. Edited by Norman Kemp Smith. London: Thomas Nelson & Sons, 1947.

Jacob, Margaret C. *The Enlightenment: A Brief History with Documents*. Boston: St. Martin's Press, 2001.

Jesurathnam, K. "Towards a Dalit Liberative Hermeneutics: Re-reading the Psalms of Lament." *Bangalore Theological Forum* 34, no. 1 (2002): 1-34.

Jones, Gregory L., *Embodying Forgiveness: A Theological Analysis*. Grand Rapids: Eerdmans, 1995.

————. "The Judgment of Grace: Forgiveness in Christian Life." *Theology Matters* 3, no. 4 (July/August 1997): 7-16.

Keeler, C. J. "Eichmann in All of Us: Thoughtlessness and the Banality of Evil in *Sophie's Choice*." *Perspectives on Evil and Human Wickedness* 1, no. 3 (2003): 96-105.

Kerr, A., T. Shakespeare, and S. Varty. *Genetic Politics: From Eugenics to Genome*. Cheltenham, England: New Clarion Press, 2002.

Kilby, Karen. "Evil and the Limits of Theology." *New Blackfriars* 84, no. 983 (2003): 13-29.

Kleinman, Arthur, and Byron Good, eds. *Culture and Depression: Studies in the Anthropology and Cross-cultural Psychiatry of Affect and Disorder*. Berkeley: University of California Press, 1985.

————, Veena Das, and Margaret Lock, eds. *Social Suffering*. Berkeley: University of California Press, 1997.

Lammers, Stephen E., and Allen Verhey. *On Moral Medicine: Theological Perspectives in Medical Ethics*. Grand Rapids: Eerdmans, 1987.

Landsman, Gail. "'Too Bad You Got a Lemon': Peter Singer, Mothers of Children with Disabilities, and the Critique of Consumer Culture." In *Consuming Motherhood,* edited by Janelle Taylor, Danielle Wozniak, and Linda Layne, pp. 100-121. New Brunswick: Rutgers University Press, 2004.

Larrimore, Mark, ed. *Problem of Evil: A Reader*. London: Blackwell Publishers, 2004.

Lewis, C. S. *The Weight of Glory and Other Addresses*. New York: Collier Books, 1980.

Lipowski, Z. J. "Physical Illness, the Individual, and the Coping Process." *Psychiatry in Medicine* 1 (1979): 91-102.

Locke, John. *Essay Concerning Human Understanding*. Oxford: Clarendon Press, 1894.

Luther, Martin. "An Introduction to St. Paul's Letter to the Romans." In *Dr.*

Martin Luther's Vermischte Deutsche Schriften. Translated by Robert E. Smith. Edited by Johan K. Irmischer. Erlangen: Heyder and Zimmer, 1854.

MacIntyre, Alasdair. *After Virtue: A Study in Moral Theory.* Notre Dame, Ind.: University of Notre Dame Press, 1981.

Macmurray, John. *The Form of the Personal,* Volume 1: *The Self as Agent;* Volume 2: *Persons in Relation.* London: Faber, 1961; reissued 1991.

Marquard, Odo. *In Defense of the Accidental: Philosophical Studies.* Translated by Robert M. Wallace. New York: Oxford University Press, 1991.

Mason, T., J. Richman, and D. Mercer. "The Influence of Evil on Forensic Clinical Practice." *International Journal of Mental Health Nursing* 11 (2002): 80-93.

McFadyen, Alistair. *Bound to Sin: Abuse, Holocaust, and the Christian Doctrine of Sin.* London: Cambridge University Press, 2000.

McFarland, Ian A. *The Divine Image: Envisioning the Invisible God.* Minneapolis: Fortress Press, 2005.

Meilaender, Gilbert. *Bioethics: A Primer for Christians.* Grand Rapids: Eerdmans, 1996.

————. "Learning from Pieper: On Being Lutheran in This Time and Place." *Concordia Theological Quarterly* 63, no. 1 (1999): 37-49.

Mercer, D., T. Mason, and J. Richman. "Good and Evil in the Crusade of Care: Social Construction of Mental Disorders." *Journal of Psychosocial Nursing* 37, no. 9 (1999): 13-17.

————, J. Richman, and T. Mason. "Out of the Mouths of Forensic Nurses: A 'Pathology of the Monstrous' Revisited." *Mental Health Care* 3, no. 6 (2000): 197-200.

Merton, Thomas. *Raids on the Unspeakable.* New York: New Directions, 1966.

Migliore, Daniel L. *Faith Seeking Understanding: An Introduction to Christian Theology.* Grand Rapids: Eerdmans, 1991.

Miller, Patrick D. "Current Issues in Psalms Studies." *Word & World* 5, no. 2 (1985).

Mohrmann, Margaret E., and Mark J. Hanson. *Pain Seeking Understanding: Suffering, Medicine and Faith.* Cleveland: The Pilgrim Press, 1999.

Morton, Nelle. *The Journey Is Home.* Boston: Beacon Press, 1985.

Nelson, S. "Facing Evil: Evil's Many Faces; Five Paradigms for Understanding Evil." *Interpretation* 5, no. 4 (1 October 2003): 398-413.

Nouwen. Henri. *Out of Solitude.* Notre Dame, Ind.: Ave Maria Press, 1974.

Ogletree, Thomas W. *Hospitality to the Stranger: Dimensions of Moral Understanding.* Louisville: Westminster/John Knox, 2003.

Pascal, Blaise. *Pensées.* Translated by A. J. Krailsheimer. London: Penguin Books, 1966.

Patton, J. *Is Human Forgiveness Possible? A Pastoral Care Perspective.* Nashville: Abingdon, 1985.

Peck, S. M. *People of the Lie: The Hope for Healing Human Evil.* London: Arrow Books, 1990.

Poling, James. *Deliver Us from Evil: Resisting Racial and Gender Oppression.* Minneapolis: Fortress Press, 1996.

Post, Stephen. "Alzheimer's and Grace." *First Things* 142 (April 2004): 12-14.

————. *The Moral Challenge of Alzheimer's Disease: Ethical Issues from Diagnosis to Dying.* Baltimore, Md.: Johns Hopkins University Press, 2000.

Prins, H. "Psychiatry and the Concept of Evil." *British Journal of Psychiatry* 165 (1994): 297-302.

Ramsey, Paul. *The Patient as Person.* New Haven: Yale University Press, 1970.

Reinders, Hans S. *The Future of the Disabled in Liberal Society: An Ethical Analysis.* Notre Dame, Ind.: University of Notre Dame Press, 2000.

Richman, J., D. Mercer, and Y. Mason. "The Social Construction of Evil in a Forensic Setting." *The Journal of Forensic Nursing* 10, no. 2 (1999): 300-308.

Ricoeur, Paul. "Evil, a Challenge to Philosophy and Theology." *Journal of the American Academy of Religion* 53, no. 3 (1985).

Rothman, B. K. *The Tentative Pregnancy: Prenatal Diagnosis and the Future of Motherhood.* New York: Penguin Books, 1987.

Russell, Letty M. "Practicing Hospitality in a Time of Backlash." *Theology Today* 52, no. 4 (January 1996): 476-85.

Scarry, Elaine. *The Body in Pain: The Making and Unmaking of the World.* Oxford: Oxford University Press, 1985.

Singer, Peter. *Practical Ethics.* Second edition. New York: Cambridge University Press, 1993. First edition, 1979.

————. *Rethinking Life and Death: The Collapse of Our Traditional Ethics.* New York: St. Martin's/Griffin, 1996.

————, and Helga Khuse. *Should the Baby Live? The Problem of Handicapped Infants.* Oxford/New York/Toronto: Oxford University Press, 1985.

Smedes, Lewis. *Forgive and Forget: Healing the Hurts We Don't Deserve.* New York: Harper and Row, 1984.

Soelle, Dorothee. *Suffering.* Philadelphia: Fortress Press, 1975.

Stevenson-Moessner, J. *The Spirit of Adoption: At Home in God's Family.* Louisville: Westminster/John Knox Press, 2003.

Strozier, Charles B., and Michael Flynn, eds. *Trauma and Self: Essays by Robert J. Lifton.* Oxford: Rowman & Littlefield, 1996.

Styron, W. *Sophie's Choice.* Third edition. London: Picador, 1992.

Sullivan, Andrew. "When Grace Arrives Unannounced." *Time,* 28 March 2005. www.time.com/time/magazine/article/0,9171,1039693,00.html

Surin, Kenneth. *Theology and the Problem of Evil.* Oxford: Blackwell, 1986.

Swinburne, Richard. *Providence and the Problem of Evil.* Oxford: Clarendon Press, 1998.

Swinton, John. *From Bedlam to Shalom: Towards a Practical Theology of Human*

Nature, Interpersonal Relationships, and Mental Health Care. New York: Peter Lang, 2000.

————. *Resurrecting the Person: Friendship and the Care of People with Severe Mental Health Problems.* Nashville: Abingdon Press, 2000.

————, ed. *Critical Reflections on Stanley Hauerwas' Theology of Disability: Disabling Society, Enabling Theology.* New York: Haworth Press, 2005.

Taylor, Charles. *Multiculturalism.* Edited and introduced by Amy Gutman. Princeton: Princeton University Press, 1994.

Thompson, P. "The Evolutionary Biology of Evil." *The Monist* 85, no. 2 (2002): 239-59.

Tilley, Terrence. *The Evils of Theodicy.* Washington, D.C.: Georgetown University Press, 1991.

Torrance, T. *Divine and Contingent Order.* Oxford/New York: Oxford University Press, 1981.

Tutu, Desmond. *No Future without Forgiveness.* New York: Doubleday, 1999.

United Nations. *Convention on the Status of Refugees 1951.* New York: United Nations, 1951.

Verhey, A. "Hospitality Remembering Jesus." *Reformed Review: A Theological Journal of Western Theological Seminary* 57, no. 2 (Winter 2003-2004). http://216.239.59.104/search?q=cache:jitBSwUcwwoJ:www.westernsem.edu/Pub/04Winter/Verhey.htm+%22allen+verhey%22+hospitality+pohl&hl=en

Volf, Miroslav. "To Embrace the Enemy." *Christianity Today,* 17 September 2001. http://www.christianitytoday.com/ct/2001/138/53.0.html

————. *Exclusion and Embrace: A Theological Exploration of Identity, Otherness, and Reconciliation.* Nashville: Abingdon Press, 1996.

————, and Dorothy Bass. *Practicing Theology: Beliefs and Practices in Christian Life.* Grand Rapids: Eerdmans, 2001.

Wadell, Paul J. *Becoming Friends: Worship, Justice, and the Practice of Christian Friendship.* Grand Rapids: Brazos Press, 2002.

Waller, J. *Becoming Evil: How Ordinary People Commit Genocide and Mass Killing.* New York: Oxford University Press, 2002.

Weems, Ann. *Psalms of Lament.* Louisville: Westminster John Knox, 1995.

Wells, Sam. *Improvisation: The Drama of Christian Ethics.* Grand Rapids: Brazos Press, 2004.

Westermann, Claus. *Praise and Lament in the Psalms.* Atlanta: John Knox Press, 1981.

Wiesel, Elie. *Inside a Library and the Stranger in the Bible.* Hebrew Union College–Jewish Institute of Religion, 1980.

————. "Jenseits des Schweigens." In *Das Gegenteil von Gleichgultigeit Ist Erinnerung.* Edited by Dagmar Mensink and Reinhold Boschki. Mainz: Matthias-Grunewald Verlag, 1995.

Wilson, Bryan R., ed. *Rationality*. Oxford: Basil Blackwell, 1977.

Work, Telford. "Advent's Answer to the Problem of Evil." *International Journal of Systematic Theology* 2, no. 1 (March 2000): 100-111.

Yoder, John Howard. "Trinity versus Theodicy: Hebraic Realism and the Temptation to Judge God." Unpublished paper, 1996. http://www.nd.edu/~theo/research/jhy_2/writings/philsystheo/THEODICY.htm

Zaner, Richard M. *Troubled Voices: Stories of Ethics and Illness*. Cleveland: The Pilgrim Press, 1993.

Index

phers, 40-44; idolatrous nature of,
42n.18, 42-43; as intellectual enterprise, 12n.3, 14n.6, 14-15, 42; as jus-
tifying/rationalizing evil and suffering, 17-21; as meaningless, 13;
necessity of, 2-3, 38-40; and original
sin doctrine, 21n.19, 21-26, 23nn.25-
26, 24n.27; and pastoral perspectives on problem of evil, 9-29; pastoral problems with, 3-4, 12-15, 17-
28; as potential source of evil, 13,
26-28; and practical impact of evil
on people's lives, 14-15; reframing
of, 15-17, 28-29, 44-45, 76-77; as second-order activity, 4, 16-17. *See also*
Evil; Problem of evil
Thessalonians, Paul's Second Letter
to, 35-36
Thoughtfulness, 179-212, 245; Arendt
on, 179, 183; and the banality of evil,
181-83; and critical thinking, 180,
183; and God's love, 210; and image
of God as relationship, 204-5; and
interconnected Christian practices,
200-205, 210-12; and moral significance of love, 198-200; and politics
of recognition, 218; and practice of
adoption, 205-10; and renewing the
mind, 179-80; as resistance, 183-91;
and thoughtlessness/inattention,
180-83, 218. *See also* Personhood
Tilley, Terrence, 27, 43, 77n.9
Timothy, Paul's First Letter to, 61
Torrance, Tom, 66
Tragedy: Christian communities' responses to, 90-93, 113, 119-21; and
evil, 61-66; and the tragic structure
of creation, 62-65
Tragic Vision and Divine Compassion
(Farley), 62

Tutu, Desmond, 91, 201-3, 204n.40

United Nations Refugee Convention
Relating to the Status of Refugees,
230

Verhey, Allen, 238, 240, 241
Victims of grace, 132, 167-68, 169
Volf, Miroslav: on Christian practices,
82, 83; on forgiveness, 140-41, 158,
168-69, 174-75; on imprecatory
psalms, 174-75; on reconciliation,
168-69; on repentance, 140-41; on
revenge, 135

Wadell, Paul J., 169-70
Waller, James, 146, 156-57
Warren, Rick, 151-52
Weems, Ann, 126-27
Wells, Sam, 56, 57
Western culture: friendship and rela-
tionships in, 220, 227-28; and neces-
sity of theodicy, 2, 2n.2, 3, 38-40;
and personhood, 194-95, 200, 203
"What Is Enlightenment?" (Kant), 32
"When Grace Arrives Unannounced"
(Sullivan), 151-52
Wiesel, Elie, 97
Work, Telford, 36n.11, 36-37

Xeno-racism, 232-37, 238n.32; dual
meaning of *xenos,* 238; as idolatry
and selfishness, 236-37; and myths
about refugees and asylum-seekers,
233-34, 234nn.23-24; as racism
against God, 234

Yoder, John Howard, 42n.18

Zaner, Richard, 27